Serials Librarianship

Handbooks on Library Practice

SERIALS LIBRARIANSHIP

EDITED BY
ROSS BOURNE

THE LIBRARY
ASSOCIATION
LONDON

© The Library Association 1980. *Government department libraries.* Crown Copyright. Published by permission of the Controller of Her Majesty's Stationery Office. Published by The Library Association, 7 Ridgmount Street, London WC1E 7AE and printed in the USA by Vail-Ballou Press, Inc., Binhamton, New York.

First published 1980

British Library Cataloguing in Publication Data

Serials librarianship. — (Handbooks on library practice).
  1. Serials control systems
  I. Bourne, Ross   II. Library Association
  III. Series
  025.17'3   Z692.S5

  ISBN 0 85365 631 2 (boards)
  ISBN 0 85365 721 1 (paper)

Contents

v

Contents

Contributors

R. BAKER
Head of Acquisition, Science Reference Library, Bayswater Branch

ROSS BOURNE BA ALA
Head, Serials Office, British Library Bibliographic Services Division

D.W. BROMLEY MA ALA
Deputy Director, Sheffield City Libraries

JOHN COWLEY BA FLA
Head of Library Services, Middlesex Polytechnic

R.H. DE VERE MSc
Planning Officer, Science Reference Library

JEAN DOWNS ALA
Assistant Librarian, University of Aston, Birmingham

B.G. DUTTON BSc PhD
Information Unit Manager, ICI Ltd (Mond Division), Runcorn,
Cheshire

FEONA J. HAMILTON BA ALA
Information and Press Officer, The Library Association

Contributors

GEOFFREY HAMILTON FLA
Librarian, British Library, Library Association Library

PROFESSOR K.G.E. HARRIS MA FLA
Librarian, Newcastle-Upon-Tyne Polytechnic

STELLA KEENAN ALA
Lecturer, Department of Librarianship, University of Technology, Loughborough

CATHERINE OLVER BA ALA
Sub-Librarian, University of Reading

ADRIAN PEASGOOD BA ALA
Sub-Librarian, University of Sussex

JEAN PLAISTER BSc (ECON) FLA
Director, London and South Eastern Library Region, London

MALCOLM SHIFRIN ALA
Central Library Resources Services, Inner London Education Authority, London

A.T. SMAIL
Agent for the Copyright Libraries, London

F.R. TAYLOR MIInfSc FLA
Scientific and Technical Librarian and Information Officer, Central Library, Manchester

P.A. THOMAS
formerly School of Library, Archive and Information Studies, University College, London

A.J. WALFORD MBE PhD FLA

D.P. WOODWORTH BA ALA
Senior Lecturer, School of Librarianship, Loughborough Technical College

Introduction

The last few years have been a vintage period for books about serials librarianship, reflecting, it would seem, renewed interest in what has so often been a Cinderella area in our profession. One might perhaps attribute this to the growth of national and international standards, the use of the computer for routine processes, the development of centralized services, or any number of other things; be these as they may, serials librarianship is a practical discipline in which a considerable amount has been taking place in recent years. This book sets out to capture some of these happenings; its intention is to act not only as a practical manual from which serials librarians and others concerned with the use and deployment of serials in libraries might learn something to help them in their work, but also as a state-of-the-art. For this reason, our concern is with the present and to a limited extent the future, but not the past. The history of the learned journal is not to be found here, but those who need it could do a lot worse than read Andrew Osborn's account in his excellent book.[1] Neither is the book comprehensive: the reader will look in vain for a description of the work of the British Library Lending Division, probably one of the most far-reaching developments in post-war British librarianship, and especially so for serials librarians. It was felt by the Editor that this information is readily available elsewhere, for example in W. L. Saunders's *British librarianship today,* one of the Library Association's centenary volumes[2], but that what would be more useful would be to read about its effect on different types of library and library processes. Again, it would simply not have been feasible to commission a chapter on every type of library, since this would have resulted in a book of unmanageable length; so, alas, county libraries and the libraries of nationalized industries and government research establishments had to be dropped from the editorial plan of the book. What remains will be, the Editor trusts, helpful to those whom he sees as the target audience: senior- and middle-management librarians, serials librarians (naturally), non-librarians who want to gain an appreciation of the problems faced in maintaining serial collections, and perhaps even the teaching profession who are to educate the serials librarians of tomorrow.

Part 1 deals with library processes and provides most of the book's practical information, for example in Ray de Vere's chapter on *Checking and claiming*, where he abides by his own injunction to use the imperative. Part 2, on the other hand, examines serials librarianship from a number of different viewpoints, those of different types of library. It was originally feared that a certain amount of repetition might result, but this does not seem to have taken place; indeed what repetition there is may not be altogether a bad thing if it produces more than one perspective on a particular aspect of the work. But this section of the book does include some valuable information, such as Tom Smail's account of the workings of our national libraries, a subject on which he, as the Agent for the Copyright Libraries, and formerly of the National Library of Scotland, is uniquely qualified to write. Likewise, Adrian Peasgood's questionnaire to university libraries has uncovered some interesting facts which academic librarians would do well to consider in respect of their own serials collections. Finally, Part 3 does a little crystal-ball gazing, and is neatly rounded off by David Woodworth who describes one of the few courses in serials librarianship available in this country.

And this, it is hoped, is the book's message. While on-the-bench training will and obviously should continue, our library schools are not doing all that much to provide future librarians with the basic knowledge that will enable them to manage serials collections. Yet while I write these words, I can almost understand why this is so. Serials are not just another type of library material, like films or maps or gramophone records; they pervade all of these, but are only managed separately from other printed material or audio cassettes or whatever because they *continue*, and hence present very real practical problems, for example in the payment of subscriptions. The division between serials and other library collections, then, is a practical not a theoretical one. And from an educational point of view, how does one impose a teaching framework on something whose major characteristic is its unexpectedness and variability? To its credit, Loughborough tries, and perhaps others will follow.

A final comment: I do not intend to define what a serial is, except that the following ISO definition was suggested as a guide to contributors:

A publication, in printed form or not, issued in successive parts usually having numerical or chronological designations and intended to be continued indefinitely. Serials include periodicals, newspapers, annuals (reports, yearbooks, directories, etc.), the journals, memoirs, proceedings, transactions, etc. of societies, and monographic series.[3]

The reason for my reluctance is that it seems that in practical situations, a serial is whatever you want it to be — and no amount of theorizing on my part is going to persuade the libraries of the United Kingdom to give up their cherished working definitions. For those who must have a definition, may I recommend Osborn[1] and Davinson[4]. But the lack of such a discussion, will not, I hope, deter readers from dipping into this Handbook. M. Jourdain was no worse off for not knowing that he had been speaking prose all his life — in fact, his troubles began after he had realized!

REFERENCES

1. Osborn, A.D. *Serial publications: their place and treatment in libraries.* 2nd ed., revised. Chicago, American Library Association, 1973. 20–41.
2. Line, M.B. 'The British Library Lending Division', in Saunders (ed), *British librarianship today.* London, Library Association, 1976. 86–107.
3. International Organization for Standardization. *Documentation-International Standard Serial Numbering (ISSN).* ISO 3297, Geneva, ISO, 1975.
4. Davinson, D. *The periodicals collection.* Revised and enlarged ed. London, André Deutsch, 1978. 7–15.

Part 1
PROCESSES AND OPERATIONS

1

Bibliographic Sources And Data Bases

A. J. Walford

PUBLISHED LISTS AND THEIR USES FOR SELECTION

Ideally, a selected list of serials should be grouped by subjects (preferably in classified rather than alphabetical order of subjects, so as to associate affinities). For each serial it should state aim, audience and level of appeal, contents, subject coverage, availability of an index or indexes, publisher, frequency, price and whether covered by any of the major abstracting and indexing services.

A primary selection tool, particularly for American periodicals, is the third edition of *Magazines for libraries*, by Bill Katz and Berry Gargal (New York and London, Bowker, 1978, xix + 937pp.), with sub-title, 'for the general reader, and school, junior college, college and public libraries'. It has 100-word annotations for over 4,500 titles, in subject categories A/Z, with title index. Data on each title include circulation, availability of samples, microforms and reprints, where indexed/ abstracted, inclusion of book reviews (length and whether signed), audience and evaluation. Some Canadian and British periodicals, with a few 'exceptionally important' foreign titles, find a place.

D.P.Woodworth's *Guide to current British journals* (2nd ed., London, Library Association, 1973, 2 vols.) is a pale reflection of *Magazines for libraries*. True, vol.1 has 4,585 entries in UDC order, but information on each title is skeletal and only four indexing services are quoted, including the redoubtable *IBZ*. A new edition, however, is in active preparation.

The *British national bibliography* records the first issue of new British periodicals and also the first issue of British periodicals that appear under a new title. The author and title index to the *BNB* includes a list of these titles under the heading 'Periodicals'. Such entries become subsequently available on the UK MARC data base.

Too much importance can be attached to mention by indexing and abstracting services as a claim to selection. Again, using the hypothesis that citation of a document indicates use of that document by the citing author, Martyn and Gilchrist started with a check list of 1,842 British journal titles; it was found that 590 (32 per cent) were cited.[1] The last of five tables lists the top 165 titles, with their publishers.

A current selection tool is the quarterly *Serials Review* (Ann Arbor, Mich., Pierian Press, 1975–), which aims to review 'both new and well-established periodicals, providing in depth evaluations and comparisons'. In 1975 59 journals and 41 reference serials (including a number of indexes) were reviewed. In general, this is a field in which the British effort falls well behind the American.

A selection tool may be concerned with a specific audience in mind, and here we are on surer ground. E. I. Farber's *Classified list of periodicals for the college library* (5th ed., Westwood, Mass., Faxon, 1972, 449 pp.) chooses 937 titles, recommending 367 for initial purchase. *Periodicals for schools,* compiled by C. A. Wait (London, School Library Association, 1969, ix + 45 pp.) has brief evaluative annotations on 117 titles, indicating suitable age-category, price, average pagination, and size. Arrangement is in eight topic groups, subdivided, and there is an index of titles, subjects and organizations.

The Subject Approach

Guides to the literature of particular fields or subjects, at their best, draw attention to the leading periodicals concerned. A good example is Carl M. White's *Sources of information in the social sciences: a guide to literature* (2nd ed., Chicago, American Library Association, 1973, xviii + 702 pp.) which in each of its nine divisions lists under 'Sources of scholarly contributions' the leading journals, stating where each is indexed and/or abstracted.

Medical bibliography is specially rich in selected lists of serials. *British medical periodicals: a select and annotated list* (5th ed., London, British

Council, Medical Department, 1977, 36 pp.) lists 219 titles A/Z, with brief notes on contents, and a subject index. Asterisked entries are for abstracting journals or those carrying bibliographies. *British medicine: a monthly guide* (1972–) provides updating in its section 'New periodicals or changes in titles'.

The *Bulletin of the Medical Library Association* (New York) carries, at intervals, a 'Selected list of books and journals for the small medical library'. The seventh revision (*Bulletin* 65 no.2 April 1977. 191–215) includes a list of 138 journals, American and British, of which 53 titles are asterisked as suggestions for initial purchase.

In the field of the arts there is Clive Phillpot's rewarding article, 'Art periodicals, indexing and abstracts, and modern art: an annotated topography'.[2] He picks out for comment 29 journals on contemporary art, titles that all 'just about fulfil the criteria of regular appearance and international outlook'.

A final example may be taken from the multi-disciplinary subject, geography. Chauncy D. Harris's *Annotated world list of selected current geographical serials in English, French, and German: including serials in other languages with supplementary use of English or other international languages* (University of Chicago, Department of Geography, 1971) selects, with brief annotations, 316 current geographical serials from among the 2,415 available. The basis for selection is given as the quality of geographical material; frequency, regularity and longevity of publication; citations in international bibliographies and availability in major libraries. Thirty-seven countries are covered, arrangement being by language.

Published Lists and their Uses for Bibliography

The main function of the published list of serials is to provide identification: exact title and variants, publisher and place of publication, frequency and price. For the purposes of brief identification, the more titles that are listed, the better, and such compilations as *New Serial Titles* and *BUCOP* spring to mind. But they do not meet other necessary requirements.

Ulrich's international periodicals directory: a classified guide to current periodicals, foreign and domestic (18th ed., 1979/1980) has bibliographical data on 62,000 periodicals published throughout the world. Each entry details title, publisher, price, date commenced, frequency, where indexed/abstracted, and ISSN. Subject arrangement, under 256 categories A/Z, makes *Ulrich's* a valuable aid for the librarian attempting to build in a particular subject area. Each major category has a subheading 'Abstracting. Bibliographies. Statistics', with cross-references from 'Abstracting and indexing services' and 'Statistics' as form headings — an innovation. The directory is adequately equipped with an index of titles and subjects, plus a list of cessations since the 17th edition. *Ulrich's quarterly* (1977–, vol.1–) provides supplements between the biennial editions.

The companion, *Irregular serials and annuals: an annual directory* (5th ed., 1978), similarly arranged, lists some 32,000 serials, annuals, continuations, conference proceedings and other irregular serials or those issued less frequently than twice a year. *Sources of serials: an international publisher and corporate author directory to Ulrich's and Irregular serials and annuals* (Bowker, 1977) locates 50,000 publishers of the titles listed and is particularly valuable as a key to corporate authorship.

Serials for libraries: an annotated guide to continuations, yearbooks, almanacks, transactions, proceedings, directories, services, compiled by Joan K. Marshall (New York, Neal/Schuman, 1979, xv + 494pp.) has five main classes, with descriptions of about 2,000 annuals and other serials 'suitable for collection by public, school and undergraduate libraries'. An appendix states month of publication, under both title and month/season, for some 880 of the titles. This guide, a companion to *Magazines for libraries,* is equally US-slanted but less easy to use because of its cumbersome arrangement.

The International Serials Data System (ISDS) is an intergovernmental organization established within the framework of the Unesco UNISIST programme. It aims to provide a reliable registry of world serials publications and contains essential information for the identification and bibliographic control of serials. The *ISDS Register,* supplemented at two-monthly intervals by the *ISDS Bulletin,* is available on microfiche from the ISDS International Centre in Paris.

CONSER (CONversion of SERials) is a data base of serials, contributed to by a limited number of participants and controlled bibliographically by the Library of Congress and the National Library of Canada, and a data base eventually building up to about 250,000 titles is envisaged. CONSER records are currently available on LC MARC(S) tapes.

6

Form and Subject Bibliographies of Serials

Given a special period, a compiler may hope to provide a near-exhaustive bibliography of serials. *The Waterloo directory of Victorian periodicals, 1824-1900* (Phase 1, ed. by Michael Wolff, and others; sponsored by the Research Society for Victorian Periodicals and Waterloo Computing in the Humanities, Montreal, Wilfrid Laurier University Press, 1976, xxvii + 1, 187 pp.) is an A-Z listing of 28,995 newspapers and periodicals published in England, Ireland, Scotland and Wales between 1824 and 1900. Phase 2 will be an extended version of Phase 1.

Directories of 'fringe' periodicals include: *The international directory of little magazines and small presses* (annual, 15th ed. Paradise, Calif., Dustbooks, 1979; edited by Len Fulton and Ellen Ferber), a list of more than 2,000 titles, noting editorial policy, contents, features, payment rates, back-issue prices, etc.; J. Noyce's *The directory of British alternative periodicals, 1965-1974* (Hassocks, West Sussex, Harvester Press, 1979), a descriptive record of 1,256 titles, mostly short-lived, with an index of personal names, place-names, organizations and subjects; and the triennial *Gebbie house magazine directory* (New York, Gebbie Press, 1952-), a guide to the leading American house-magazines. These help to supplement *Ulrich's*.

The numerous national annual directories of current newspapers and periodicals sometimes go beyond national boundaries. Thus, *Benn's newspaper press directory, 1978* (126th ed., London, Benn, 1977) devotes vol.2 to *Overseas* for the first time. *Willing's press guide* (105th annual ed., Croydon, Skinner's Directories, 1979) devotes a sizeable section of its 13,000 titles to European and US newspapers and periodicals. So, to a lesser degree, does the *Annuaire de la presse* (Paris, 1880-), although it is primarily a key to the Paris and French national and provincial press.

Among subject bibliographies of serials, the fourth edition of Unesco's *World list of social science periodicals* (Paris, Unesco Press, 1976, 382 pp.) represents the first application to the social sciences of the International Serials Data System, adding ISSN to titles already registered in the third edition of the *World list*. The scope now extends to secondary-source serials, review journals, abstracting and indexing services, catalogues, current-contents listings, etc. But the *List* does not include publications appearing less than once in a fortnight.

A. M. Woodward's *Directory of review serials in science and technology* (London, Aslib, 1974, iv + 57 pp.) lists some 500 titles of 'regular and quasi-regular publications containing state-of-the-art and literature reviews'. Coverage is claimed to be comprehensive for USA, UK, France, Germany and the Netherlands. *BIOSIS list of serials* (Philadelphia, Pa., BioSciences Information Service, [1977?], 251 pp.) lists 8,458 serial titles published in 117 countries and other areas that are actively covered by *Biological abstracts* and *Bioresearch index.*

The *Catalogue of the newspaper collections in the British Library* (London, British Museum Publications, 1975, 8 vols.) records 40,000 titles in two sequences: place of publication (vol.1: London; vol.2: England and Wales, Scotland, Ireland; vols. 3-4: Aden ... Zanzibar); and titles, A/Z. Its rough counterpart is the Library of Congress's *Newspapers in microform: United States, 1948-1972* (1973) with 34,289 titles reported by 843 libraries and 43 commercial firms; *Foreign countries* (1973) with over 8,600 titles; annual supplements. The annual *Ayer directory of publications* (Philadelphia, Pa., Ayer Press, 1880–) places emphasis on locality. Entries for the press of the USA, Puerto Rico, Virgin Islands, Canada, Bahamas, Bermuda, the Republic of Panama and the Philippines are arranged by country, state, and city or town.

Directories

An example of a well-used bibliography of directories is *Current British directories: a guide to the directories published in Great Britain, Ireland, the Commonwealth, Pakistan and South Africa* (Edition 9, Beckenham, CBD Research, 1979, xiii + 370 pp.). The strictly British directories are in two sequences: local and specialized, and data on each directory include a brief note on contents and special features. Some 3,000 directories, annuals, membership lists, etc. are covered in all, and there is a full index of titles, subjects and countries.

Monographs in Series

The Library of Congress's *Monographic series* (Washington, 1974–, 3 quarterlies; annual cumulation) lists series by titles, A/Z, using reproductions of Library of Congress cards. It includes many older works, especially foreign-language materials, and its frequency gives it a decided edge over E. A. Baer's *Titles in series: a handbook for librarians and students.* This latter (Metuchen, N.J., Scarecrow Press, 1964, 2 vols.; supplements 1–3, 1967–74) totals 66,368 titles, with indexes to authors and subjects, and to series titles, plus a directory of publishers.

Books in series in the United States: original, reprinted, in-print and out-of-print books, published or distributed in the United States in popular, scholarly and professional series (2nd ed., New York and London, Bowker, 1979) lists some 113,154 books in 10,837 series issued by about 1,270 publishers and distributors.

UNION LISTS OF SERIALS

The obvious functions of a union list of serials are to act as a vehicle for interloan or photocopying and to provide locations for periodicals or newspapers that must be consulted *in situ.* The union list has several variants: the publications recorded may be a 'world list' or be restricted to the output of a single country or area; locations are likely to be nationwide rather than worldwide, or they may be confined to a particular area or group of libraries within a business concern, government department library or libraries within a university campus. The barest details for identification, plus a statement of holdings (including details of gaps) and location code often suffice for an entry.

The *British union-catalogue of periodicals: a record of the periodicals of the world, from the seventeenth century to the present day in British libraries* (London, Butterworth, 1955–58, 4 vols.; *Supplement* (covering 1950-60), 1962; *New Periodical Titles, 1960-68* (1970) and 1969–1973 (1976), plus quarterly supplements and annual cumulations) has been the subject of consideration by a Working Party on Access to Serials since early 1977.[3] BUCOP's *New Periodical Titles* is to continue publication until the end of 1980, to be followed by a new service based on the British Library and certain other libraries chosen for either their specialist holdings or geographical location. The holdings are also to be recorded in the BLAISE MARC (British Library Automated Information Service. Machine Readable Cataloguing) files; 'an on-line service through BLAISE would include input from any libraries wishing to contribute'. The BLLD's *Current serials received* (April 1979, 455 pp.) contains about 51,500 titles; in the sense that its holdings are reinforced by a back-up service from other libraries, it constitutes a union list.

BUCOP's US counterpart, the third edition of *Union list of serials in the libraries of the United States and Canada* (New York, H. W. Wilson, 1965, 5 vols.) musters 156,449 titles that began prior to 1 January, 1950 (compared with about 140,000 titles in the *BUCOP* parent work). The *Union list*'s successor, *New Serial Titles, 1950-1970* (New York, Bowker, 1973, 4 vols.) lists 220,000 serials held by 800 US and Canadian libraries reporting to Library of Congress. *New Serial Titles: subject guide, 1950-1970* (New York, Bowker, 2 vols.) followed in 1975. *New Serial Titles* is itself updated by supplements (eight per annum, with quarterly and annual cumulations).

World list of national newspapers: a union list of national newspapers in libraries in the British Isles (compiled by Rosemary Webber under the auspices of the Standing Conference of National and University Libraries (SCONUL), in contract with the Social Science Research Council (Butterworths, 1978, viii + 95 pp.)) records 'all newspapers having national circulation' — some 1,500 titles. It omits newspapers that ceased before 1800, as well as emigré, religious and armed forces newspapers, political and cultural weeklies, and complements the *Catalogue of the newspaper collections in the British Library.*

Periodicals from Africa: a bibliography and union list of periodicals published in Africa, compiled by Carole Travis and Miriam Alman (Boston, Mass., G. K. Hall, 1977, xvii + 619 pp.) is an admirable example of a union list confined to the output of a continent. The 17,000 titles cover 'all African countries except Egypt, all subjects and languages from the earliest days of African publishing up to 1975'.[4] It records the holdings of some 60 British libraries, and entries are arranged country-by-country, with a title index.

G. Raymond Nunn's *Southeast Asian periodicals: an international union list* (London, Mansell, 1977, 486 pp.) is also arranged by country of publication. It lists over 26,000 periodicals originating from Southeast Asian countries (excluding Oceania and New Guinea). Locations attempt to be international but they are mostly American, and only the British Library is cited for UK holdings.

The Subject Approach

The *World list of scientific periodicals* — whose fate is presumably bound up with that of *BUCOP* — had its fourth edition, covering 1900–1960, in 1963–65 (Butterworth, 3 vols.). It recorded 59,961 items in 247 British libraries. Although incorporated thereafter in *BUCOP*'s *New Periodical Titles*, there is a separate annual: *World list of scientific periodicals: scientific, medical and technical entries from the British union-catalogue of periodicals: New periodical titles.*

The Institute of Advanced Legal Studies' *Union catalogue of legal periodicals: a location guide to the holdings of legal periodicals in libraries in the United Kingdom* (1978, xix + 316 pp.) lists about 3,500 titles in 114 libraries, including BLLD, although accessibility, in general, is not stated. A *Union list of statistical serials in British libraries*, published for the Committee of Librarians and Statisticians, Library Association and Royal Statistical Society (London, Library Association, 1972, 86 pp.) gives locations for some 400 titles in 270 libraries. The bulk of the titles are government publications, mostly departmental. One appendix briefly locates overseas statistics; another is a 'Subject guide'.

The Committee on Latin America (COLA) has so far produced three in its survey of holdings of Latin American periodicals in UK libraries, *Latin American serials: Latin American economic and social serials* (1969), *Latin American history, with politics* (1973) and *Literature, with language, art and music* (1977). Each records some 1,000 titles in 80–90 libraries. Entries are grouped under countries/areas, with a title index.

The National Library of Medicine is expanding to 35,000 titles its on-line serials file. 'This will include ceased titles. The new development will be known as SERLINE, and will include location information for 6,500 serials in 120 libraries, to facilitate interlibrary loans.'[5]

Local Union Lists

The value of the local — as opposed to the national — list can be appreciable. It often forms part of a local library co-operative scheme; it provides a speedy service and can use inter-library transport, as in the London Inter-library Transport Scheme.[6] The *Essex union list of serials* (no.13, Autumn 1977, Chelmsford, Essex County Library, x + 672 pp.) records over 11,000 titles at 76 localities, including the University of Essex and various college libraries. Thanks to a computer data base, revised editions appear each March and September. The Cambridge University Library's *Current serials* (1976, 2 vols.) has a main A/Z title sequence of about 35,000 titles. University Library holdings are in bold type; other holdings are for 95 departmental and college libraries. The classified list appended to volume 2 (also available separately) is followed by a subject index. A single volume covering non-current serials will also shortly be published. The University of London is also currently compiling a union list of serials in its various libraries, but it is uncertain whether this list, when complete, will be made generally available. Libraries are not necessarily the main repositories of local newspapers. *Newspapers first published before 1900 in Lancashire, Cheshire and the Isle of Man: a union list of holdings in libraries or newspaper offices within that area*, edited by R. E. G. Smith (London, Library Association, Reference, Special and Information Section, 1964, 47 pp.) lists holdings of no less than some 400 newspapers for more than a hundred locations. Arrangement is by towns, with an index of titles and all towns mentioned in titles or sub-titles.

REFERENCES

1. Martyn, J. and Gilchrist, A. *An evaluation of British scientific journals.* London, Aslib, 1968. vii.
2. *ARLIS Newsletter* no. 19 June 1974. 11–21.
3. 'Eventual successor to BUCOP'. *British Library News* no. 31 July 1978. 1.
4. *African Research & Documentation* no. 15 1977. 12.
5. *Information Hotline* 10 no. 2 Feb. 1978. 7-8.
6. 'Transport of inter-library loans'. *British Library News* May 1978. 1.

2

Acquisition Methods

R. Baker

INTRODUCTION

The study and re-evaluation of existing acquisition methods should be a continuing task of any periodicals librarian. Changes in existing methods of supply for established serials should be avoided where possible, since the initiation of such changes is a time-consuming exercise fraught with risks of breaks in supply or the receipt of duplicates. It is better, if the service is poor, to do all that can be done to improve it, by tidying up routines or bullying an agent or publisher to give a better service.

The methods available for acquiring serials can be discussed under three headings: purchase, exchange and donation. Which method is best in any particular case depends upon the nature of the serial itself, the publisher and the library. Libraries with substantial holdings of serials inevitably find themselves using a variety of methods.

PURCHASE

The librarian who needs to purchase has the following options. He may approach the publisher or his distributing agent directly, he may place a subscription with a local distributor, or he may use a library subscription agent.

Dealing with the Publisher

There are so many publishers that if a library with a significant holding of current serials deals directly with each it will be involved in a proliferation of correspondence and cheque writing. Subscription agents flourish because they have organized themselves to take some of this load off the library's staff.

However, direct orders are advisable for many serials and necessary for some. Some publishers will not deal through an agency; others discourage the use of agents by offering no special discounts or offering the direct subscriber better terms. Many of the bigger publishers, such as Pergamon Press, McGraw-Hill and Academic Press, have set up well-organized distribution services so that the library which takes several serials from such a publisher may find it convenient to deal direct. There may sometimes be an advantage in dealing direct for highly-priced serials if the agent is charging for his services at a fixed percentage of the subscription rate. However, if the agent has determined his percentage charge to a library having taken account of the need for these higher-priced serials he may need to increase his percentage mark-up if these are taken away from him. Agents do not gain greatly from handling low-priced and irregular serials. Sometimes publishers of such serials respond better to queries from librarians than they do to those from agents, and then it may be better to deal direct.

Memberships

There are some society, trade association or institutional publications which are only available to members, and there are others where members are offered preferential terms. In such cases a membership may be taken out in the name of the library, its parent organization, or an individual. Most organizations of this kind are willing to accept a library as a corporate member.

Local Distributors

The man in the street who wishes to buy a newspaper, or a mass circulation periodical, automatically turns to a local newsagent. The distribution of such serials is geared to operate most efficiently through such outlets and, in consequence, use of them will ensure the most rapid supply. Servicing the initial order can be almost instantaneous if the serial concerned is handled by the chosen supplier. Initiating an order in any other way takes time.

In dealing with local suppliers the price charged will normally be the publisher's cover price. Discounts to suppliers of such serials are usually reasonably generous, so one may get a better financial deal through a library subscription agent who may pass on some of this discount.

Library Subscription Agents

Most libraries with significant holdings of serials use one or more subscription agents.[1] The agent stands between the librarian and the publisher, serving them both. In the words of the Bookdealer-Library Relations Committee of the American Library Association 'Agents accept the responsibility of providing centralized placement of orders and payments and helping to insure prompt and continuing supply of serials ordered by libraries.' The prompt and continuing supply can only be maintained with the co-operation of the publisher; 'publishers' activities are beyond the control of the agent, but the agent is in the best position to obtain and forward information in either direction'.[2]

Payment for the agent's services can come from both sides: from the publisher as discounted prices which are not available to the direct subscriber, and/or from the library in the way of charges added to the subscriptions paid. In the past discounts were sufficiently generous to enable the agent to offer serials to the library at the publishers' prices and still cover his own costs. If the list contained a substantial proportion of mass circulation periodicals where discounts were high the agent might be in a position to bargain for the library's custom by passing on some of the discount. Nowadays discounts are being squeezed and the agent has to look to the librarian for a greater proportion of his costs.

The librarian has to weigh up any extra subscription costs involved in using an agent against the convenience and saving in staff costs that ensue. The major saving in staff effort comes from the reduction in the number of invoices to pay, since the agent will combine in one bill invoices for numbers of serials from many publishers. Most agents will present their invoices to the librarian for payment according to the librarian's convenience. This can mean that all subscriptions are covered in one major payment or that invoices are spread throughout the year. If an attempt is made to combine all subscriptions in one annual bill it is usually necessary to send a number of small adjustment invoices later since the agent cannot always know what changes in publishers' subscription prices will arise, and it is normal practice to bill for new subscriptions separately. The librarian should be able to trust the agent to renew with the publisher in good time and therefore should not need to keep a record to check when payments for individual serials become due.

A record of payment for each serial is needed and this is best kept on the serial's check-in record. Then the check-in clerk can be aware of the state of payment when he considers what action to take if there is a break in supply.

It should be most efficient for a library to place all its purchased serials with a single agent. Most libraries will, however, spread their custom to cushion the risk of an agent going out of business and to gain experience with more than one agent. If foreign serials are required care should be taken to use an agent with the capability and experience to service serials from the country concerned. If only well-known commercial journals are wanted then there is every likelihood that the agent dealing with the library's home-produced serials would cope well enough. He should be able to deal with foreign currency payments and correspondence in foreign languages. However, when there are a number of serials from a particular country (some of which may be irregular) and the library also buys books from that country, a foreign agent can be a distinct advantage. He should have an instinctive feel for the ways of the publishing country and be better placed to sort out bibliographic problems, to locate publishers and obtain answers from them. Once having decided to use a foreign agent it is best to place all the library's subscriptions from that region with him.

In some situations it is useful to have an overseas agent who will collect issues of serials locally and send them in batches to the library. He will be able to chase missing items locally more promptly. In the Science Reference Library many Japanese serials come this way and it is found useful to have a German agent collect parts of those German serials that are issued irregularly and priced separately.

Choosing an Agent

If one has to choose a new agent the best first step is to consult with other libraries with a similar serials list to one's own. Ask them about the agents they use, whether they deal in the range of journals that one wishes to place with them, whether they answer letters promptly, whether their invoices are easy to understand and check, and whether their charges are reasonable. In the United States guides to subscription agents have been published, the most detailed being that by Bill Katz and Peter Gellatly.[1] This book contains a considerable amount of detailed information about agents' services, obtained by sending questionnaires to both librarians and agents. A particularly relevant section to the selection of agents is that which gives a check list of the services provided. The questions asked of the agents provide a useful guide to the type of question that a librarian should put to the representatives of prospective new agents. The book is restricted to coverage of agents operating in America, including most of the major agents operating in the United Kingdom, but British agents who do not serve American libraries are not listed. A more recent check list of questions to be considered in evaluating or comparing agents' services has been compiled by Kuntz.[3]

Agents' Invoicing Practices and Charges

Agents vary in the ways in which they collect their charges, in the amounts they charge, and in the degree of openness that they display in clarifying their charges to their customers. Many agents calculate their charges as a direct percentage of the price that they pay the publishers. The agent then gets a better return from the higher-priced serials which are normally more reliable and involve less work for the agent than the low-priced serials which may be fighting for survival and are more prone to changes in title or publication pattern. The agent would be justified in charging a higher percentage to the library with a subscription list of low-priced serials than to one with mainly high-priced periodicals. A few agents levy a fixed charge per serial, which may seem fairer, but it is not satisfactory from the agent's point of view because, when the charge has to be increased to meet rising costs, the increase is less acceptable to the client than the automatic increase in revenue that ensues from a fixed percentage of rising serial subscriptions. Some agents operate complex charging schemes involving a minimum charge for low-priced serials, a percentage charge for average price serials and a scaled-down percentage for expensive subscriptions; Swets Subscription Service do this.

Many agents still quote cover prices on their invoices to libraries and add a service charge on top of this. This service charge may be noted separately for each serial or, in some cases, it may be added to the end of a listed invoice. In either case it is difficult to ascertain, from the invoice alone, what the charging policy is. Ebsco Subscription Services, for example, quote cover prices on customers' invoices, but calculate their mark-up as a percentage of the total of the prices that they pay the publishers, this percentage varying with the average value of the subscriptions listed on the invoice.

For foreign serials some agents collect part of their charges by using generous exchange rates. This can be justified in times of fluctuating exchange values when payments to the publishers are not simultaneous with payments from the library.

Time to Establish the Supply of a New Serial

The *ALA guidelines*[2] advise that orders for new serials be placed 'generally three months before the date of the first issue required'. A similar timescale is suggested by agents' literature. A routine order through an agent has to be processed and recorded by the library, sent to the agent, recorded and processed by the agent and sent to the publisher. The publisher will check the order and may demand prepayment if the agent has not already anticipated this; he will then have to organize the printing of the library's address on his distribution list and a label for the first issue to be sent will be included in the next label run.[4] The post is involved three times, in the transfer of the order, from the library to the agent and from the agent to the publisher, and for the serial part, from the publisher to the library. Time can sometimes be saved by missing out the agent, but the greatest delays are usually with the publisher. The agent probably has more experience with the publisher, which may enable him to expedite the order more quickly. Use of the phone to transmit orders can also help to save time in some cases. Particular care must be taken in timely ordering if the library wishes its holdings to start at the beginning of a volume. Commercial publishers do not these days always retain back issues of their serials so that missed issues may have to be sought from another source.

Bibliographic Services of Agents

The agent is ideally placed to gather information about the vagaries of periodical publications. He is obliged to maintain up-to-date information about serial titles and publishers' addresses and, from feedback from his library customers, can be as aware as anyone of any breaks in publication, changes of title and so on. Some agents publish lists of serial titles with their prices.[5,6,7,8] Many of these can be obtained by libraries not using the agent concerned (after all, it may encourage new business). Those agents not publishing lists will often be able to provide, from their own records, help in identifying titles or filling out other information necessary to place an order.

Some agents also produce regular news bulletins which give information about new titles, the demise of old ones, changes of title, and the latest issues of irregulars.[9,10,11] Their use can sometimes save the fruitless pursuit of non-existent serial issues.

EXCHANGES

When a library's parent body has a substantial publication programme of its own, it appears an attractive proposition for the librarian to barter with copies of these in order to obtain publications issued by other corporate bodies. The librarian can usually call upon his own organization's publications without there being any drain on his acquisitions budget. The direct cost to the organization as a whole appears small since there are usually spare copies on the print run. The setting up of an exchange involves more staff effort, and probably at a higher level, than that required to set up a purchased subscription. Once the arrangement is running, it should — if it concerns only regular serials — require less effort to keep it running since there are no payments to be made.

When a library does not have free access to publications it is still possible to enter into exchange deals using purchased material to send to the exchange partner. Such exchanges are uneconomic and direct purchase is to be preferred where this is possible. There are, however, many foreign serials which cannot be obtained through commercial channels and the librarian must forgo these altogether if he will not resort to exchanges. The types of material involved often include academic, university and library publications, dissertations, theses, reports and official publications.[12] Many librarians in countries where hard currency is in short supply need to organize exchanges to obtain serials from Western sources.

The British Library Lending Division, who have few publications of their own and regard exchange as a last resort acquisitions method, receive over 13,000 of their current intake of 50,000 serials on exchange. They pay for British serials to be sent overseas. When this is done, it is best to ask a subscription agency to service the subscriptions to serials being sent abroad. The subscription agent pays the publisher, deals with enquiries about delivery of parts, and invoices the home library as required.

Exchanges of Duplicates and Other Unwanted Material

What is being disposed of by one library may well be needed by another. If such material is passed on the major cost involved is that of transporting the material. A difficulty exists in identifying a library in need when there is material for disposal. In the United Kingdom the British Library Lending Division's Gift and Exchange Section[13] acts as a centre where duplicate material can be sent. The Centre accepts donated material and circulates, both domestically and internationally, lists of what is available. It may sometimes be possible to pick up wanted back-runs from this source.

Other countries operate similar co-operative schemes. In the United States, for example, the major scheme is the Universal Serials and Book Exchange, but more limited schemes include the ALA's Duplicate Exchange Union, the Medical Library Association Exchange and the Science Book and Serial Exchange.

The international co-ordination of exchanges has been an interest of Unesco since it came into being. Considering the exchange of literature to be an essential form of international scientific and cultural co-operation, they have encouraged the setting up of national exchange centres and prodded governments into exchanging official publications. In the United Kingdom the British Library's Reference Division acts as the centre for the exchange of official publications while the Lending Division's Gift and Exchange Section carries out some of the other duties that might fall to a national exchange centre. A list of the exchange centres in countries throughout the world is given in the Unesco *handbook on international exchange*,[14] which also gives a wealth of information about the history of exchanges, the types of exchange, the international framework, the functions of exchange centres and so on.

Balancing Exchanges

The Unesco *Handbook*[14] says 'a generous attitude should always be adopted ... some kind of balance is desirable, in order to preserve the difference between exchange and a mere gift'. Overmuch bickering about exchange balances can be costly in terms of staff time. Scientific and other learned bodies, whose main interest is in disseminating knowledge about their own work and keeping up to date with other work in the same field, can afford to overlook any question of balance in financial terms. At the other end of the spectrum, the librarian who has entered into an exchange agreement in order to obtain publications not available to him in any other way may be under pressure to keep a watchful eye on balancing costs. If the material is commercially priced then the commercial value may be used to evaluate a balance. Alternatively, a piece-by-piece or page-by-page comparison can be made.

DONATION

Most libraries receive unsolicited donations. When an issue of a new serial arrives in this way the librarian has a decision to make. If the serial looks to be of value to the library, a letter should be sent asking the donor to continue the supply. If the original had been sent in the hope that a new subscription would be placed this will quickly be made clear. Often, however, a continuing donation will ensue because the donor is pleased that his publication should reach the library's readers. If the donated material is not wanted it can be thrown away either immediately or after displaying it for a while for readers to see. Whatever decision is made, it should be recorded so that if later issues arrive the check-in staff will know what to do with them and not waste time searching in vain or referring for a decision.

It is well to remember that there are many organizations who may react favourably to a direct request for the donation of their publications. When asking for the supply of publications from any organization that is not a commercial publisher, it often pays to make the first approach direct, expressing interest and asking for issues to be sent. One may finish up having to pay for a subscription in the normal way, in which case the renewal can be transferred to an agent. If the organization is overseas one may well finish up with an exchange, but a straight donation is always a possibility.

REFERENCES

1. Katz, B. and Gellatly, P. *Guide to magazine and serial agents.* New York and London, R.R. Bowker Company, 1975.
2. *Guidelines for handling library orders for serials and periodicals.* Chicago, American Library Association, 1973.
3. Kuntz, H. 'Serial agents: selection and evaluation'. *Serials Librarian* 2 no. 2 Winter 1977. pp. 139–50.
4. Greenfield, S. R. '. . . and the subscription agent'. *Special Libraries* 63 no. 7 July 1972. 293, 298–304.
5. Dawson Subscription Service. *Guide to the press of the world, 1978, Little Red Book.* Folkestone, Wm Dawson and Sons Ltd, 1978 (almost 5,000 titles).
6. *Librarians' handbook 1978-1979.* 2 vols. Birmingham, Alabama, EBSCO Subscription Services, 1978 (approximately 100,000 titles).
7. *1977 Librarians' guide.* Westwood, Mass., F.W. Faxon Company Inc., 1977 (over 80,000 titles).
8. *Librarians' periodical guide.* vol. 3. North Cochocton, N.Y., Moore-Cottrell Subscription Agencies Inc., 1978 (over 30,000 titles).
9. *Faxon's serials updating service.* Westwood, Mass., F.W. Faxon Company Inc.
10. *Stechert Macmillan News.* New York, Stechert Macmillan Inc.
11. *Swets Info: information on current periodicals/serials.* Lisse, Swets Subscription Service.
12. Gombocz, I. 'Economic aspects of the exchange of publications'. *Unesco Bulletin for Libraries* 25 no. 5 Sept.-Oct. 1971. 267–332.
13. Allardyce, A. 'International exchange of duplicate publications at the Lending Division'. *Interlending Review* 6 no. 2 60–1.
14. Vanwijngaerden, F. (ed.). *Handbook on the international exchange of publications.* Paris, Unesco, 1978.

3

Checking and Claiming

R. H. de Vere

hecking and claiming and the associated process of renewing subscriptions provide the means of maintaining the completeness of a serials collection; and the serials receipt records form a detailed account of the collection which can be used to provide statistical data as well as to answer enquiries about the holdings. This chapter sets out to explain these processes; it is devoted to manual systems since these predominate at present, but some references to computer-aided systems additional to those provided in Chapter 18 are also given.

Other general treatments of the subject are to be found in Brown,[1] Davinson,[2] Osborn,[3] and Woodworth.[4]

RECORD SYSTEMS AND DATA

The chief factor governing the choice of recording system is the size of the collection. For small collections there is little to choose between them since the time spent manipulating the records is so short that differences are negligible; this is not so for large collections and the choice of system becomes important.

A system suitable for serials control must be easy to search, easy to update and hospitable to new records. In practice, the available systems are:

(i) Conventional card files: hospitable to new records but not always easy to search, and cards have to be withdrawn for updating, with the risk of re-filing errors.

(ii) Rotating drum file: here the above criticisms are overcome to some extent since all the cards are securely locked in and fall flat for writing on as the drum is turned.

(iii) Visible strip index: probably the most widely used system today. Cards are securely hinged into the sides of a shallow tray so that they lie flat, one upon the other; each is displaced relative to the card beneath it to reveal about 1 cm of the bottom edge of the lower card — the visible strip which bears the entry term. A standard size of cabinet holds 18 trays, each containing 70 records. Cards are easy to locate, new ones may be inserted quickly and they are easy to write on. A disadvantage is that two people cannot use one cabinet simultaneously, so one person can block 1,200 or so records. The visible strip may be a separate piece (often coloured) sliding into a transparent slot on the card holder; in addition to the entry term it may also carry data codes and a sliding marker to indicate when action (e.g. receipt of a part) is due.

(iv) Loose-leaf ledgers: easy to use, hospitable to new records, and neighbouring volumes can be used by two people simultaneously without conflict. A visible index version has the records staggered vertically so that the bottom edge of each record protrudes below that of its predecessor; on opening, several forms are presented and the page has the appearance of a list. Each 'page' is backed by a stiff divider to provide support for writing. A typical file has 15 records per page and 35 pages per volume.

Serial Receipt Records

Regardless of the nature of the system used, each record has to accommodate permanent (i.e. rarely changed) and variable (i.e. frequently updated) statements. In some cases simple codes may be used.

Permanent data:

(i) Title. Titles provide the principal means of access to the records. They may be strict catalogue entries and so have the support of the catalogue should a receipt record prove hard to find; but very long entries are difficult to contain in a limited space. An alternative is to use apparent title, i.e. as seen on the covers by the recording clerks; but not everybody 'sees' the same title, and problems arise when staff leave or cover formats change; and the catalogue can provide no help in problem cases.

(ii) Catalogue entry. A fairly full entry is required in the record if the check-in procedure is to detect potential catalogue changes. A duplicate catalogue card filed with the record is a simple way of achieving this.

(iii) ISSN may in future form the main entry term to a serials record system, but many more serials need to be numbered before that can happen, and ready access to a catalogue will still be required for coping with problems arising from duplicate numbers and misprints. Meanwhile ISSN serve as useful checks in the case of difficult titles, e.g. similar titles, or works printed in non-roman scripts.

(iv) Location. This must be precise so that each new part may be correctly addressed.

(v) Title pages, indexes and contents lists. Their existence should be indicated and notes provided on when and how they are to be obtained.

(vi) Type of serial, e.g. periodical, newspaper, monograph series, etc.

(vii) Special physical form, e.g. microfilm, microfiche, videotape, film, sound recording, etc.

(viii) Source. Main sources of supply may be indicated by a simple code; names and addresses are required for the lesser-known suppliers.

(ix) Method of acquisition. Annual subscription, standing order, order when published, institutional membership, exchange, donation, etc. Enter details of exchange arrangements in the notes.

(x) Purchase fund.

(xi) Country of origin.

(xii) Language.

(xiii) Frequency of publication should be visible at a glance since it is a factor in implementing claims procedures. Colour-coded visible index strips are very effective here.

(xiv) Notes. Brief notes are required for (v) and (ix) above, and for any other special problems or special actions.

Variable data

(xv) Registration. Considerable space is required to register the receipt of each serial part. Year, month, volume, part, date of receipt must all be neatly recorded and clearly distinguished. The format of these records is determined by the frequency of publication. Forms and cards may be purchased ready made, but many libraries prefer to design their own. Examples are shown in Figs. 3.1–4.

(xvi) Payment. Space is required for details of parts renewed, price, location of invoice and date.

The simplest filing order is a single alphabetical sequence — with several work stations for the larger collections. Separate sequences may offer some advantages (e.g. to separate regular from irregular publications, or titles from different countries, etc.), but these advantages may be discounted by the more complicated preliminary sort required. In order to slim the active file, closed titles and full records may be kept in a separate sequence, but summarize the full card on the new one first. Many libraries discard such records (when all relevant problems have been dealt with) but others, particularly those with research collections, prefer to retain them for future reference — for date of receipt, or for details of deficiencies, losses, etc.

There is no 'right' size for the record but experience shows that 8″ × 5″ is comfortable and that 3″ × 5″ is not.

Accounts Records

Two files are required to control invoices:

(i) Suppliers' file — to register receipt of invoices and to record broad payment details. A record is required for each supplier, with space for invoice number, date of receipt, amount due, amount paid, cheque number and date paid. File the records first by year, then by suppliers' name; in this way they are easily located, whilst keeping the current file small.

(ii) Invoice file. Keep invoices for seven years; file these also by year and supplier.

Binding Records

These are usually maintained separately, but binding details are sometimes entered on the receipt record.

PROCEDURES

Opening and Sorting Mail

Open the mail carefully and insert the envelopes and wrappers into the parts for possible future consultation. Sort the mail into working order.

Preliminary Examination

Compare each serial item with the receipt records to determine whether it is a continuation of an established title (including changes of title), the first part of a title on order, or an unsolicited item. Also at this stage examine each part for imperfections (e.g. missing or mutilated pages, illegible printing, etc.) and inserts (e.g. supplements, advertisements, errata slips, etc.), and initiate the appropriate action.

Recording Continuations

For straightforward continuations enter details of the individual parts (year, volume, part number, etc.) and date of receipt; record receipts in strict order of numeration so that skipped issues may be detected. The dates provide a receipt pattern on which a claims programme can be based; they also help answer enquiries about expected issues. After registration, pencil the location on the cover or title page, discard the wrappers, and send for shelving.

New Titles

On receipt of the first issue(s) of a new title create a temporary receipt record (to handle continuations whilst the earlier parts are processed) and pass the part(s) on for further processing. When all the necessary data (i.e. approved title, location, catalogue entry) are to hand, upgrade the record to permanent status.

If the work is rejected at this stage, no further documentation is

Figure 3.1 Serials receipt record — weekly card for bi-weekly publication.

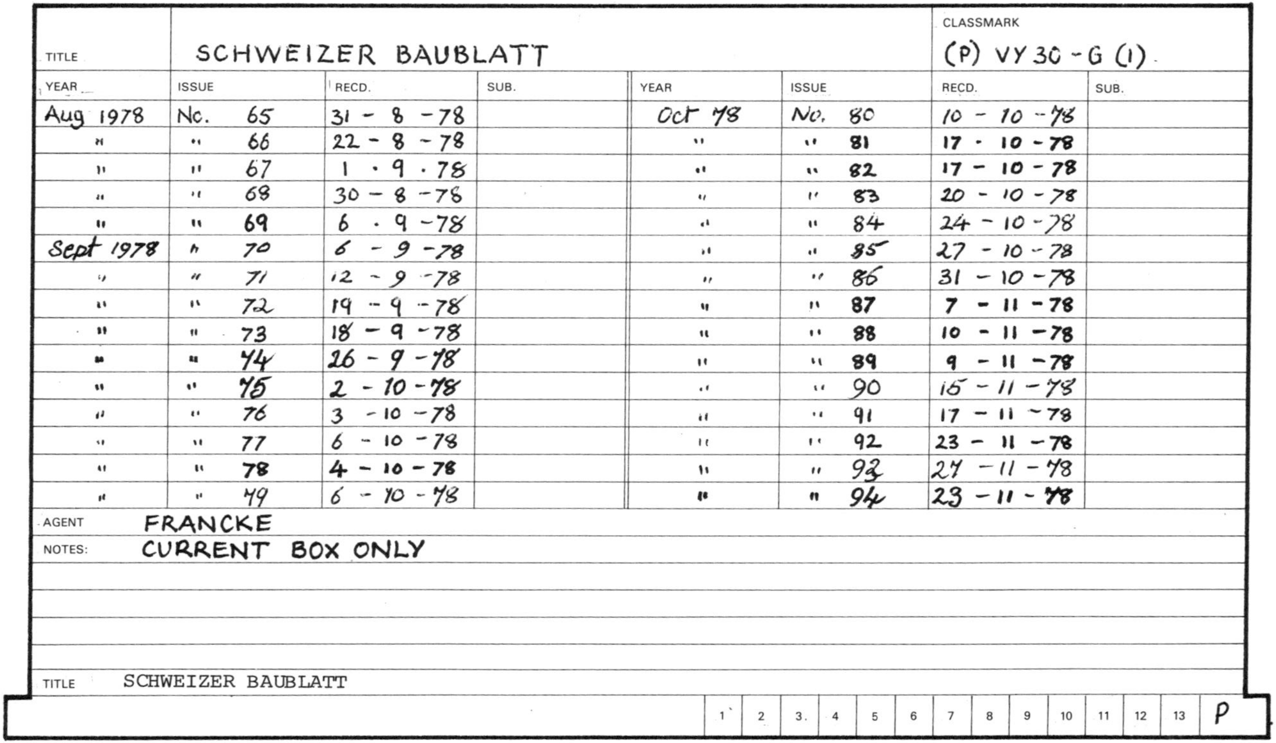

TITLE SCHWEIZER BAUBLATT — CLASSMARK (P) VY 30 - G (1)

YEAR	ISSUE	RECD.	SUB.	YEAR	ISSUE	RECD.	SUB.
Aug 1978	No. 65	31 - 8 - 78		Oct 78	No. 80	10 - 10 - 78	
"	" 66	22 - 8 - 78		"	" 81	17 - 10 - 78	
"	" 67	1 · 9 · 78		"	" 82	17 - 10 - 78	
"	" 68	30 - 8 - 78		"	" 83	20 - 10 - 78	
"	" 69	6 · 9 - 78		"	" 84	24 - 10 - 78	
Sept 1978	" 70	6 - 9 - 78		"	" 85	27 - 10 - 78	
"	" 71	12 - 9 - 78		"	" 86	31 - 10 - 78	
"	" 72	19 - 9 - 78		"	" 87	7 - 11 - 78	
"	" 73	18 - 9 - 78		"	" 88	10 - 11 - 78	
"	" 74	26 - 9 - 78		"	" 89	9 - 11 - 78	
"	" 75	2 - 10 - 78		"	" 90	15 - 11 - 78	
"	" 76	3 - 10 - 78		"	" 91	17 - 11 - 78	
"	" 77	6 - 10 - 78		"	" 92	23 - 11 - 78	
"	" 78	4 - 10 - 78		"	" 93	27 - 11 - 78	
"	" 79	6 - 10 - 78		"	" 94	23 - 11 - 78	

AGENT FRANCKE

NOTES: CURRENT BOX ONLY

TITLE SCHWEIZER BAUBLATT

1 2 3 4 5 6 7 8 9 10 11 12 13 P

Figure 3.2 Serials receipt record — monthly.

CLASSMARK

TITLE: THE SOUTH AFRICAN BUILDER

(P) W MOO—E (12)

SUB.	£3·49 (1976)	85/76 £4·56	50/77 £5·15 (1975)	41/78 £5·15
VOL.	53	204/75 54	55	56
YEAR	1975	1976	1977	1977
JAN 1	1- 24-3-75	1- 3-10-76	1- 24-2-77	1-17-3-78
FEB 2	2- 15-4-75	2- 1-4-76	2- 1-4-77	2-21-4-78
MAR 3	3- 9-5-75	3- 5-5-76	3- 24-4-77	3-4-7-78
APR 4	4- 30-6-75	4-10-6-76	4-21-6-77	4-12-6-78
MAY 5	5- 15-5-75	5- 12-7-76	5-28-6-77	5-22-8-78
JUN 6	6- 8-8-75	6-29-7-76	6-22-7-77	6-22-8-78
JUL 7	7- 3-9-75	7- 31-8-76	7-31-8-77	7-21-9-78
AUG 8	8- 3-10-75	8-23-9-76	8-22-9-77	8-23-10-78
SEP 9	9- 5-11-75	9-	9-22-11-77	9-1-12-78
OCT 10	10- 9-12-75	10-	10-29-12-77	10-15-12-78
NOV 11	11- 2-1-76	11- 7-1-77	11- 1-3-78	suppl-19-1-79
DEC 12	12- 12-2-76	12-11-2-77	12-16-3-78	11-2-3-79
13			21/77 + INV £1·54	12-21-2-79

T.P.I.

AGENT: STOBART. 534.

NOTES: Please also see 1968 — 1974 Complete.

TITLE: SOUTH AFRICAN BUILDER

S. AFRICA

J F M A M J JY A S O N D P

29

Figure 3.3 Serials receipt record — quarterly.

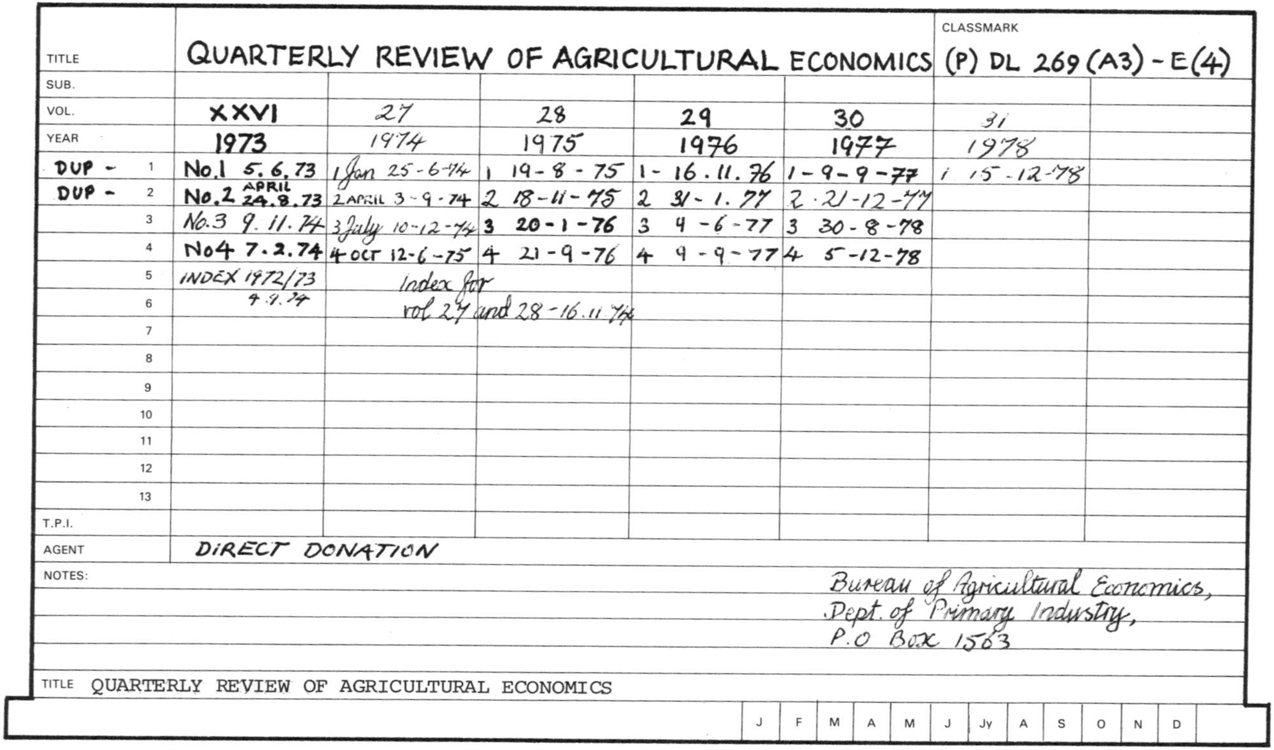

TITLE		QUARTERLY REVIEW OF AGRICULTURAL ECONOMICS					CLASSMARK (P) DL 269 (A3) - E(4)	
SUB.								
VOL.		XXVI	27	28	29	30	31	
YEAR		1973	1974	1975	1976	1977	1978	
DUP -	1	No.1 5.6.73	1 Jan 25-6-74	1 19-8-75	1- 16.11.76	1-9-9-77	1 15-12-78	
DUP -	2	No.2 APRIL 24.8.73	2 APRIL 3-9-74	2 18-11-75	2 31-1.77	2 21-12-77		
	3	No.3 9.11.74	3 July 10-12-74	3 20-1-76	3 4-6-77	3 30-8-78		
	4	No4 7.2.74	4 OCT 12-6-75	4 21-9-76	4 9-9-77	4 5-12-78		
	5	INDEX 1972/73	Index for					
	6	4.9.74	vol 27 and 28 - 16.11.76					
	7							
	8							
	9							
	10							
	11							
	12							
	13							
T.P.I.								
AGENT		DIRECT DONATION						

NOTES:

Bureau of Agricultural Economics,
Dept. of Primary Industry,
P.O Box 1563

TITLE QUARTERLY REVIEW OF AGRICULTURAL ECONOMICS

J	F	M	A	M	J	Jy	A	S	O	N	D

Figure 3.4 Serials receipt record — annual.

TITLE	ANNUAL REPORT: PRAIRIE FARM REHABILITATION AND RELATED ACTIVITIES. CANADA							CLASSMARK (P) DL70 (P) - E (1)	
YEAR	ISSUE	RECD.	SUB.	YEAR	ISSUE	RECD.	SUB.	RECD.	SUB.
1966 - 67	✓	*(stamp)*							
1967 - 68	✓								
1968 - 69	✓								
1969 - 70	✓	15 - 4 - 71							
1970 - 71	✓	15 - 3 - 72							
1971 - 72	✓	22 - 3 - 73							
1972 - 73	✓	9 - 5 - 74							
1973 / 74	✓	6 - 5 - 75							
1974 / 75	✓	18 - 5 - 76							
1975 - 76	✓	8 - 7 - 77							

AGENT   Direct Donation   CURRENT BOX ONLY

NOTES: Information Services
Department of Regional Economic Expansion
401 Motherwell Building, Regina, Saskatchewan. Canada

TITLE	ANNUAL REPORT: PRAIRIE FARM REHABILITATION AND RELATED ACTIVITIES. CANADA										
	J	F	M	A	M	J	JY	A	S	O	N	D

31

required; cancel the order and annotate the order cards with the reason for the rejection and date, and file for reference in case the title is reconsidered at some future date; add instructions for dealing with continuations should they continue to arrive.

Changes of Title

The serials collection is never static; serials close, re-open, merge, split, or titles simply change; additionally there are changes of author or publisher, of frequency of publication, or of numeration; the possibilities are legion. When such changes are detected amend the serials record immediately (to aid recording future continuations). A temporary annotation (and re-filing if necessary) will suffice until the new permanent record arrives. Then notify cataloguing and binding sections of any action required on their part.

Untraced Items

There are items which arrive for no apparent reason, e.g. the first issue of an unsolicited donation or specimen copy, the first part of a changed title; or the recording clerk may simply have not found the entry. Whatever the reason such items must be re-checked at a more senior level and sutiable action initiated.

Duplicates

The difficulty here is that an apparent duplicate may in fact be part of a second set, a replacement part (whose order has not been entered on the receipt record), an extra part with the same numeration, a revised edition, or the previous part may have been recorded incorrectly. The only safe solution is to compare each duplicate at the shelf with the part already received. Genuine duplicates should be sent for disposal, although in the case of very expensive items it is a courtesy to offer to return them to the supplier.

Should a particular title continue to arrive in duplicate, note the fact (in pencil) on the receipt record, and also write to the publisher enclosing an incorrectly addressed wrapper asking him to amend his mailing list. The results are not always encouraging since publishers often consider it easier to continue sending duplicates than to modify their lists; and there is always the risk of them deleting both addresses from their lists.

Procedures

Back-runs and Replacements

A note of orders for back-runs and replacement parts must always be pencilled on the receipt record so that the parts can be correctly processed when they arrive. On their arrival, record their receipt and attach an instruction slip to notify cataloguing and binding section of action required. Deficiencies should be recorded permanently on the receipt record together with the reason, e.g. out of print.

Special Actions

Not all serials are straightforward; many require special treatment, such as supplements, superseding volumes, 'selected issues only', circulation prior to shelving, and so on. In each case a note is required on the receipt record outlining the nature of the problem and the action required.

Claims

For many reasons parts of serials fail to arrive; they may be lost in the post, sent to the wrong address or not sent at all. Whatever the reason libraries have to detect these lacunae and try to fill them.

A skipped issue is relatively easy to spot when registering the latest part; irregular titles present difficulties and only experience and careful housekeeping can help. A title which ceases to arrive can be found only by systematically examining every serials receipt record several times a year — a tedious job which is rarely done satisfactorily in large collections. Invoice checks will discover the titles affected, but often too late for a claim to be effective, and not at all for titles acquired by exchange or donation.

Claims should not be made too early since the missing parts may merely be delayed in the post and a claim will be ignored; nor too late since modern print-runs tend to be short, and stocks soon run out or are sold off to secondhand dealers, and the claim will fail. Defer claims if it is known that deliveries are delayed by factors beyond the publisher's control, e.g. postal strikes.

Not every claim elicits a response, and it is often necessary to send a second or third. The timing of claims is crucial, complicated as it is by such factors as frequency and regularity of publication, and country of origin. The following timings may serve as a guide — and be amended to meet particular cases.

Frequency of publication	Claim
Weekly	after 1 month then at monthly intervals
Monthly	after 2 months then at 2-monthly intervals
Quarterly	after 4 months then at 4-monthly intervals
Annual Semi-annual Biennial	after 6 months then at 6 monthly intervals
Irregular	within 6 months of previous issue or quoted date of publication, then at 6-monthly intervals or as soon after publication date as possible

When claiming, pencil in details on the receipt record, i.e. parts claimed, date of action, number of claim. Pre-date and file duplicate copies of the claims in a bring-forward file. Examine the file regularly and send the duplicates to the suppliers on the due date. When a claim is successful, remove the duplicates from the file, and upgrade the temporary entry on the receipt record.

The first two claims may be sent automatically (although any claim is worth a moment's thought). If these produce no satisfactory response seek further information from editorial matter in recent issues, from *BUCOP, NST,* etc., or from other libraries. Subsequent action may be to write to the publisher, to declare the missing parts deficient, or to close or delete the title.

It is usual to send claims to subscription agents (when used), since this reduces the cost and effort of mailing, and keeps agents informed of delivery problems. Most agents forward claims within a day or so of receipt. Many agents provide claims forms, but libraries often prefer to design their own. They may be simple letters or they may have a more stylized format with prepared answers. For foreign suppliers, use translated versions or multi-lingual forms. The address for reply should be impersonal (i.e. to a section) so as to avoid complications when staff change jobs. Multiple forms using NCR paper (less messy than carbon paper) will save writing second and third copies.

Increasingly subscription agents are informing their clients of delays in publication, closures, changes of title, etc. — a useful addition to, but not a replacement for, local effort. Some agents offer to collect and forward serial parts and also record receipts and claim missing issues on their clients' behalf. This has its attractions but it can introduce extra delays and will not guarantee that the parts actually reach the library, nor does it absolve the library from the responsibility of examining each issue.

Invoices, Payment, Renewal

Each year a library has to renew its serials subscriptions. This is done via subscription agents (if used) or directly with the publishers. With direct purchase, renewal is certain only when the publisher has received the approved invoice (publishers do not, as a rule, accept standing orders); agents on the other hand will often renew standing orders on their clients' behalf before their invoices are returned.

It is good practice to settle accounts promptly. In the case of direct purchase it will ensure continuity of supply; when agents are used it will help maintain good relations and avoid incurring penalties for failing to pay within a prescribed period. In spite of this injunction, always check invoices against the records before settling, and resist the temptation to pay first and check later; it is not always possible to retrieve payment made for items not received, or paid for twice. If on occasion it is necessary to break this rule, always check expensive items.

Always be on the look-out for invoices/renewal notes tucked into odd issues of journals. If these are missed or accidentally discarded the journal will stop coming. The claims procedure will eventually detect these titles, but often too late to obtain the early parts of the new volume. And always be aware that the form of a title on an invoice may differ from that used by the library.

In passing, remember that title pages, indexes and contents lists are not always part of the subscription and are sometimes invoiced separately — and sometimes have to be ordered separately. The basic steps in processing invoices are:

(i) Record receipt of an invoice on the supplier's record, i.e. invoice number, amount and receipt date.

(ii) Check the invoice against the serials receipt file to ensure for each title that:

it is part of the library's holdings — be particularly careful with similar titles.

it has not been renewed already.

it has not been cancelled recently.

it is still extant.

it has arrived satisfactorily during the current year.

the price is acceptable. A large increase for a particular work is a signal to reconsider its value to the library.

as each title is approved, enter on its receipt record against the volume renewed the invoice number, price and date — to warn against sending claims for titles which have not been renewed. When all items on the invoice have been accounted for pass the invoice for payment.

Usually payment is made by a central accounts department to whom future disputes may be referred. Alternatively, relevant information for each invoice (i.e. sum paid, cheque number, date of payment) may be fed back from the accounts section and entered on the suppliers' records.

By these means invoices are controlled, proper payments only are made, information is readily available for handling disputed payments, and claims for unrenewed titles may be avoided.

Should problems arise while processing an invoice (e.g. titles invoiced twice, no parts received during current year, etc.) delete the items and authorize payment of the revised total; but write immediately to the supplier to explain why.

Information

Providing details of holdings to readers, staff and other libraries is an important aspect of serials management. In small libraries the receipt records may be kept in the reading room for consultation by readers; intensive staff use makes this impossible for large collections, and questions are answered by staff from records kept behind the scenes.

ORGANIZATION OF WORK

Staff

The number of staff required to control a serials collection increases in proportion to three factors:

    (i) Size.

    (ii) The proportion of difficult titles (i.e. of irregular titles, exchange items, titles from difficult areas or in difficult languages).

    (iii) The degree of control required — not every library needs to pursue relentlessly every missing item, or catalogue immediately every deficiency or change of title.

Generally speaking, a difficult collection under maximum control requires one recording clerk for every 1,500–2,000 titles; in less demanding libraries, one clerk can cope with around 3,000 titles. McGregor[5] has recently published the results of his survey into the staffing of serials acquisitions sections in 48 American libraries. His survey included ordering, but it is possible to analyse his data to obtain figures for checking and claiming only. It appears that check-in and claims staff in the larger libraries can handle about 4,000 titles each, but that this figure falls to around 2,000 when the holdings fall markedly below 5,000 titles. However, the scatter in the data is large, so too much reliance cannot as yet be placed on this unexpected phenomenon.

Recording receipts is not a simple task. To the clerk's usual attributes of accuracy, neatness and concentration must be added a certain skill with languages and a basic knowledge of librarianship. Senior supervisors require a professional knowledge and must have a professional approach.

Allocation of Work

As far as possible each clerk should have full responsibility for the titles in his charge. This is relatively easy with small collections and can even include other aspects of serials processing such as ordering, but for larger collections some separation of function is inevitable. Claiming is sometimes treated as a separate operation, but this approach removes a certain element of self-correction; a better candidate is invoice processing since invoices can then be checked quickly and accurately without the distractions of other demanding work; and an invoice in one pair of hands is less likely to wander than one passed from station to station.

Written Instructions

Ensure that each member of staff has an up to date copy of the procedures. Write procedures in the imperative mood; leave no loose ends, and instruct staff to refer upwards when in doubt. Including a short preamble describing the aims of the section and relating its work to that of the library as a whole will help staff appreciate the value of their work; it will also help them to deal more effectively with problems originating outside their section.

REFERENCES

1. Brown, C.D. *Serials: acquisition and maintenance.* Birmingham, Alabama, EBSCO Industries Inc., 1973. 13–53, 127–32, 133–46, 147–54.
2. Davinson, D. *The periodicals collection.* 2nd ed. London, André Deutsch, 1978. 191–98.
3. Osborn, A.D. *Serial publications: their place and treatment in libraries.* 2nd ed., revised. Chicago, American Library Association, 1973. 121–89.
4. Woodworth, D.P. 'Bibliographic control', in Paul Mayes (ed.) *Periodicals administration in libraries.* London, Clive Bingley, 1978. 67–77.
5. McGregor, J.W. 'Serials staffing in academic libraries'. *The Serials Librarian* 1 no. 3 Spring 1977. 259–72.

REFERENCES TO COMPUTER-AIDED SYSTEMS, ADDITIONAL TO THOSE CITED IN CHAPTER 18

Buckeye, N.M. 'The OCLC serials subsystem: implementation/implications at Central Michigan University'. *The Serials Librarian* 3 no. 1 Fall 1978. 31–42.

Corey, J.F. 'OCLC and serials processing: a state of transition at the University of Illinois'. *The Serials Librarian* 3 no. 1 Fall 1978. 57–67.

De Gennaro, R. 'Wanted: a minicomputer serials control system'. *Library Journal* 102 no. 8 15 April 1977. 878–9.

De Varennes, R. 'On-line serials systems at Laval University Library'. *Journal of Library Automation* 3 no. 2 1970. 128–41.

Evans, 'G.T. Periodicals control: state of the art review', in H. William Axford, (ed), *Proceedings of the LARC Institute on Automated Serials Systems, 24-25 May, Chase Park Plaza, St Louis, Missouri.* Tempe, Arizona, LARC Association, 1973. 7–14.

Fayollat, J. *Technical processing system procedures and documentation manual: on-line serials and cataloguing modules.* Biomedical Library, University of California, Los Angeles, 1976.

Kamens, H.H. 'OCLC's serials control system: a case study'. *The Serials Librarian* 3 no. 1 Fall 1978. 43–55.

OCLC Newsletter no. 108 April 1977. 4–6; no. 115 April 1978. 3.

Silberstein, S.M. 'Computerised serial processing at the University of California, Berkeley'. *Journal of Library Automation* 8 no. 4 Dec. 1975. 299–311.

Willmering, W.J. 'Northwestern University Library's NOTIS 3 automated serials control system', in B.M. Fry (ed.), *Information management in the 1980s: proceedings of the 40th ASIS Annual Meeting, vol. 14, Chicago, Illinois, 26 Sept.-1 Oct. 1977.* Part 1 (printed volume) abstracts; part 2 (microfiche) full pages. White Plains, N.Y., American Society for Information Science, 1977. Part 2, fiche 10, frame D7.

4

Cataloguing

Jean Downs

The necessity of providing a library catalogue at all has been queried in a provocative article by Grose and Line.[1] They argue that it is feasible to arrange books and periodicals alphabetically by title and that then, since the user need only go straight to the shelves to ascertain whether what is required is available or not, a catalogue is superfluous, as circulation records will show what is on loan. It is true that in certain situations, for example where the number of periodicals taken is low, the catalogue may be dispensed with and the receipt record used in its stead, but their thesis, as applied to periodicals, assumes at least that volumes are not removed from the shelves to other locations within the library without some indication being given; that the title for which the reader is searching is that by which it is shelved, while arrangement by title is of little use to anyone who wishes to find out what material the library has on a given subject. Recourse to subject bibliographies or to the staff for help would be necessary for this, which in turn presupposes that the reader is aware of the existence of subject guides and that staff are always available to provide help.

The reasons quoted by Osborn[2] for cataloguing serials are mainly administrative and it has been said that catalogues are primarily used by library staff. Even if a catalogue is not provided for public use, in all but the smallest libraries, it will be necessary to construct one, to provide for staff use a list of what the library has in order to ensure that material is not duplicated unintentionally when ordering back-runs or new subscriptions, checking duplicates lists or accepting donations.

On the basis that records should not be duplicated unnecessarily, it is sensible that a catalogue should be provided to serve the needs of both readers and staff. It gives a statement of the library's serials collection and acts as a key to it, listing and describing the library's holdings in such a manner as to enable the user to find the material wanted from any one of a number of access points and to locate it within the library. What is arguable is not so much the provision of a catalogue but the amount of detail provided in that catalogue. It has been truly said that 'the concerns of full bibliographic description simply do not apply to most serials listings'.[3] The full detail which should be provided in a bibliography issued by a national library which will be used as a reference tool is quite irrelevant for a library which has only a small collection of periodicals, or indeed in most libraries, unless specializing in a certain subject field where the catalogue may have the additional function of providing a bibliography of serials in a particular subject. The amount of detail supplied must vary according to the type of library; the size and complexity of its serials holdings; the needs and sophistication of its users; and the other serials records kept within the library. It is interesting to see this need for differing levels of information being recognized in the second edition of the *Anglo-American cataloguing rules*.[4]

Another factor which fundamentally affects the production of a serials catalogue is the chameleon-like propensity for change displayed by serials. Unlike monograph cataloguing, where an entry once made usually remains static, virtually any or every characteristic of a serial may alter during its lifetime. Thus, almost as much effort is expended keeping pace with these changes as in cataloguing titles which are new to the library. This changeableness leads one to question whether it is necessary to record all these alterations in the catalogue, and if it is not, to decide what steps can be taken to minimize the amendments needed. How should changes in titles or in corporate-body headings associated with serials be handled? As far as the first is concerned, it seems practicable to omit from the catalogue those bibliographic details which may readily be found in published bibliographies and guides or in other records maintained by the library. Such details include the collation, which is rarely required in practice; the imprint, except where this is necessary to distinguish titles otherwise identical; and frequency of publication.

Various solutions to the problem of what to do when a title changes have been proposed over the years: entry under the earliest title; the latest title; successive titles. The first, entry under the earliest title, was advocated by the AA Code of 1908.[5] This method has the disadvantage that considerable time may be expended in establishing the earliest form of the title, which may not be well known (how many people would think of looking for *The Times* under *Daily Universal Register?*), which the library may not hold in any case and which results in a catalogue which is frustrating to use as anyone who consults the early volumes of the *British union-catalogue of periodicals* up to 1960 soon finds. Entry under the latest form of title involves much recataloguing and while both of these solutions provide in one place a bibliographic history of the title for those who may be interested, neither is very convenient when it comes to their application to the practicalities of shelf arrangement. By far the most satisfactory is the practice recommended in AACR2[4] of making a separate entry under the new form whenever the title changes. Whilst this goes against the cataloguing dictum of bringing all editions of a work together, it is doubtful whether this comparison with the editions of a book can be said to apply to serials. The successive entry principle does have the practical merit of meeting the commonest form of approach by the reader who is usually in quest of a particular reference, which will cite the title contemporary at the time it was made.

Keeping up to date with changes in the names of corporate bodies represents more of a problem. For one thing it all depends on how serials issued by corporate bodies are catalogued, a question which has occasioned considerable and continuing discussion.[7] In recent years, many libraries have abandoned the precepts in AACR1[6] in favour of cataloguing serials under the title as it appears on the piece, this being the form in which the title is usually cited in the literature and consquently sought by the reader. This practice is that favoured by AACR2[4].

Another point to be considered when producing a serials catalogue is whether there should be a separate catalogue or whether entries should be included with those for all other library materials in one sequence. There is much to be said for the latter practice. It is convenient, for example, to have everything in one place when searching for material on a given subject. Users of the catalogue often have difficulty in distinguishing clearly between serials and monographs especially when it comes to the fine distinctions that divide publishers' from monographic series. A title such as 'Advances in …' may be the proceedings of a conference or it may be a serial publication, or it can be both, and from the retrieval point of view it would be easier to find it in a single sequence. Nevertheless it has to be said that a small catalogue is easier to search than a larger one.

If it is decided to maintain a single catalogue, then it is important that consistency of presentation should be maintained. In those libraries where serials are treated as just another part of the material added to stock and their cataloguing is the responsibility of the cataloguing section, this should be a routine matter, but where there is a separate section dealing with all aspects of periodicals then the serials and cataloguing sections must liaise closely to ensure consistency.

FILING

If a separate listing is decided upon, then some attention should be given to filing title sequences, in relation to the question of filing of initials and the filing of those titles commencing with a generic word. The usual rules of filing, letter by letter or alternatively, word by word, e.g.

> *Journal and Proceedings of the Institute of Sewage Purification*
> *Journal — British Waterworks Association*
> *Journal of Materials*
> *Journal de Physique*
> *Journal für die Reine und Angewandte Mathematik*
> *Journal of the American Medical Association*

do not result in sequences which are helpful to the user, unless the exact details of the title are known. This is seldom the case: the approach is often from a title abbreviation, usually incorrect, and experience is necessary to decide whether, to take an example, *Rev. chim.* means *Revue de Chimie* or *Revista de Chimica*. (Incidentally, one suspects that a serials catalogue arranged by citations, with explanatory entries for those ubiquitous 'journals' *Ibid., Loc. Cit.,* and *Op. Cit.*, might prove to be a boon to readers.) The alternative is to ignore insignificant words in the title, e.g.

> *Journal (of the) American Medical Association*
> *Journal — British Waterworks Association*

Journal (of) Materials
Journal (de) Physique
Journal (and) Proceedings (of) the Institute (of) Sewage Purification
Journal (für die) Reine (und) Angewandte Mathematik

This produces a more useful arrangement. It can be said that it is an artificial arrangement. Alphabetical arrangement is, however, anything but simple as reference to the *ALA rules for filing catalogs*[8] will demonstrate. How to file titles commencing with or containing initials is another problem area. Should they be filed at the beginning of a sequence or should they be treated as though they formed a word? Neither solution is entirely satisfactory although the latter is preferable.

The British Library Lending Division's list of current serials[9] is arranged on principles similar to those used for the *World list of scientific periodicals,* except that periodicals beginning with the words Bulletin, Journal or Report, if associated with the name of a corporate body, are filed before such periodicals with a distinctive title commencing with one of those words. The rules adopted for arranging the *British union-catalogue of periodicals* since 1960 refine further on this kind of arrangement since cognate forms in the same and different languages are interfiled as are singular and plural forms, initials being filed as though they represented a word. Personal experience of the *BUCOP* system used for filing titles in a separate serials catalogue indicates that it is easily comprehended even by the more unsophisticated user.

TRADITIONAL AND MODERN METHODS OF CATALOGUE PRODUCTION

The requirements of the physical format of a catalogue are that it should be flexible so as to allow the easy insertion, deletion or amendment of entries; be accessible and convenient to use; be economic to maintain and economical of space; and be cheap and simple to reproduce where multiple copies are required.

None of the most widely used forms of catalogue devised to date, those on cards, in printed form or visible indexes, fulfils all these criteria. The printed form is the least flexible, being out of date the minute it is printed. It is virtually impossible to amend, except by cumbersome methods, and is usually kept up to date by frequent revision or by issuing supplements which entail repeat checking to ensure that all the required information has been found. Methods of reproduction vary. Conventional letterpress is usually too expensive unless the number of copies required is sufficient to justify the cost of setting up type. Duplication of lists on offset litho masters, especially when produced by means of a tape-typewriter is, however, feasible, since the paper tape can be updated fairly easily.[10] If the collection is small, then it is simple and cheap to produce from the stock cards onto which the catalogue entries are drafted, a typed and duplicated list. The frequency with which a printed list will need to be updated will depend on the number of alterations that have to be made to serials records, but on average, three to four times a year should suffice.

Where only a single-entry title plus holdings and location listing is required, then a visible index is a format to be considered. Entries are typed on strips which are inserted into holders, which may be of metal, plastic or stout paper. Those held in metal frames are usually suspended from racks fixed to a wall, or attached to a free-standing spindle. Those inserted in plastic or paper holders are usually inserted into binders. Both forms are easily kept up to date and have the advantage of providing a basis for a printed list by means of facsimile reproduction.

By far the most widely used is the card catalogue whose main advantage is the ease by which it can be amended. Unlike a printed list it is, provided that filing is done promptly, always up to date. Where more than one copy is necessary, additional sets of catalogue cards can be reproduced by tape-typewriter or by spirit or stencil duplication, or, if no more than six copies of an entry are required, by an ordinary typewriter, though this last has the disadvantage that all copies of the card have to be checked for accuracy. In addition to this, the card cabinets required to house the catalogue are expensive to purchase as is the upkeep of the catalogue in terms of filing costs.

Increasingly over the past 15 years, libraries have turned to computers to facilitate routines and the production of serials listings has been one of the more popular areas chosen for an initial essay into mechanization.[11] The constant changes necessary to records for serials due to their proclivity for change makes the prospect of updating by alteration of one central record and all those stemming from it enticing.

The input to a machine file can be by various methods. The cataloguing data is first written down onto input forms, which are then encoded into machine-readable form by one of several techniques.

Punched paper tape is one of the most widely used media, because it is both cheap and reliable, as are punched cards, although these are not quite so suitable for processing the variable length text fields commonly found in cataloguing applications. Alternatively, using a magnetic encoder, the catalogue record can be written onto magnetic tape. Encoders have the advantage that various checks can be made on the data being input to ensure accuracy and any mistakes noticed can be corrected, but the capital cost is higher than for either of the other two methods. Once in machine-readable form, the input is usually dealt with on a batch process basis, on-line processing being, at present, too costly, although it is being used when data are being edited. The master catalogue file is usually held on magnetic tape, or if very large or on-line access is required, on magnetic disc.

As far as output is concerned, this may be conventional catalogue cards, computer printout, microfiche or microfilm (i.e. COM), or a printed catalogue. The form chosen will depend on the size of the catalogue and the number of copies required. Since one of the benefits accruing from the use of a computer is the elimination of manual filing, to choose to have the output in the form of cards is to nullify this advantage. If a printed list is required, then if only one copy is wanted, the line-printer output is adequate and inexpensive. For up to four copies, line-printer output on paper interleaved with carbon paper is satisfactory. Between four and 100 copies, the most economic method is either to reduce the printout to A4 size and print by xerography, or to have the output printed directly onto offset-litho masters. For large numbers of copies, phototypesetting is a possibility. COM, microfiche or microfilm, is economic at any number of copies and is convenient to use, although the capital cost of providing readers has to be taken into account. In deciding between the two, the cost of maintaining the machines has to be considered. In this respect, microfiche readers are less troublesome, having fewer moving parts to go wrong, but in general there is little to choose between the two. Direct on-line access to catalogues is in use in America and will probably become more common as costs come down.

The emergence of national and international standards and of a bibliographic format are relatively recent developments in the field of serials cataloguing. With experimentation has come the realization that if duplication of time and effort is to be avoided then it is best to obtain common agreement as to what the elements to be contained in a given record are and to standardize their coding. The user of the machine record may then select as many or as few of the data elements as required and manipulate them as preferred. The various standards and formats so far developed are fully described in Chapter 17 and it is not proposed to discuss them here.

There is as yet no national service in the serials field comparable to that provided by the British Library MARC tapes for monographs. Any entries for serials contained on those tapes are for newly-published titles or changes in title. In most cases, however, new subscriptions taken out by libraries include not only newly-published journals but also journals which may have been established for a considerable time, unlike book acquisition where the majority of the material being acquired is that currently being issued. Relative to the number of books issued, the number of serials published is not large, and the likelihood of a number of libraries subscribing to a given title and thus able to share the costs of cataloguing it by utilizing a machine record is much higher than for monographs. Future developments in serials cataloguing would seem then to lie in the establishment of networks. In this country, one such already exists in BLCMP. The serials union catalogue contains upward of 20,000 titles comprising the holdings of three university libraries, two polytechnics and a public library. BLCMP has published its own format, MASS (MARC-based Automated Serials System),[12] which is based on the Library of Congress MARC format for serials,[13] which was first issued in 1970, and has endeavoured to ensure that it is compatible with ISBD(S). Because of the similarity between the MARC formats used for serials and monographs, the serials catalogues produced for each library may either be integrated with the monographs catalogue or may be produced as a separate listing. Other libraries, notably Loughborough University of Technology[14] and the University of London[15] have used MASS in establishing their own serials systems. London University is using BLCMP's file and the MASS format in establishing a union catalogue of the holdings of all its constituent schools and colleges. Newcastle University, having designed and implemented its own system,[16] is now collaborating with the University of Durham and the public and polytechnic libraries of Sunderland and Newcastle[17] to produce a union list, as is the University of Sheffield with Sheffield City Library, Sheffield Polytechnic and SINTO.[18] The latter will be based on Sheffield University's own locally developed periodicals listing system.

This chapter began by considering the necessity for a serials catalogue.

That need continues, but what should diminish, given current developments,[19] is the amount of time spent in individual libraries chronicling the busy lives of serials, with a consequent improvement in the service to the user, who can only benefit by the introduction of some standardization in the cataloguing of serials.

REFERENCES

1. Grose, M. W. and Line, M. B. 'On the construction and care of white elephants'. *Library Association Record* 70 no. 1 Jan. 1968. 2-5.
2. Osborn, A. D. *Serial publications.* 2nd ed. Chicago, American Library Association, 1973. 199.
3. Gorman, M. 'International standard bibliographical description and the new ISBDs'. *Journal of Librarianship* 10 no. 2 April 1978. 131-7.
4. *Anglo-American cataloguing rules.* 2nd ed. London, Library Association, 1978.
5. *Catalogue rules: author & title entries.* London, Library Association, 1908, Rule 121.
6. *Anglo-American cataloguing rules.* British text. London, Library Association, 1967, Rule 6.
7. e.g. Soper, M. E. 'Entry of serials'. *Serials Librarian* 1 no. 1 Fall 1976. 23-37; or Henderson, K. L. 'Serials cataloguing revisited', in W. C. Allen (ed.) *Serial publications in large libraries: papers presented at an institute conducted by the University of Illinois Graduate School of Library Science, 2-5 November, 1969.* London, Clive Bingley, 1971. 48-9.
8. *ALA rules for filing catalogues.* 2nd ed. Chicago, American Library Association, 1968.
9. *Current serials received.* Boston Spa, British Library Lending Division, 1979.
10. Wyatt, R. W. P. 'Producing a serials catalogue on tape'. *Library Association Record* 71 no. 7 July 1969. 210-11.
11. Wainwright, J. *Computer provision in British libraries.* London, Aslib, 1975.
12. *BLCMP MASS manual: input procedures for serials cataloguing.* Birmingham, BLCMP, 1973.
13. *Serials: a MARC format.* 2nd ed. Washington, Library of Congress, 1973.
14. Wall, R. 'Automation at Loughborough: a status report'. *Program* 6 no. 2 April 1972. 127-39.
15. Rodgers, L. and Wainwright, J. 'The University of London union list of serials project'. *Education Libraries Bulletin.* 19 no. 2 Summer 1976. 25-31.

16. Jeffreys, A. E. 'Newcastle University Library serials catalogue'. *Program* 12 no. 4 Oct. 1978. 175-84.
17. 'Union serials catalogues'. *VINE.* (17) Jan. 1977. 33-4.
18. 'Sheffield union serials catalogue'. *VINE.* (20) Feb. 1978. 28.
19. *Access to serials: report of a working party convened by the British Library.* British Library, 1978.

5

Retention, Disposal and Cancellation

Catherine Olver

Expected use will determine the choice of treatment for any unit entering the library. Seeking the appropriate future for a varied intake of purchased and free serials, the librarian will try to judge the permanent relevance of the material in the collection, how much it will be read, and for how long. He will want to collect evidence of wear, and for less-used titles he will want information on who uses the set, and whether alternative locations are available to potential readers. Circumstances alter. Space, money and time shrink. Advisers change. Reader habits shift. Alternative sources of literature or information become available. Decisions on the immediate and long-term treatment of periodicals will change in response to conditions. The Atkinson report alters the expectation of libraries, which had been accustomed to view themselves as permanent historical collections, by removing the prospect of automatically available expansion space as it becomes needed. By sharpening public awareness of the capital cost of elastic space, Atkinson introduced a new sense of the need to justify the retention of material. That shift in attitudes, along with the growing awareness of collections management as a vital tool in the maintenance of a reader-accessible library, is in itself a change in the circumstances determining the choice of treatment of material.

The choices are Rejection, Immediate discard, Deferred discard,

Retention, Reduction, Relegation, Disposal, and Cancellation. These responses are not clear-cut. They form a chain. At any time as circumstances change substitutions may be made, to save space, time or money — or to render more permanent material which proves to be disintegrating or disappearing.

REJECTION AND DISCARD

Rejection of material, which we should with more space have accepted, is a primary form of collection control. Every serials librarian is familiar with the miscellaneous batch of cupboard clearings and shelf sweepings that comes in after moves or retirements. As lack of space bites, it becomes imperative to insist that the giver should be thinking, not 'This might be useful to you in the library', but 'This will be useful to me in the library'. The deposit of live material or coherent collections is acceptable. The use of the library as a wastepaper basket is not, and the librarian will risk the loss of the odd useful item to avoid the time-consuming sifting for it. Firmness is very much more difficult to apply to executors anxious to find a useful home for apparently valuable journal collections. Here, a knowledge of young libraries, and libraries specializing in the offered subjects, can help. Executors would often rather give material than sell it to a dealer. The advising librarian can point out that dealers exist to redistribute material to buyers, who prove their need by their willingness to pay. He can warn prospective sellers to expect few, and low, offers. He should never accept duplicate material to be sold and the proceeds devoted to the library. Few donors should be offended by a grateful but reasoned refusal, especially if an alternative course of action can be suggested.

Immediate discard is the space-saving solution for material that arrives at the library, unasked, regularly. Many libraries basket their junk serials on opening. The alternative is to display for a week or until replaced, preferably in a low priority corner where they take little space and make as little mess as possible. Overseas readers do like to see their own embassy newsletters; and it is quicker to assume that every pressure group has its adherents than to discriminate among them.

Deferred discard has been habitually practised by public and special libraries who have not regarded themselves as permanent historical repositories as have academic libraries. One-to-five-year files are normal.

Serials designed to meet an ephemeral need are produced to be discarded. These include current awareness tools, 'soft' news media from organizations, directories and yearbooks, newspapers, consumer magazines and many technical periodicals. But a library keeps the papers that other people throw away. However, limited space and rising storage costs combine with the quantity of twentieth-century publishing output to force rapid recognition of the principle that although 'everything should be kept, it shouldn't be kept everywhere'. And once selection for permanent storage is accepted, the bulk-to-information ratio of technical journals makes them immediate candidates for a deferred discard that is intended from the time of their arrival in the library. In those subject areas in which the library feels a special historical responsibility, it may feel compelled to retain its technical weeklies and monthlies. But most should go. They exist as news-media. They are financed by and designed for advertisers rather than libraries. Their margins are narrow, and their paper impermanent. Their content dates rapidly. Hard copy is cheap because of the advertising, and the microform alternative for the same reason costly. Unless the journal is of such critical importance within the institution that the permanent storage cost of hard copy or microform is justified, bundling and deferred discard are the only sane solutions.

RETENTION

However many titles we may try to class as temporary, in an academic or research library permanent retention is the expected destiny of most material that has passed the tests for purchase and a place on the shelves. We are preparing for use. In many cases we are preparing for abuse. And we are preparing to give our readers rapid access to a wide range of scholarly material of all periods. Our estimate of their use will determine whether we box, bundle or bind.

Whether material is sent out to commercial library binders, or sent to a bindery on the premises, the binder cannot know the special problems peculiar to the library or the journal, and the librarian cannot know the technical problems or the technical solutions available, without consultation. A good co-operative working relationship with an ingenious, skilful binder is a constant joy. New problems arise daily — paper refuses to absorb glue; margins narrow beyond the guillotinable;

technical pagination instructions evolved for earlier volumes cease to apply or are found to have been fatally misleading; inserts overweight their guards; and overlays slip from their pockets. The pleasure of solving with the binder each day's batch compensates for the frustrations of theft and mutilation which make so much binding a two-stage operation, with binding itself possible only after prolonged 'search-and-complete' exercises. Obviously this kind of consultation is easier if the bindery is on the premises or if complex work is sent to a specialist. But the large commercial binders, in spite of the fact that they must bind as a factory operation to keep costs down, are most careful consulters, and bring to the solution of technical or lettering problems an experience based on a greater number of examples than is available to any on-site binder.

The decisions on whether and how to bind, however, are not technical but political. We compromise between the integrity of the publication and the shortages of staff time, shelf space and money. We want instructions to be as uniform and straightforward as possible, but we must respond to every peculiarity of each title or volume. We want to cut staff time spent on binding preparation. On the other hand, any abnormality left unremarked and without a specific instruction will lead to delay if the binder queries the anomaly, or disaster if he does not. The niggling checking that leaves only missing gatherings for the binder to discover, and makes provision for every loose sheet, is costly in staff time and training. The results of imprecise instructions, however, surface years later as unfulfilled reader needs. We choose also between the waste of binding time and shelf space. Great bulk may drive us to excise all advertising even when it is paged in, while erratically positioned advertising may fail to repay in saved space the time spent searching it out for discard. Cedric Chivers of Bath offers a special rate if they can bind everything without collation, which indicates the cost of normal preparation and pre-sewing collation operations. Lettering we can also pare. As costs per line increase spines can be simplified, and lettering reduced to that minimum which will allow unique identification and the reliable establishment of correct order on the shelf.

For some exceptionally heavily-used and mutilated titles, the staff time spent in binding preparation may be so heavy that a second subscription to a closet copy for binding may prove the only economic solution. Other core titles may suffer heavy use prolonged enough to justify the binding of two copies. This kind of undergraduate source will be bounced on the

Xerox machine and battered until its pages slither on their stitches. Choice of binding style will be governed by the probable need for rebinding; and traditional sewing, which offers flat opening, can be succeeded eventually by a more standard method with reduced back margins and a stiffer opening. For the more normal run of research titles, modern binding methods, which shave off the spine and secure the single leaves by sewing and flexible glues, are strong and practical — so far. At least they seem a reasonable response to rising costs, given the probable life of the material. For single units, cheap reinforcement and plasticization techniques provide floppy volumes with stiffening and a readable spine, and, when the existing spine can be preserved, save lettering decisions. And when, occasionally, the value or rarity or condition of a set requires that we should allow the physical integrity of the volumes to determine binding policy, preliminary consultation with the binder is vital. Treatment can only be worked out in terms of cost; and while the exercise of skill on a non-routine job is a pleasure, especially for the library's own binder, he alone is able to advise the librarian on the comparative costs of the less than perfect solutions, and guide towards the most appropriate treatment within the limitations. It is then up to the informed librarian to insist, for instance, on complete de-acidification and reinforcement, or on total re-sewing and rebinding when he judges it necessary. It is a policy judgement that transforms wastepaper into a rarity.

Binding periodicals is expensive. It is more expensive in time and skill than most administrators realize. In a busy library, the protection it offers delays wear and discourages theft, and it provides a uniform system for the arrangement of variable material on the shelf that renders it findable and shelvable.

We can decide not to bind, and elect instead to box or bundle. For some titles where a predominantly repository function can be identified and the library can see that it is laying down historical evidence for occasional future use, the protection of binding is unnecessary. Boxing can be extended into a greater range of smaller research journals, especially the publications of local history bodies and the specialized micro-bodies in the natural sciences. Even if the decision should need to be reversed, multiple volumes can be bound together. Hull[1] records in its report for 1972-73 a fully-consulted decision to cease binding 120 titles. It is a saving that constructively reacts to increased binding costs by a planned, publicized, lowering of standards.

RELEGATION

Permanent retention of library material has in the past been the normal expectation. The new orthodoxy preaches the slimline library with a working collection of constantly moving books, and the moribund relegated to closed storage or pulped. Where the ideal of immediate, delayed and remote access to information can be appropriately realized, it is hoped that accessibility can be improved by the separation. At the same time, the increasing value of their vulnerable stock compels librarians to weed as much for security as for obsolescence. Individual circumstances and changes in building and transport costs will determine the choice between large-scale co-operative deposit, middle-distance converted warehouse or nearby purpose-built bookstore. Whatever the local conditions, relegation is now an essential tool of library management. Cheap practical methods of separating low- and high-use stock are needed yesterday. They are of special interest to serials librarians. Because a greater yardage of relocation can be effected with fewer record changes if serials are moved rather than books, long back sets regularly recommend themselves for removal to shelving supervisors in crisis.

In the search for a strategy, Rice[2] in her state-of-the-art bibliography gives immediate access to the story to date. Seymour[3] gives a well-balanced review of the weeding problem up to 1972. She points out that most weeding studies have been undertaken in science collections, with results that would not necessarily hold good in other subject areas. Having summarized the alternative methods for evolving a weeding strategy, including borrowing records, citation levels, and dates of publication, her final paragraph emphasizes the uniqueness of each library and its individual combination of loan and consultation within the library, and recognizes consultation as the truer indicator of use. In medicine, the subject area most closely studied, Newcastle[4] found that when they compared use in the library, recorded in a re-shelving survey, with circulation, they could derive the following rule:

> For a particular title, if all volumes of that title which were published during the last fifteen years have not been borrowed during the last five years then that title is a candidate for relegation, unless it is a current subscription with a back-run of five or less volumes.

Using this rule alone, a few titles would have been moved which on evidence of consultation would not have been. As a basis for a relegation strategy in other libraries, their rule seems extremely useful. The object first of all is to identify those titles which are to remain fully accessible, and then to divide the remainder into certains and doubtfuls. The doubtfuls can be tested for consultation within the library, and readers can be consulted, or observed, if this seems wise.

Every subject and every collection will be used differently. There is always the temptation to plump for relegation by gross characteristic as a saving in record changing and reader confusion. 'Pre-World War II' may indeed help some libraries. But 'pre-World War II except for ...' rapidly erodes simplicity. Two counter-considerations need to be stated. Low-use material relegated becomes no-use material; it is the curious and eclectic reader who is most impatient of restricted access, and those who have most time to explore are most inexpert in their use of the catalogue. And we have over-emphasized the specific reference in research. The study of trends or historical developments requires browsing; and a reader often discovers a journal the entire back set of which illuminates.

In fact relegation normally corresponds untidily to the rate of acquisition and shelf overflow in different sectors of the library. We select the required footage of the least inconveniencing rejects. A reasonable rule-of-thumb on the Newcastle model combines with the exigencies of space to necessitate title-by-title decisions at the shelf. They can be surprisingly rapid. The correctness of our choices is measured by the consequent fetching and carrying; but the inevitable loss of access can be tempered, as far as is compatible with security, by humane lending policies, and the widest possible distribution of catalogues and guides. Where it can be proved that relegation best exploits limited storage resources, with the least possible delay in access, the policy can be made acceptable.

REDUCTION

Reduction, the holding of serials in microform, is an early alternative to binding, and later an alternative to relegation. Acceptance has been slow for both these purposes. As a substitute for reprints, microform rules. Increasingly, concurrent fiche is becoming a desirable alternative for paper, as more publishers grasp that librarians can understand that first-copy costs must be distributed among subscribers, whatever the substrate, and switch from as-well-as to instead-of schemes. But as a substitute for hard-copy already in the library, the microform alternative appears to be marginally uneconomic and marginally inconvenient unless some additional compelling factor reinforces the arguments. Partly, University Microfilms' hardsell has been off-putting. But, for popular titles, paper is tough and readable. A bound volume can be found, photocopied, borrowed. Microforms are more costly to reproduce; while the unbound parts, retained in theory for the period of maximum use, invite theft and concentrate controversy. Recording the arrival of microform is roughly equivalent in time to preparing binding. The space savings, however, according to the British Library Lending Division in their excellent summary of the case for and against, published as Annex F in the Atkinson report, are estimated to be about 65–70 per cent.[5] The balance is fine; and as space becomes scarcer, it is increasingly more easily tipped towards microform as a binding substitute. Each library has its examples. Newspapers are kept on microfilm because newsprint is impermanent and the hardcopy is impossible to bind. Heavily mutilated weeklies may be worth the microfilm investment to save disproportionate binding preparation costs. Compact arm's-length reference convenience can determine the choice of microform for heavy abstracts. And microform may suit the special library serving a small highly-paid on-site daytime readership.

Similarly compelling special conditions affecting any given library may recommend microform storage as a substitute for material already fully incorporated as hard copy in the library's stock. Marian Chinn,[6] describing the jacket fiche system used at the Consumers' Association library in central London, shows how in-house reduction can relieve pressure for a unique collection of scrappy material in an inelastic library. Microform is an excellent solution for rare material printed on disintegrating paper. If the pages will turn once more with care, the audience should be a camera. It should only be the library's own camera if no commercial version is available; and this can be difficult to determine, since in the micro-bibliographic jungle a listing often expresses a mere intention, and no sign of a listing is no proof of non-existence. For normal back sets, however, where use has fallen off, the cost of micro-substitution as against relegation makes the purchase of microform as a storage policy an ineffective contender for current funds.

Relegation and eventual disposal will inevitably be the choice if substitution microform competes directly with new material.

Relegation in hard copy offers the chance occasionally to reverse a mistaken decision. More importantly, it offers the opportunity for relegation to metamorphose into disposal. If a case can be made for a five-year store, that store must be managed in such a way that the institution can know the cost of housing distant access material at its own expense, as against the cost of borrowing it — or of shipping the reader rather. than the material. Closed access facilitates accurate monitoring. And where use can be proved to be low and the costs of storage can be identified, a strong factual case can be made for disposal. Or retention. Or, while we are in 1984, more money for terminals.

DISPOSAL

Disposals are a means of making space not money. Having said that, selling periodicals is so rare and difficult that a bookseller's offer is an immense reward and encouragement for the serials staff, and worth concentrating some skill on achieving. A file of booksellers specializing in serials and in subjects will help direct the library's own offers, and those of its friends whose material it is unable to accommodate. Booksellers are only interested (apart from the occasional foray for 'odds') in continuous complete sets. They have a canny expert knowledge of what will sell, and their accountants have a sharp awareness of the costs of warehousing and insurance, and the cost of money tied up in stock. Retiring professors, offering complete founder members' sets of journals relating to disciplines they isolated in their prime, all retire together. And since microform back sets are cheaper than hard copy, the bookseller's market for paper has shrunk. If the librarian has a good back set for disposal, however, he should try booksellers first. But he should not allow his library committee at any time to delude itself into thinking that selling back sets of periodicals will make any significant contribution to the library budget. After failing to sell, it may be possible to offer material to a young library, or to a library with a strong collecting interest in the subject field of the disposables. Connections with teaching staff moving to third-world research stations can give rise to the occasional placement of material. And short specialized lists of material for disposal can be more accurately aimed at likely libraries and more rapidly scanned by a higher level of staff than would be normal for a blunter list. The British Library Gift and Exchange Section has plans for the possible compilation of a subject specialist guide to libraries, derived from its own experience. This would be invaluable in providing direct friendly access for mutual help between librarians in a variety of institutions with meshing interests. Wants and offers occur together in fields of active collection building.

For routine disposal, the British Library Gift and Exchange Section acts as a clearing-house for wants and offers that provides discarding librarians with the hope of a future life for unwanted material. If the offering library is unable to house it, the British Library will take delivery and shelve volumes during the period of offer. Records of these are merged with records of material held in the disposing library, and regular monthly serials lists are circulated. A response is received on about a third of the entries. Further lists for circulation abroad are compiled from whatever remains unrequested, and a third of these entries elicits a further response. After the fixed period during which volumes await foster-libraries, they are crated. In science and technology, the British Library Lending Division, with its system of back-up libraries, has achieved such comprehensiveness of coverage that only very rarely are discards absorbed into their stock. In the social sciences, a small amount is creamed off. In the humanities they have many needs but receive few discards. The secondhand market in the humanities remains lively. Earlier impressions that discards contributed to the strength of the BLLD are now largely outdated in serials. (The same is by no means true of books.) Nevertheless, for the serials librarian hoping to make constructive and useful discards, the BLGES provides a rapid, comprehensive advertising service with satisfactory penetration of the potential market. Moreover, since the service has a strict time-limit, the decision for final disposal can be regularly brought forward, and unwanted offers can be pulped.

CANCELLATION

Cancellation of periodicals subscriptions has been the main non-routine activity in British periodicals departments during the mid-1970s. Serials prices were rising so much more quickly than book grants that existing current orders, if they were left as they were, would come to consume an unacceptably high proportion of total funds. Librarians would have no budgeting freedom and would overspend by inertia. Throughout the academic serials buying world, cancellation projects were initiated in the attempt to control serials commitments before they took over. Accounts of three such exercises, at Hull,[7] Glasgow[8] and Auckland, New Zealand,[9] outline a variety of strategies for the determination of candidates for cancellation, but all stress the amount of work involved, the amount of potential ill-feeling generated, and the importance of close co-operation between the library staff and the teaching staff in bringing about an acceptable list. In almost all communities, co-operative efforts to contain periodicals spending brought about new and better relationships between the library and its public. If marginal titles could be shaken out, and those read only by ghosts could be eliminated, scarce resources could be more usefully allocated. Problems of equity in sacrifice were posed openly, and faculty committees showed themselves experienced maverick handlers. Instead of the animus against the library which had been generated during the preceding period of new order embargo, there arose an understanding of the library's problems in the provision of material. The book grant, formerly an undifferentiated lump characterized in institutional politics only by the librarian's habitual assertion of its inadequacy, particularized itself, title by title, in terms of periodicals the loss of which could vividly be imagined. Cancellations shocked. In many organizations, cancellations, actual or imminent, precipitated reinstatement grants and revised levels of funding. When a non-librarian lobbies his MP on university grants by saying 'We are having to cut periodicals', a new era begins for the serials librarian.

Several writers have said that cancellations exercises cost more than the savings effected. Elizabeth Rodger points out that 'the savings are recurrent whereas the costs are not'.[8] Major serials scrutiny provides a basis for permanent review. Once it has been established that the relative importance of periodicals changes through time, so the need for continuous adjustment of the list becomes a permanent responsibility for the serials librarian. Expensive but questionable subscriptions can be watched, and observed use can replace avowed use as a basis for negotiation. The case for detailed justification of new orders is strengthened if specialized periodicals are likely to be cancelled when their specialist leaves. The increased awareness of serials costs can also be used gradually to bring about a rationalization of scattered literature spending through the institution as a whole. The interdisciplinary relevance of serials was consistently revealed and remarked on in all accounts. As cuts bite deeper, the centralization of stock, or at least its co-ordination, becomes increasingly imperative. The library may well have to accept greater flexibility of reading points to facilitate use. But it is nonsense for the library to cut unique subscriptions while departments continue similar and often duplicate commitments from university funds. Further advantages of the testing and questioning of recent years arise from the consciousness that if one is to apply the slogan 'Every journal a wanted journal' to purchased titles, the same criteria must be extended to gifts. Lapsed gifts, if there is no evidence of demand, remain unrequested, with a consequent concentration of effort on the essential. More and more often when it is recognized that a gift would nowadays not have been added to the collection, the entire back set is discarded. The dusty to the dustbin.

Cancellations and rejected new order requests have undoubtedly included essential titles too costly to justify for purchase. Since middle-sized research libraries cannot hope to be comprehensive their readers must expect to visit specialist libraries. And in many cases, standing interloan requests for all issues have been adopted as a palliative. The extensive photocopying necessarily then practised within research teams contravenes copyright. And publishers become understandably anxious, claiming that readily available interloan erodes sales. But publishers have also been affected by cancellations. Suddenly they made effective efforts to hold prices. The Pergamon two-column journal typifies a movement. Moreover, as inflation strained the financial and informational links between writer, publisher, buyer and reader, the different groups increasingly recognized their interdependence. They began to talk to each other. Although mutual abrasiveness continues, more participants understand each other's problems than before, and there has been an increasing frankness about finance on the part of the publisher. The interloan file's evidence of unpurchasable regular needs exposes the unworkability of present high-cost research publishing and low-level research library funding. And while the solution is certainly not inevitably an increase in library funds, the library can help by acting as a reminder of the problem, to create a writing/reading public educated by their involvement in cancellation projects, sharply aware of the competition for literature resources, and encouragingly receptive to new publishing experiments. The cancellations debate continues.

The library and its community have been forced by inflation to work together to revise subscriptions lists in order to spend limited funds more wisely. The entire community, and not just its finance committee, has gained practical experience of the unity of library resources. The understanding so gained can now inform decisions which urgently need to be made in response to the shortage of money for space. No finance committee needs to be reminded that it is all the same money. The reader required to approve the pulping of a title he might occasionally read to make space for current arrivals, will need helping towards understanding — especially if the current arrivals are someone else's. To the professor of linguistics, all economics journals are inessential. And while no community expects to be called upon to make its librarian's professional mind up for him, it does expect to be consulted. As the gap between resources and needs widens, the choices become harder, and the conflicts of interests more difficult to reconcile. It was the concreteness of the choices that was so educative in the great cancellations exercise. The same kind of specific decisions will arise in the solution of storage problems. To achieve a public informed enough to be worth consulting, the librarian must translate the costs of new material and the storage of existing stock into the same terms, so that they are clearly competing for the same money. That will not reconcile conflicting aims, but it can bring about wider understanding of those aims. Moreover, when additional funds are not available, the more the librarian can communicate the costs of their needs to his public, the more he can rely on their goodwill. It may not be possible to persuade readers that the least undesirable course is actually desirable; but it should be possible to convince them that it is the best in the circumstances.

REFERENCES

1. University of Hull, the Brynmor Jones Library. *Report 1972-3.* 10.
2. Rice, B.A. 'Weeding in academic and research libraries: an annotated bibliography'. *Collection Management* 2 no. 1 Spring 1978. 65-71.
3. Seymour, C. A. 'Weeding the collection: a review of research on identifying obsolete stock, Part I: Monographs. Part II: Serials'. *Libri* 22 1972. 137-48; 183-9.
4. Taylor, C. R. 'A practical solution to weeding university library periodicals collections'. *Collection Management* 1 nos. 3-4 Fall-Winter 1976-1977 27-45.

5. University Grants Committee. *Capital provision for university libraries: report of a working party.* Annex F, British Library Lending Division. *Microfilm as an alternative to hard copy storage.* London, HMSO, 1976.
6. Chinn, M. 'Consumers' Association library and microfiche — a success story?' *Assistant Librarian* 69 no. 6 June 1976. 108–11.
7. Brennan, M. M. 'Periodical cancellations: what happened at Hull'. *BLL Review* 5 no. 2 April 1977. 67–73.
8. Rodger, E. 'Pruning periodical subscriptions at Glasgow University Library'. *ASLIB Proceedings* 30 no. 4 April 1978. 145–53.
9. Durey, P. 'Weeding subscriptions in a university library'. *Collection Management* 1 nos. 3–4 Fall-Winter 1976-77. 91–4.

Part 2

LIBRARIES

6

National Libraries

A. T. Smail

HISTORY OF LEGAL DEPOSIT

The concept of legal deposit originated in France in the first half of the sixteenth century with a decree made by King Francis I. This decree required every printer and publisher in France to forward a copy of every newly-published book to the Royal Library at Blois, and the penalty for failure to comply with this requirement was confiscation of the whole edition of the work and a heavy fine. This legislation was effective in creating a national collection which comprehensively recorded the publishing history of the country, and, gradually, other countries adopted their own forms of legal deposit.

A form of deposit was introduced in England in 1610 by an agreement, between Sir Thomas Bodley and the Stationers' Company, which entitled the library of Oxford University to receive a free copy of every new book published by members of the Company. Although this private agreement briefly received the support of the Star Chamber in 1637-40, it was not until 1662 that the first of the Licensing Acts made statutory provision for the deposit of copies, the libraries so designated being the Royal Library and the libraries of Oxford and Cambridge Universities. These Acts were in force from 1662 to 1679 and from 1685 to 1695. The famous Copyright Act of 1709, following the Union of Scotland and England, extended the legal deposit privilege to nine libraries, increased to eleven by the Act of 1801, and reduced to five by the Act of 1836, until the Copyright Act of 1911 (1 & 2 Geo. 5, c.46) settled on six libraries. These were the British Museum, founded in the middle of the eighteenth century and based on the collections of the Royal Library which were transferred to the nation by George II; the Bodleian Library, Oxford and the University Library, Cambridge, being the libraries of the two great English seats of learning; the library of the Faculty of Advocates at Edinburgh, the sole survivor of, at one stage, five deposit libraries in Scotland; the library of Trinity College, Dublin, first granted the privilege of legal deposit at the beginning of the nineteenth century; and the National Library of Wales, granted its Charter of Incorporation in 1907 and situated at Aberystwyth. When the British Library was established in 1973 it incorporated the library departments of the British Museum and assumed their legal deposit entitlements. In 1925 the transfer of all non-legal material from the Advocates' Library to form the basis of the National Library of Scotland included the transfer of the legal deposit privilege to the new library. The six libraries are generally known as the Copyright Libraries, although it would be more correct to call them the Legal Deposit Libraries.

The Copyright Act of 1911 has been extensively amended by subsequent legislation, but the Section relating to legal deposit (Section 15) has only been the subject of minor amendments covering the transfers of privileges already mentioned and is still the current legislation.

A more detailed history of legal deposit can be found in a two-part article by Bell,[1] while the standard work on the subject is still Partridge,[2] albeit 40 years old.

THE LEGAL DEPOSIT OF SERIALS

The publisher of every book published in the United Kingdom is obliged by Section 15 of the Copyright Act 1911 to supply, within one month of publication, a free copy to the British Library. The other five legal deposit libraries are required to make written demands for copies within twelve months of publication, although the Act allows such demands for serials to include all subsequent numbers or parts.

The British Library, in terms of the Copyright Act, should, if publishers are punctilious in observing these terms, receive every serial that is published (as indeed it nearly always does). The other libraries, because of the different basis of their entitlement, can decide to claim only certain serials. In practice, they exercise the power of selection only within a narrow range of very ephemeral material. They try to ensure that all subjects within the scope of British serial publications are fully covered, and even in the case of very ephemeral material at least one library is likely to take a copy if the others do not, thus ensuring that there is a second copy outside London to provide a safeguard against loss or damage of the copy presumed to be in the British Library. The arguments for continuing to have more than one legal deposit collection were strengthened by the extensive loss of material which occurred when the British Museum was damaged by bombs during the London blitz.

All the Copyright Libraries are aware of their responsibility to anticipate the needs of readers in the future. They are constantly reminded of the dangers of a limited selection policy by the gaps in their holdings of many older 'popular' magazines, which were considered as inappropriate for their collections at the time of publication, but are now of interest to scholars, particularly in the field of social history. It is important, therefore, that the Copyright Libraries should collect the type of publication which other libraries are liable to overlook or ignore, in particular ephemeral and obscure periodicals. The National Library of Scotland, in addition to receiving the wide range of British serials already mentioned, tries to seek out and claim all other Scottish serials, however localized or ephemeral, and it extends this intensive interest in some degree to the North of England as well. The National Library of Wales searches out Welsh serials, and indeed most serials of Celtic interest, in a similar way.

Irish publications, including serials, are deposited with the British Copyright libraries under the terms of the Irish Copyright Act 1963, which is similar to the British Act in most respects, although Irish publishers are required to deposit with a total of 11 libraries, including all six covered by the British Act.

The legal deposit requirements only cover serials which are available to the public and are not considered to cover publications which are distributed only to members of a society or similar restricted body. However, it is unusual for any such publications not to be available to non-members on request, and they can therefore be considered for deposit. In fact, the editors of such magazines are usually surprised, and often delighted, that their efforts should be considered worthy of retention by the Copyright Libraries, and they readily agree to deposit copies. Another important category excluded from the Act is microform publications. If a journal is published in both printed and microform editions, the Libraries are only able to claim the printed edition. However, more and more material is being originally published in microfiche or microfilm alone, and in most cases these are not being deposited in the national collections. If the law is not altered in the near future, a significant gap in the records of British publishing, as represented by the collections of the Copyright Libraries, will result. The Gregory Committee on Copyright[3] considered this point in its Report published in 1952, and recommended that new publications in microform should be clearly included within the scope of the Act, and, more recently, the Whitford Committee[4] endorsed the principle as a valid one which should be considered. Some of the Copyright Libraries also recommended to the Whitford Committee that future legislation should cover material published in the Isle of Man and the Channel Islands, at present exempt.

CONTROL OF DEPOSITED SERIALS

Serials deposited with the British Library are directed initially to the Copyright Receipt Office, where they are recorded in ledgers arranged by publisher, and after stamping they are then distributed to the appropriate departments of the library. The first part of a serial received is acknowledged, subsequent receipts only being issued on an annual basis in most instances, and it is then passed to the UK National Serials Data Centre for the possible allocation of an International Standard Serial Number (ISSN). New serials received by the British Library are catalogued within the Bibliographic Services Division, and many of these are listed in the *British National Bibliography.*

The four libraries with identical privileges — namely the libraries of the Universities of Oxford and Cambridge, the National Library of Scotland and Trinity College, Dublin — employ an Agent to act on their behalf in respect of claiming copies under the Copyright Act. Section 15(2) of the Act requires the Libraries to maintain a depot in London to which publishers can deliver copies for all the libraries, and the office of the Agent, often called the Copyright Agency, serves this purpose. To enable the Agent to claim copies of serials only for the libraries which specifically require them, a list of new titles compiled from information supplied by the Libraries themselves, and by the Agent, is circulated to them for the selection of titles for claim. It is interesting to note that the two University Libraries obtain much of their information regarding new publications from their staff and students, whereas the National Library of Scotland relies far more on research by library staff, including the perusal of newspapers and relevant journals, for this information. The exchange of information between the four libraries therefore provides a good coverage of new titles, and there is also a further exchange of information with the British Library which benefits all concerned.

The records of the Copyright Agency are arranged by publisher to enable each publisher's serials to be checked and, if necessary, claimed at the one time. The control of multiple copies, varying between one and four depending on the decision of the Libraries, requires careful monitoring and presents problems which are seldom faced in an individual library.

None of the Copyright Libraries has yet developed an automated control system for its serials, although there are plans for possible co-operation in the future.

OTHER SOURCES OF SERIALS

Legal deposit only provides a proportion of the serials holdings of the Copyright Libraries, and one of the advantages of legal deposit is the release of funds for the purchase of foreign publications to enhance the national collections. In addition to the purchase of serials to augment the intake of the Reference Division, the British Library subscribes to a high proportion of the 51,500 current serials which are taken by the Lending Division (BLLD) at Boston Spa. All the Copyright Libraries act as back-up libraries in the Inter-Library lending system, and as such they provide photocopies of articles from serials, but only in strict accordance with the copyright regulations.

The Bodleian Library subscribes to almost as many serials as it receives by legal deposit, and the other libraries also use large proportions of their purchase funds on serial subscriptions.

The Copyright Libraries also receive donations of current serials and sets of back issues from various sources. The problems of storage faced by many libraries have forced them to adopt policies of zero-growth, whereby they must dispose of earlier holdings to allow space for current material. It is to be hoped that such material will be offered to the Copyright Libraries in the first instance, so that gaps in their holdings can be filled. The Libraries also receive serials as a result of exchange agreements with libraries and institutions in other countries.

In the National Library of Scotland, severe space restrictions before the opening of the present building prevented the comprehensive collection of Scottish newspapers. For a number of years now, the Library has been endeavouring to fill these gaps in its newspaper collections by microfilming publishers' files of their newspapers or files held by local libraries. The National Library of Wales has a similar project for obtaining microfilms of early Welsh newspapers.

STATISTICAL INFORMATION

It is not possible to present comparative statistics of the serial holdings of the Libraries as they all have their own definition of serials and this is reflected in their statistics. However, the following statistics of serials received from all sources may serve to illustrate the size of the handling and storage problems which the Copyright Libraries must face.

The Copyright Receipt Office of the British Library handles some 250,000 serial parts annually, and the 1978/79 annual report of the British Library shows that the Science Reference Library alone takes 33,700 current serial titles. The Annual Report does not give a figure for all serial parts received by the British Library, but they must account for a high proportion of the approximate total of two million items recorded by the Library in 1978/79.

The Bodleian Library received over 218,000 current serial parts, representing some 37,000 titles, in the year 1978/79, and Cambridge University Library received over 33,000 current serials. The National Library of Scotland, which is in process of gradually extending its serials recording system (previously covering periodicals in the narrower definition) to include all serial titles, at present records over 10,500 current titles. The National Library of Wales records about 6,000 current periodicals.

CONSERVATION AND STORAGE

The problems of storage and conservation of their serial holdings is of constant concern to the Copyright Libraries. Although there is nothing in the Copyright Act to prevent the Libraries from disposing of any of their holdings, the Libraries accept that the intention of the Act is for all material deposited to be preserved indefinitely and that there is a moral obligation on them to do so. All the Libraries have found it necessary to acquire new stack space in recent years, and in most cases they have introduced mobile, or compact, shelving to make the best possible use of the space available.

The practice in the Libraries is generally to store the unbound issues of a serial with the bound volumes of the same serial. The exceptions to this rule are the National Library of Scotland and Cambridge University Library, where the unbound parts of all bound serials are kept in the one area of stackage adjacent to the working area where the serials recording is carried out. In the National Library of Scotland, about 70 per cent of their periodicals, including all newspapers, are bound, the exceptions being items which are unsuitable for binding due to their format or infrequency of issue. The storage of all unbound issues in the one area convenient to serials staff allows for the systematic selection of volumes for binding and for easy checking of gaps in holdings which can never be done with an absolute degree of certainty from the records alone.

There are several methods of conserving serials in use at the Libraries. Serials which are used frequently are normally bound in buckram or cloth at all of the Libraries. Less-frequently-used serials and others considered unsuitable for binding are normally stored in closed cardboard pamphlet boxes or, in some case, in parcels.

The use of microfilming as a means of conservation of newspapers and other serials has been the subject of considerable debate in recent years. There are several factors to be considered as far as the Copyright Libraries are concerned. As already mentioned, publishers are only required to deposit printed editions, and the Libraries are not in a position to request the deposit of microfilm or microfiche editions where these exist. It would therefore be necessary for the Libraries to accept the printed editions and to microfilm them at a later stage, with the publisher's permission if still in copyright.

If it is decided to microfilm files of journals and newspapers already deposited in the Libraries, it would then be necessary to decide whether or not to retain the originals as a safeguard against the possible deterioration of the microfilm. The permanence of various types of microform has only been tested over a relatively short period, compared to the life-span of the early books and manuscripts which are preserved in the collections of the Libraries.

The use of microfilm would not be as suitable for journals which contain photographs or where the text or illustrations are other than monochrome. There is also the question of the intrinsic interest of the book form. Microform copies provide acceptable sources of information, but consideration must also be given to the preservation of serials and books as items of historical interest in their own right. Most people would find it far more rewarding to read a contemporary report of an important historical event in an actual newspaper of the time, in the same way that they would prefer to see the actual exhibits in a museum rather than just photographs of them.

There are, however, very strong arguments in favour of the microfilming of certain types of serial, particularly newspapers. The space saved by the retention of microform copies would be considerable and they would probably be less liable to damage from regular consultation. In any case, the retention of a master copy of each microfilm would lessen the consequences of accidental damage to the reference copies. It would also be far easier to provide copies, either on microfilm or as photocopies, from a microfilm rather than directly from the original. There are photocopiers which provide instant copies from microfilm, whereas many large format serials are not suitable for normal photocopying processes.

In 1977, the British Library issued a Consultative Paper[5] on the use of microfilm as the principal medium for newspaper storage, conservation and use within the Library. This paper was intended to stimulate the development of constructive views which could be taken into account before a final decision on the transfer of all the Library's newspapers to microfilm was made. It should be noted that the British Library's definition of a 'newspaper' includes most serials which are published fortnightly or more frequently, and therefore includes publications such as *The Autocar, Popular Gardening* and *Woman's Own* as well as all national and local newspapers of the more accepted definition. The British Library's newspaper collections are housed in the Newspaper Library at Colindale in North London, and consideration of the statistics of periodicals held here certainly illustrates the economic appeal of microfilming. The Library already contains about half a million volumes and parcels of newspapers and periodicals, and this total is being added to at the rate of about 5,500 a year. In fact, over 4,000,000 printed pages are received by the Newspaper Library annually. If the policy of retaining all accessions in printed form is continued, the existing bookstacks at Colindale will be full by the mid–1980s, and it is estimated that it would cost around £2,000,000 to construct a suitable bookstack for a further twenty years' accessions.

The solution to the problem of newspaper conservation may be found in co-operation between the major libraries of the country. If at least one printed copy of each periodical were retained indefinitely, perhaps in the major library closest to the place of publication, other libraries could hold microfilm copies for consultation. This would certainly be a compromise worth considering, and the general reaction to the British Library consultative paper certainly suggests that there is opposition to the retention of microfilm copies only.

The British Library Board in considering the responses to the consultative paper, has decided to undertake an enlarged programme of microfilming at its Newspaper Library, but will not discard any newspapers after microfilming. It hopes to extend its coverage of British national newspapers and to build a new extension at Colindale. It has also been agreed that a Working Party on Access to Newspapers should be set up to consider the most suitable arrangements for the co-ordination and dissemination of information about the storage, microfilming and availability of newspapers.

REFERENCES

1. Bell, R. 'Legal deposit in Britain'. *Law Librarian* 8 no. 1 April 1977. 5–8; 8 no. 2 August 1977. 22–6.
2. Partridge, R. C. Barrington. *The History of the legal deposit of books throughout the British Empire.* London, Library Association, 1938.
3. *Report of the Copyright Committee.* Cmd. 8662. London, HMSO, October 1952.
4. *Copyright and designs law.* Cmnd. 6732. London, HMSO, March 1977.
5. *The newspaper collections and the future.* London, British Library, 1977.

7

Public Libraries

F. R. Taylor

SERIOUS PROVISION OF SERIALS

The problems of serial provision in public libraries are more varied and complex than in most other categories of library, mainly because of the very diversity of their clientele and the multiplicity of their objectives. Basically their aim is to provide the serials necessary to serve the needs of their readership in exactly the same way as other types of libraries. Contrast, however, the difficulties of attempting to fulfil this seemingly simple task with those presented in the academic, industrial, government or special research library. In these latter cases, the coverage is usually strictly limited both as to subject field and standard of provision, and the number of clients is similarly limited. The term 'limited' is, of course, a relative one and I can imagine university librarians thinking, quite rightly, that their responsibilities are very broad. Even in these cases, however, the numbers of students and staff are finite, as are the subject fields of the various faculties. Public libraries, on the other hand, have no generally accepted sets of aims which can be applied over the whole gamut of them, and often feel that they are expected to be all things to all men. Certainly it is true that they are called upon to cater for the recreational, educational, vocational and general information needs of whatever sections of the public choose to use them, and from experience have found that they are often expected to provide services in depth on almost any subject under the sun, often for readers with right of access to one or more of the special types of library listed above and accustomed to receiving very sophisticated services from them which they assume the public library can duplicate.

This, then, is the size of the problem facing the public library with regard to the selection, exploitation and preservation of serial publications of all kinds. It is only possible in a short chapter to draw attention to particular differences of approach to these three facets of serials provision at the serious or research level.

The first, and most obvious one, is that of financial restraint, particularly in these days of rigid government control of public spending. The number of serial publications is legion and very stringent selection, monitoring of use and revision of subscriptions are all necessary to obtain the maximum cost-benefit out of what are strictly limited resources in even the largest public libraries with recognized regional reference and information responsibilities. No one library can hope to be fully comprehensive these days in view of the numbers of periodicals and their expense, which means that two further responsibilities have to be undertaken to correct this failure.

The first is to ensure that the library takes as many abstracting and indexing journals as it can afford in order that it shall have the keys to unlock the doors to those sections of the literature it cannot afford to buy and store. In any subject field where knowledge is advancing rapidly, such as science, technology and medicine, it is an axiom that books contain only secondhand information and the value of periodical literature cannot be too strongly emphasized. The latest research projects, detailed accounts of experiments carried out in furtherance of them and the actual practical applications of the results are described in the relevant specialist journals within a relatively short space of time. This information does not appear in book form until a much later date, and much of it never appears at all in full but merely in the form of references to the periodical articles in question. These facts make it imperative that the library has these abstracting and indexing tools to back up the numerous citations of periodical literature in textbooks mentioned above.

The second is the role the library will be called upon to play as a referral centre at local, regional and national levels. In the same way as it is necessary to have a large abstracts collection to signpost bibliographically the material which exists, so it is equally vital to make available as many location guides as possible where the files containing the references may be consulted or approached for loans or photocopies. Such guides as *BUCOP* and *World list of scientific periodicals* and the like are sufficiently well known not to need emphasizing, but locally compiled lists are invaluable for arranging speedy matching of reader with reference. Co-operative schemes to do just this and much more have existed ever since SINTO pioneered this work in Sheffield, to be emulated in many areas and forms since, and are sufficiently well documented elsewhere[1,2] as not to require repetition here.

Official standards for serial provision in public libraries do exist in the Library Association *Standards for reference services in public libraries* which were approved by the Council on 7 November 1969 and published in February 1970.[3] These were prepared on the initiative of the Reference Special and Information Section and drawn up by a Working Party of that Section strengthened by representatives of the erstwhile County Libraries Section, the Library Advisers of the Department of Education and Science and a representative of the Office for Scientific and Technical Information, as it then was. The Appendix to these Standards defines 'Standards for provision of reference material' divided into 15 categories, of which Periodicals, Directories and Guides, Timetables and Statistics fall within the definition of serials we are considering. An attempt is made to lay down minimum levels, both numerically and qualitatively, of provision in these categories. For example, the largest reference library dealt with, that serving a population in excess of 300,000, the recommendation was for a minimum of 1,500 periodicals (excluding donations) plus major newspapers both national and foreign. In practice, the major reference libraries with regional responsibilities and catchment areas of two to three million normally take close on 5,000 titles at an annual cost approaching £100,000, quite apart from their not inconsiderable expenditure on directories and the other categories mentioned above. Financial restraints again, with a vengeance! The Standards are currently being revised after the passage of ten years and the upheaval of Local Government Reorganization and they should be promulgated anew before the ten-year period has elapsed in 1980. The intention is that the Appendix should follow a similar pattern of groupings under types of material and should be equally valuable for guidance purposes. A blanket recommendation of particular importance is that devoted to Local Material where it is urged that all libraries collect local material comprehensively for the area within their boundaries, with the larger libraries assuming responsibility for their region. It puts the onus fairly and squarely on the library to preserve locally published periodicals including parish magazines, newspapers, electoral registers, telephone directories, council minutes, local acts, publications of societies and firms and ephemera such as theatre programmes, invitations to functions and sales catalogues. Indeed, if the public library does not carry out this responsibility, who will? If it neglects it, much valuable and unique material will be lost for ever by default.

DIRECTORIES

Directories are a specialized form of serial publication which can be of great value to the clientele of a public library for a number of reasons. They have been sufficiently written up elsewhere[4] not to require more than a passing reference here. Usually issued at annual intervals they take a variety of forms from professional lists, trade or town directories and telephone directories to international directories in particular fields. Trade directories are appearing in increasing numbers of specialized facets, as are numerous bogus ones issued for no other reason than to earn money for the publisher by the sale of advertising space.

Directories being notoriously expensive both to produce and to buy, financial restraint rears its ugly head once again in connection with a collection of them. In addition to the initial expense, they have got to be replaced at frequent intervals to keep their contents both relevant and accurate, which gears up the already high cost of such a collection considerably. The smallest library should attempt to have a basic collection of all directories of local town or area, of any relevant local trades or industries, the local chamber of commerce, and a selection of the basic professional lists with emphasis on any local factors such as a large medical or other faculty at the local university. In the large city reference libraries with regional responsibilities this will grow to collections of 4,000-5,000, backed up by company and investment material and stock exchange services of various kinds. The City Business Library in London[5] and the Commercial Library at Manchester[6] are probably the two leaders in this country and have rendered very readable accounts of their services through the pens of their librarians.

POPULAR PROVISION OF SERIALS

The old stereotype of the public library reading room, so beloved of fiction writers and film makers, no longer exists in any numbers.

Festooned with 'Silence' and 'No Spitting' notices, peopled with a sprinkling of decrepit readers leafing through *Punch* or the *Illustrated London News*, or worse still using these magazines and the daily papers as cover for a quiet snooze in a warm room away from the elements, this type of establishment has long joined the Cotgreave Indicator in the dustbin of library history, but problems of newspaper provision still exist.

The main one, as ever, is to ensure a fair political balance between the major political parties to avoid any allegation of bias in their selection. This has become, if anything, more difficult as the extremists do not want a fair balance to be maintained. They believe, or profess to believe, so vehemently in their own extreme doctrine that they want to prevent anyone reading the opposite political viewpoint and try to involve the library actively in their struggle through the selection of newspapers and journals. One of the favourite ploys is to offer to supply a particular paper or journal free in exchange for an undertaking that it shall always be on display. Further complications arise in areas where immigrant communities exist, especially where their origins are from regions antagonistic to each other, this often leading to friction if one group or another feels that organs published by the other faction are being displayed without their side being similarly provided for.

As a general rule I would say the objective should be to provide a good cross-section of national newspapers, with the added proviso that the library should regard it has a duty to take any locally published newspapers and preserve them permanently, either by binding or on microfilm, for future use as primary source material in their Local Studies Library. The question of permanent preservation of national dailies is not as vital as it used to be, except that it is still useful to have as many full retrospective files as funds permit. This aim is more easily fulfilled in these days of relatively cheap microfilm sets and reading equipment.

The Library Association Standards[3] have something to say on the provision for even the smallest library, as have Donald Davinson[7] and Malcolm Campbell[8]. The first puts the minimum number of periodicals at 60 excluding donations, ranging upwards to the 1,500 titles mentioned earlier, and the general recommendation is that the majority of such periodicals should be permanently filed. This has to be reconsidered bearing in mind the availability of back-up stocks at the British Library and elsewhere now available, but the value of a good collection of serials on the spot has been discussed previously.

PROCESSING OF SERIALS

As far as the acquisition, processing and preservation of periodical and serial holdings are concerned, these functions need be performed no differently in public libraries than in libraries of other types of similar size. They can range from the simplest manuscript accession records to the most sophisticated forms of computer control, according to the size and complexity of the records involved. Indeed, many methods pioneered and refined in industrial and academic libraries have been quite happily adopted by public libraries once the snags have been ironed out for them. The reverse is, of course, equally true. The only acid test is whether the system is efficient and capable of producing whatever details are required from it speedily and accurately.

One small, but significant, difference in processing after receipt stems from the very public access to the collections implied in the name public libraries and is an important one in the scientific and technical field. This is the necessity to mark permanently on individual numbers of periodicals the date of receipt in such a position that it will be retained throughout the life of the journal and after it has been bound. This is vital for legal cases involving patent law, where what are known as 'prior art' searches loom large. In a nutshell, if it can be proved, when objecting to the granting of patent rights, that a particular point at issue had been generally known previously, the patent application usually fails. The fact that a journal containing the information had been generally available to everyone in a public library is usually held to constitute prior publication and librarians are often called upon to provide affidavits to this effect and produce the relevant periodical complete with date stamp affixed or a photocopy of same. The point is that it has to be in a library open to all the public, not restricted to one particular section as in an academic or industrial library.

Another problem not exclusive to public libraries, but particularly widespread there, is that of parts being removed, leaving the files incomplete when they are due for binding for permanent preservation. The part is often irreplaceable and out of print by the time for binding, with all the frustrations of incomplete volumes in the set. This is yet another reason to be thankful for definitive sets maintained for permanent reference at the British Library and elsewhere. If I were asked what had been the biggest single factor in revolutionizing the availability of periodical literature it would have to be the excellent resources and services developed at Boston Spa. Be that as it may, however, it cannot be too strongly emphasized that the existence of the British Library Lending Division's holdings, or the existence of on-line retrieval facilities (of which more later) does not absolve any library and particularly no public library, from its obligation to provide a representative collection of serials both for current awareness and retrospective research purposes. Availability is the key-word here and the additional resources listed above should only be regarded as back-up services to reinforce the facilities available locally. The value of regular access on a continuing basis to a carefully selected collection of periodicals as they appear is immense. The number of readers who demand specific references only is a small minority, and their demands would quickly dry up altogether if they read nothing else on a regular time scale.

The whole question of what periodical files should be kept permanently is a thorny one, particularly in the light of these modern developments. It has always been a choice between how such valuable storage space, usually in expensive prime city-centre sites, can be monopolized by back-runs, balanced against the staff time and resources necessary to undertake the obtaining of all needs from other sources, with all the carriage and postal charges involved. Not to mention the question of whether such a service is equally valuable to the reader.

Attention has been focussed on this dilemma ever since the excellent services of Boston Spa first became available, and it is likely that more and more demands will be made on this central store as libraries of all kinds cancel subscriptions to journals either out of financial necessity or conscious choice. A further fillip will be given to this process by the widening use of on-line retrieval, particularly BLAISE through which an increasing number of data bases will become available as time goes on. A Utopian, if somewhat glib, school of thought seems to be developing which envisages the library of the future without any current or back files of periodicals at all to back up their book-stock, not even indexes and abstracts. The BLAISE terminal would be there, or some other visual display unit, giving instant access to all the many specialist data banks from medicine to engineering. The staff would merely interrogate the machine to obtain a list of relevant references, which could then be ordered from Boston Spa by pressing the appropriate key and the items would arrive by post the next day! Librarians have been heard boasting that they had financed the acquisition of a terminal by cancelling so many standard and abstracting journals which they now no longer need, but had they really thought it through logically?

The majority of specialist periodicals already exist on a knife-edge of sales, and wholesale cancellations if this attitude were to spread will drive them into oblivion. It should never be forgotten that each cancellation of a journal subscription could be the last straw to break that particular camel's back and thus lead to an actual diminution of a primary information resource. Similarly, or more acutely, with the abstracting services. Many of the specialized data bases which the terminals interrogate are themselves produced as a by-product of the hard copy abstracting journals (or vice versa according to your viewpoint) and financed largely by the subscriptions to these very journals. Again, large-scale cancellations could result, not only in the loss of the bath water of the abstracting journals, but of the baby of the computer data bases along with it, and where would the A.D.2001 scenario be then? That the publishing authorities for some of these journals are aware of the danger is evidenced by the fact that some of the abstracting journals will only allow access to their data bases to subscribers to their journals. Experience in industrial libraries using on-line retrieval extensively has also shown that it is a positive advantage to have the hard copy abstracts available both to back up the references retrieved and to enable the readers to browse more widely among related topics. This browsing facility, particularly in conjunction with a good book-stock, has long been recognised in academic and research circles as one of the most fruitful both for current awareness and extending a reader's interests and grasp of the subject in question.

No one is more aware than me that it is impossible to deal in depth with all the aspects of serial provision in public libraries in a chapter of this length, and so it has proved. The problems will continue, not least those of financial restraint; the option which many libraries seem to regard as a soft one in hard times is to cancel periodical subscriptions. This inevitably produces more problems, not only at the library making the cancellations and thereby reducing its own services, but at other libraries such as the nearest regional reference library onto which the demand is thrown either unwittingly or, all too often these days, quite deliberately. All this apart from the manifold problems discussed previously. If the arguments have only convinced a few that a good serials collection is a vital part of the public library service, which should be maintained at the highest standard commensurate with the funds available, it will have been worth writing.

REFERENCES

1. Taylor, F.R. *'Public library technical services'* in P.H. Sewell (ed.) *Five Years Work in Librarianship 1951-1955.* Library Association, 1957. 135-46. (32 references.)
2. Taylor, F. R. 'Library service to industry in Great Britain and on the Continent'. *Library Trends* 14 no. 3 Jan. 1966. 306-31. (60 references.)
3. 'Standards for reference services in public libraries'. *Library Association Record* 72 no. 2 Feb. 1970. 53-7.
4. Henderson, G. P. 'Directories and company information sources', in M. J. Campbell, *Manual of business library practice.* London, Clive Bingley, 1975. Ch. 5 63-78.
5. Campbell, M. J. 'The public provision of business information: consideration of some problems encountered in establishing and maintaining the City Business Library'. *Library Association, Reference, Special & Information Section, Conference Proceedings* 1976. 51-8.
6. Smyth, A. L. *Commercial information, a guide to the Commercial library.* 3rd ed. Manchester Public Libraries, 1969. 32 pp.
7. Davinson, D. *The periodicals collection.* Revised and enlarged ed. London, André Deutsch, 1978.
8. Campbell, M. J. 'Periodicals, newspapers and other ephemera', in M. J. Campbell, *Manual of business library practice.* London, Clive Bingley, 1975. 127-38.

8

University Libraries

Adrian Peasgood

INTRODUCTION

The archetypal serials section of a British university library in the late 1970s would administer expenditure of £75,000–£100,000 per annum and handle 2,000-3,000 current titles. (A small minority of these would be duplicated, or be received as gifts, or within exchange programmes.) Such a section would operate without a working distinction between 'serials' and 'periodicals'. It would use a subscription agent for the majority of existing and new business, business which would have increased significantly in relative value since the early 1970s to about 55 per cent of the library's overall expenditure on stock. No net increase in the number of titles received would have been recorded, however. The section would produce a printout list of the complete serials stock of the library, but less than once a year; although there would be only an even chance of the holdings' being notified elsewhere a fair number of outside users would be consulting them.

The operations of this archetypal section would be centralized in one office dealing with receipt and claims, binding, and public enquiries. Latest parts would be separately displayed, and not available for loan. Bound volumes would be kept separately from the monograph stock in either an alphabetical or a classified sequence, and would be loanable, probably for more than a week. A fairly constant proportion of stock, about a fifth, would be retained in unbound form, most commonly in boxes. Various separate sequences of serials stock would be maintained: only a small minority of titles would be involved, normally in a closed access store within the library building. Less than 5 per cent of serials stock would be in microform; it would be kept with other non-book materials. Few, if any, changes in the arrangements for display, loan, or storage, would have been made in the 1970s.

The section would typically be circulating parts of titles in bibliography and librarianship among library staff, and be sending copies of contents pages to a few academic users. It would be receiving little regular information about the use of holdings, but rather more about requests for inter-library loans. Formal external relationships of the library would include a library committee, dealings with academics acting as library liaison officers, and the activities of its own subject librarians; new subscriptions, cancellations, and loans policies would all be discussed at some point within this framework. However, the effective decision about new subscription proposals would usually be taken by a member of the staff.

The composite description above is based on the answers of 51 university and college members of SCONUL (Standing Conference of National and University Libraries) to a questionnaire sent out in July 1978. The overall response rate, 85 per cent, did not conceal poor returns from any particular group of libraries, so the survey can be regarded as comprehensive. The high response rate to a long questionnaire, and the extent to which respondents accepted an invitation to describe their own situations in more detail than the pro forma allowed, seem to testify to an increasing awareness among university serials librarians of the complexity and importance of their activities, an awareness also exemplified by the scale of their response to Blackwell's periodicals conference of April 1975 and the subsequent creation of the UK Serials Group. The information generously provided by colleagues has allowed me to provide in this chapter an authoritative description of many aspects of current British academic serials librarianship; where I criticize particular features I do so in full awareness of the fact that colleagues were not in their replies necessarily themselves approving the situations described. The results of a similar survey in the USA are reported in an article by Geraldine Murphy Wright.[1]

The libraries discussed not infrequently fall into groups within which particular characteristics predominate. By 'new universities' I mean those wholly new institutions established in the 1960s, and by 'technology-based' I refer to the other new universities of the 1960s, those developed from colleges of advanced technology and similar institutions. Other named groups do not require definition. Libraries referred to by abbreviations are SOAS (School of Oriental and African Studies), SSEES (School of Slavonic and East European Studies) and BLPES (British Library of Political and Economic Science), all part of the University of London, and UWIST (University of Wales Institute of Science and Technology).

Two-thirds of responding libraries do not have a working distinction between 'serials' and 'periodicals'; it is hence impractical to attempt one in this chapter, and the use of one term rather than the other at any particular point is without significance.

Totals of answers to different questions vary because not all libraries could answer all questions in the terms proposed.

FORMAL RELATIONSHIPS AND POLICY-MAKING

It is probably impossible to ask questions about formal relationships and policy-making which will receive consistent and unambiguous replies. Names common to several institutions may not denote common responsibilities, and the perception of where effective power lies in relation to a given decision will often vary within the same institution according to the position (and interests) of the observer. My questions on these subjects were intended to be as hospitable as possible to the various answers respondents needed to give; none the less these questions gave respondents more problems than any others.

All libraries have library committees (though several are advisory only) and almost everywhere individual academic staff act as library liaison officers. Well over half the libraries (but noticeably fewer in the technology-based institutions) have staff with subject responsibilities. Rather less common, especially in Scotland and Wales, is the practice of having library staff serving on academic committees: barely half the libraries have this sort of contact with their parent institutions. Of the four main kinds of formal relationship libraries involved in all four total 20, including all but one of those in the new universities, founded as these were in a period when principles of open/collective management were in fashion. Twenty-three libraries are involved with three of the four. Disproportionately many of the technology-based libraries are among the eight which reported involvement with only one or two. Possible reasons for this bear thinking about: historical accident? recruitment difficulties? deliberate decision? The likelihood, or otherwise, that they will gradually adopt majority practice is another matter for speculation.

That one or more of the formal relationships is nearly always invoked when decisions about new subscriptions or cancellations are to be made is no surprise. Less expected, particularly in view of the direct effect upon users of decisions in the area, is the fact that barely half the libraries expect to discuss loans policies in such forums. (The numbers are very small, but it is striking that six libraries of the eight which adopt the minority practice of lending current parts are in this category, as are two-thirds of the libraries adopting the minority practice of not lending bound volumes as a matter of routine.) Perhaps it is more surprising that 13 libraries refer questions of binding policy to one or more of the elements mentioned: it should be added, though, that the policies reported by these libraries do not differ significantly from those of the majority. No library volunteered a comment on the formal relationships involved in decisions about relegation to store, evidence, perhaps, of tacit hopes that the need for them will not materialize.

Effective decisions about new subscription proposals are taken in one of three main ways, each adopted by about one-third of reporting libraries. The chief librarian tends to have responsibility in London and in technology-based institutions; other library staff are responsible in almost all the new universities and in a few others; library or academic committees are likely to be responsible in Scotland and in the redbrick universities. Given the generally larger size of these last it is likely that library committees rather than librarians have been determining the majority of the rather small number of new subscriptions recently possible.

ACQUISITION ACTIVITIES

The annual expenditure on serials of £75,000–£100,000 incurred by my hypothetical archetype was in fact recorded by 16 reporting libraries, mostly those created in the 1960s, whether *ab initio* or from existing institutions. Another dozen, typically the large redbrick university libraries, spent £100,000–£150,000, and seven, including three in Scotland, spent over £150,000. Only the libraries of some smaller institutions within the University of London spent less than £50,000. As percentages of overall expenditure on stock these various totals nearly all lie between 35 and 65, with SOAS and SSEES below that range and Heriot-Watt above it.

When acquisitions activity is looked at in terms of titles received rather than of money spent the distribution is rather less regular:

Number of current titles	Number of libraries receiving same
500–1,000	4
1,000–2,000	8
2,000–3,000	11
3,000–4,000	10
4,000–5,000	6
over 5,000	12

None of the new or technology-based libraries receives more than 4,000, and no university in the south of England outside London receives more than 5,000 — the assumed accessibility of metropolitan collections may help to explain this latter fact. In view of recent and continuing economic difficulties it is noticeable that the number of libraries reporting a decrease over the past five years in the number of titles received, 19, is only one greater than that of libraries reporting an increase. (Five others reported their intake as constant.) With this balance in mind it is interesting that of libraries in which the effective decision about new subscriptions was reported as being that of a library or similar committee only four recorded decreases as against seven which reported increases. Again the numbers are small, but the implication is plain: library committees tend to give serials a higher priority than do library staffs. It is not possible to tell from the questionnaire results whether they order more new titles or cancel fewer existing ones.

Use of subscription agents for serials purchases is widespread. For 26 reporting libraries agents provide more than three-quarters of their purchases, and a further 16 libraries acquire between a half and three-quarters of their purchases in this way. Almost all these 'usually' place new subscriptions through agents, so there is clearly a favourable verdict, on balance, on the services so provided. The few libraries using agents only rarely include several with atypical intakes, such as SOAS, SSEES, and Cambridge; at Cambridge, where purchases are of foreign material only, the existing low level of use of agents is being further reduced in the belief that lower prices and prompter responses characterize direct contacts with publishers.

Acquisitions other than by purchase, i.e. by gift and exchange, do not account for as large a proportion of intake as the attention often given them in professional literature might suggest. Exchange programmes in particular are little developed, with 35 libraries receiving under 5 per cent of their intake in this way, and only five libraries receiving more than 10 per cent. The libraries largely inactive in this field include all the new and technology-based institutions. Is this because, as at Sussex, the parent bodies do not produce publications suitable for inclusion in exchange programmes? The libraries particularly active include those of SOAS, SSEES, and Durham, where area studies cover countries likely to be particularly interested in exchange arrangements for one reason or another.

No such common characteristics are discernible among libraries more or less interested in gifted titles. Sixteen libraries reported under 5 per cent of retained titles received as gifts, 19 reported 5–10 per cent, and 16 over 10 per cent. Given that much gifted material arrives without particular library initiative these variations may reflect differences in retention policies rather than other, more calculated, responses to library needs. Perhaps increasing pressure on space will lead other libraries to follow Reading's increasingly critical attitude to 'marginally useful' gifts.

Duplication of titles is not widespread. Only Leeds reports having more than 10 per cent of intake duplicated, and only another four (SSEES and three large Scottish universities) have more than 5 per cent. SSEES retains some duplicates against the possibility of mutilation and the problems of subsequent replacement; some of its duplicates are sent in excess quantities by exchange partners. The other libraries with relatively heavy duplication refer to overlapping demands within decentralized library systems. Nine other libraries have to duplicate for this reason rather than because of volume of use; one hopes that the benefits of decentralization are sufficient to justify such expenditure. It is noticeable that all the new universities have to duplicate only when volume of use requires it.

ORGANIZATION OF STOCK

In only one library (BLPES, where limitations of space allow no alternative) is the majority of current parts kept with the corresponding bound volumes, though several libraries (e.g. Swansea and Sussex) observe this practice for special classes of title such as abstracting and indexing journals. Dominant practice involves the separation of all unbound parts from bound stock, and (in about two-thirds of the libraries) the separation of current from other unbound parts; in several libraries current parts are shelved with other unbound parts after a short period, perhaps a week, on separate display. One hopes that practices such as these, which are clearly convenient for library staff, do also reflect different patterns of use by readers of very recent as distinct from older issues. The experiences of libraries which have recently changed their policies in this area provide conflicting evidence: Aston and Nottingham (Law library) have for various reasons begun shelving special classes of title with bound volumes, but Nottingham's Medical library, at Queen's Medical Centre, is pleased to have been able to abandon the practice. Since occupying its new building St Andrews is able to keep current parts with other unbound parts instead of separately and is pleased with the change; Aberdeen, however, hopes to move towards separate display for an increasing number of titles. A suitable research project might provide useful guidance to librarians reviewing their own practices.

While a score of libraries has automated security systems only four protect the majority of current parts, and many protect none at all. This situation is clearly determined in part by the particular equipment associated with different systems, but must sometimes be the consequence of a freely-chosen policy. The effect upon services to readers clearly depends on particular local arrangements for balancing the needs for access and for security. At Sussex, the one reporting library to protect virtually all unbound parts, it was calculated that the cost — labour and materials — of protecting current parts would be very similar to the direct costs incurred in replacing missing current parts and in controlling the issue of other unbound parts from closed access shelves; in the first three months of operation about 10 per cent of all interceptions were of the unauthorized removal of unbound parts. Protection should largely eliminate the need for a closed access sequence and the overheads of replacing missing issues; it is surprising that it is not more widespread.

The organization of stocks of bound volumes takes five different forms, with none being noticeably more or less favoured than any other. Sixteen libraries arrange bound volumes in a classified sequence separate from that of the book stock; eleven alphabetically within subjects; nine in one alphabetical sequence; eight alphabetically within a few broad divisions; and eight in the same classified sequence as books. There is a tendency for Scottish libraries to favour one of the classified arrangements, and for libraries in London to prefer one of the alphabetical options, but the absence of any real consensus is confirmed by the variety of choices made by the new universities of the 1960s: in no other area covered by the present enquiry do their practices vary so widely. It is astonishing that so fundamental a question as the optimum presentation of a library's back-runs of journals should still be unresolved. Uncertainty in this matter is also reflected by the variety of changes made during the last five years: two alphabetical to classified, two from subdivided to single alphabetical, and one from broadly-divided alphabetical to subject-divided alphabetical. In addition, two libraries reported considering changing from a classified to an alphabetical sequence. Perhaps there is no particular net advantage in any arrangement: it would be reassuring if this conclusion were reached by an adequate research project.

Microform serials are largely excluded from the arrangements just described: in 40 libraries they are kept with other non-book materials. While this may well have been appropriate when the various microforms were occasional novelties it is surely fast ceasing to be so: with current parts of major titles such as *Dissertation Abstracts* now optionally available in microform, the advent of more specialist titles such as *Pragmatics Microfiche* published only in microform, and the increasing range of back sets so available, microform stock is surely far more appropriately housed with traditional hard copy siblings. There are difficulties, of course — the provision of reading machines over a wider area of the library, security, especially of microfiches, holders for microfiches — and it is perhaps not surprising that only five libraries (including Stirling, Sussex, Bradford and Aston) reported some kind of integration of microforms with other serials stock. (Incidentally, in these five libraries are found four different arrangements of that 'other' stock.) A sixth, Reading, hopes to move towards integration. It should be added that not all the libraries keeping microform serials separately from other non-book materials do so as a deliberate long-term policy, and the quantities involved are often very small.

Perhaps the most substantial issue in the general area of accommodation of stock — at least to judge by the quantity of discussion thereof — is the UGC's intention, following the report of the Atkinson

Committee, to enforce much greater use of store sequences as a preliminary to the discarding of less-used material. In fact 35 libraries already have separate and secondary sequences, though 15 of these are very small, not holding more than 5 per cent of serials stock, and only 11 hold more than 15 per cent. Such sequences are found in almost all English redbrick and older Welsh and Scottish libraries, but in only half the technology-based libraries, and in less than half the libraries of the new universities. The application of full Atkinson principles would lead to a marked increase in the number and scale of separate, secondary, sequences, so it is of interest to record the situation in the four libraries in which a quarter or more of non-official serials stock is so housed: at Loughborough and SSEES the proportion will fall when new accommodation becomes available, while at Cambridge the secondary sequence is of copyright intake of a largely different character from that usually administered by academic libraries. Only at Leicester, where a major reorganization in 1977 placed all pre-1960 serial volumes in a stack sequence, will there be in the immediate future experience of anything at all like the shape of library predicated by the Atkinson report, and even these arrangements are not intended to be permanent. How actively are university libraries responding to the problem of diminishing space? Five libraries reported changes in 1977 to policies for secondary sequences, as compared with seven which had made changes in the four previous years. This suggests an increasingly fast tempo, but only two libraries in addition to those already named — Warwick and Sussex — mentioned developments in this area among changes expected in the next five years; doubtless exigencies of space will oblige others to add this problem to their agendas.

An obvious major problem for most libraries in determining policies and practices for separate sequences is the inadequacy of the information most receive about the use of their stocks. Only nine claim regularly to receive information about the use of their bound stocks, and, while 24 have occasional or limited information, 16 get none at all. (Of the nine with regular information, three — Surrey, UWIST and Aston — are among the seven which also receive regular information about the use of current parts.) The variety of stock and loan arrangements described elsewhere in this chapter probably makes impossible the application of a single standard methodology for establishing levels of use, but further work on the problem would be of value to many institutions.

ORGANIZATION OF SERVICES

Loan regulations for current parts are usually prohibitive and everywhere highly restrictive. Forty-four libraries do not lend current parts at all, or lend them only on special request, and in the eight which do lend routinely a variety of restrictions is applied in addition to an almost universal 24-hour or overnight limit: status of borrower (Warwick), unavailability till week after receipt (Warwick, Reading), and unavailability of some groups of titles (Aston). Only three libraries have changed their practice in recent years. Although current and other unbound parts are almost everywhere shelved separately from other serials stock only seven libraries regularly receive information concerning their use. One might imagine that such information would have been both particularly sought in a period of financial strain and relatively easily available given the separate housing of the items. As with studies on the use of bound volumes an acceptable methodology is an urgent desideratum.

Loan regulations for bound volumes are, by contrast, more varied and more subject to change. Nine, very different, libraries have made changes in this area in the past five years, more than have changed their policies on any other issue in the survey. In seven the change was towards much shorter loan periods or a no-loan policy, and in an eighth loans on special request have given way to routine, but only overnight, loans. These results are a little surprising in view of the fact that 38 libraries still lend bound volumes routinely, the majority for a week or more. The others, which lend only on special request or not at all, are mostly libraries begun or developed in the 1960s. It will be interesting to see whether the more restrictive policies already in force in many of these newer libraries continue to spread into older, larger libraries with different traditions. It could also be interesting to consider loan policies at the same time as the availability and cost of photocopying facilities.

The separate displays usually provided of latest parts are presumably an expression of the need to facilitate 'keeping up with the literature'. If so, it is worth looking also at two other ways of doing this: circulating the parts and distributing copies of contents pages of newly arrived issues. All but three libraries circulate parts (usually only those of journals in librarianship and bibliography) to their own staffs; on the other hand, academic staff are circulated in only 11 libraries. The theoretical accessibility and retrievability of parts on colleagues' desks as compared with parts scattered around campus on the desks of academics must be the defence of this difference in scale of service. Surely, however, library staffs are uniquely well placed to inspect current parts displays, and accordingly have least need of the circulation of parts therefrom. It is surprising that more use is not made of the photocopier to make copies of contents pages for distribution within the library, yet only eight libraries do this. The sending of such copies to academic staff is clearly a question on which no consensus exists: 18 libraries do not do this at all (although two of them will circulate the actual parts), 22 do it on a very small scale, and eight fairly widely, including Aston, where the programme has been extended at the request of departments not initially served, and where requests for photocopies are sometimes direct responses to the service. The others are a heterogeneous assortment of libraries of different sizes, ages, character, and geographical distribution. Complementary information about their practice in disseminating particulars of newly-arrived books might be interesting.

LISTINGS AND NOTIFICATIONS

Only 12 libraries do not produce a list of serials holdings, half of them libraries within the University of London system awaiting lists produced within the new union list for that group. However, of the 38 lists described by reporting libraries almost half come out less frequently than annually, including six which are computer-aided in some way. It is disappointing when machine-readable files are not used to produce updated lists more frequently, and also puzzling: at Sussex about a thousand amendments are made in all to the year's two or three issues of an average-sized list of current titles only — if a similar number accumulates for less than annual lists elsewhere they must be seriously misleading for much of their life.

Twice as many lists are of complete holdings as are limited to current titles. Almost all the smaller libraries, those of new and technology-based institutions, and of the smaller London colleges and schools, have complete lists. Swansea and Hull, with lists of current titles only at present, hope to extend their coverage when resources allow.

The decision to produce a list is largely a matter for an individual library, but interest in its holdings will usually exist off campus. With all their problems union lists of serials are more practicable than union lists of other library stocks, and it is disturbing to find that British university libraries are not reporting their holdings more widely. Not quite half notify their holdings to any national office, a fact which only evidence of very considerable overlap of titles could render acceptable; apparently none of the former Colleges of Advanced Technology reports holdings nationally. This group is indeed particularly uncommunicative about its resources, including as it does six libraries of the ten which make no reports anywhere, and four more reporting only to local or regional systems. It may be a measure of the perceived value of the notification of holdings that as many libraries report into local systems as nationally, and that nine report only locally. Discussions about the future of the *British union-catalogue of periodicals*, and the uses to which its records are put, could usefully take note of these figures.

OTHER QUESTIONS OF CURRENT INTEREST

No less than 20 other topics were suggested by libraries for inclusion in this survey. The majority were mentioned once only and may well chiefly reflect particular local problems, but those mentioned more than once are presumably those on which serials librarians generally would welcome more information. The commonest concerned the relationship with book acquisition departments, in particular the delimitation of responsibility for the various kinds of serial (as distinct from periodical) publication. (This tends to confirm the discovery made when we at Sussex reviewed our standing orders procedures and list a couple of years ago, and a literature search produced virtually no relevant material.) Plenty of attempts to define serials and periodicals exist: their failure is indicated by the fact that, as mentioned earlier, two-thirds of reporting libraries do not have one as a working tool. Perhaps rationalization of practice in this area can never be complete, particularly, several libraries noted, as categorization could affect such matters as loans policies and financial control. However, some further attention to the problem would clearly be welcomed — if it were of practical application!

The second commonest suggestion was that the consequences of a decentralized or departmental structure should be examined more closely. Half the responding libraries have duplicate subscriptions because of the requirements of such a structure; one suspects that this is frequently felt to be unjustified by the volume of use. Variations in the arrangement of stock, and in loan regulations, from one sub-library to another, both found in about half the decentralized systems (though not always the same ones) may be disliked by library management as untidy but actually be appropriate responses to special needs, or be confusing to users and hence undesirable anyway. It would be good to know more about this.

Several libraries wished for information on staff numbers and grades. I fear that this would be misleading unless accompanied by rather detailed analyses of the precise responsibilities of the various periodicals sections which, as we have seen, vary widely.

A fourth subject of common concern was accounting procedures. The rapid inflation and fluctuating exchange rates experienced in a period of cash-limit budgets have exacerbated familiar problems of serials budgeting.

Among other, less frequently mentioned, subjects may be listed: back-run, relegation, and disposal policies; cancellation procedures, including requirements that existing titles are cancelled when new ones are started; the place of newspaper stocks; stocktaking and ordering of replacements; serials section housekeeping arrangements; the place of union lists in serials administration; the impact of photocopying.

THE NEXT FIVE YEARS

Few of the current problems identified above or mentioned earlier in this chapter are to be tackled in libraries' reported plans for the next five years. Most extensions of computer applications will improve serials lists or catalogues, not address the difficulties of financial analyses or control. Only two libraries outside London mention increased attention to relegation and discarding policies, so a fair-sized body of experience in this difficult area is unlikely to develop unless the programmes of librarians are determined, as they well may be, by *force majeure*. On the other hand, most London academic libraries do hope to be able to rationalize stocks and current subscriptions following production of the new London union list. No library reported an intention of studying such subjects as the optimum organization of back volumes, including those on microform, or methodologies for establishing patterns of use, possibly including the effect of alternative loan policies, especially for bound volumes.

REFERENCE

1. Wright, G. M. 'Current trends in periodical collections'. *College & Research Libraries* **38** May 1977. 234–40.

9

Polytechnic and College Libraries

John Cowley

Efficient serials acquisition within a polytechnic is linked with the academic development and activity of the institution. The effective use of resources depends on the library's awareness of academic developments and the involvement of librarians with committees and boards concerned with forward planning. Library development strategies are linked to institutional aims and this enables the librarian to create core collections, provide for new courses and options and support selected research areas within agreed budgetary limitations. This measure of support also carries with it elements of planned insufficiency for areas less in need of support, such as those in declining teaching areas or those adequately covered in other local institutions or through systems of inter-library co-operation. On the face of it such a system appears sensible and operationally sound, but experience suggests that a clear understanding of academic priorities and objectives has not always been a strong feature of polytechnic planning. It is possible, therefore, to find the library operating in something of a vacuum, on the one hand being deprived of the guidance arising from effective forward planning but, on the other hand, having no lack of rather disparate, subjective advice from individuals and departments. In such a context a well-planned strategy for serial provision has been extremely difficult to achieve.

It is also the case that the majority of polytechnics have to contend with a number of organizational and administrative features which have considerable impact on serials librarianship. There is first the multi-site problem which inevitably splits the stock between a number of libraries and causes difficulties over duplication and the proper administration and exploitation of material. Secondly, polytechnics, in recent times, have created a substantial range of new courses, most of them validated by the Council for National Academic Awards (CNAA), many of which are multi-disciplinary or inter-disciplinary in nature, thus making it difficult for the library to create collections along classic subject lines. Another influencing factor has been the polytechnic's drift towards more higher-degree and research activity, and this has had considerable impact on the nature and scope of serials provision. Collections have had to be given greater depth, with a result that costs per subscription have risen as more advanced material has been purchased. Finally, the recent period of financial stringency, which placed great pressure on all library budgets, had a harsh impact on polytechnics who were still in the initial phase of stock building. The relative newness of these institutions and their lack of extensive retrospective collections, such as those to be found in long-established universities, made the loss in purchasing power particularly hard to manage. While hesitating to say that these problems are unique to polytechnics, nevertheless they are matters which deserve further examination and comment.

The multi-site polytechnic creates demand for multiple provision of serials. Demands for six copies of a given periodical are not unknown, while purchase of two or three copies is commonplace. Means have to be found of curtailing spending on duplicate material and these have included critical appraisal of all requests for additional copies and the making available of inter-site current awareness services designed to keep the academic user informed of contents pages even though the periodicals themselves may be located elsewhere. Other economy measures have included the binding of only one copy in the system, although this still allows for the retention of unbound files of additional copies for periods of three to five years, or for as long as is judged to be useful in relation to demand. During the difficult period of the mid-seventies, investigations into the burden of multiple provision of material showed that newspapers and popular weeklies in particular were absorbing large sums of money perhaps better spent on academic material. Many polytechnics, therefore, decided to reduce provision of this kind to the minimum on the grounds that in a period of financial difficulty newspapers and the like could be purchased by the individual rather than the library. However, the problem of multiple copies will remain largely unsolved unless course locations are agreed along orthodox subject lines thus enabling related studies to be located on the one site. Failing that, the librarian may look towards advances in electronic transmission of the printed page across sites to provide the answer to this problem.

The staffing and organization of serials work is also affected by the scattered nature of the multi-site polytechnic. Most central acquisition units have been concerned with the centralization of book acquisition and the automation of cataloguing, but periodical reception and administration have been left mainly to individual sites. City of London Polytechnic, however, have centralized their serials acquisition, and the current interest in staffing economies together with the production of computerized control records suggests that the trend towards centralization may be accelerated in the next few years.

At the moment, reception of serials at sites is normally in the hands of an assistant or young professional charged with the task of ordering, claiming, receiving, recording and distributing serials. Preparation for binding is normally included in the duties and this incorporates a considerable amount of file checking and re-ordering of missing items. McGregor,[1] basing his views on American experience, suggests that each serials librarian operating in an efficient environment can process about 2,000 subscriptions annually and that individual output may improve in relation to higher volumes of throughput up to 5,000 items per year. Most polytechnics process between 1,500 and 3,000 items split between a number of reception points and are, therefore, denied these economics of scale. The typical site library will process between 400 and 800 periodicals and these absorb much of the time of one librarian. If McGregor's findings are correct the fragmented activity at sites is probably uneconomical of staff time and deserving of further investigation if the benefits of central control are to be gained.

CNAA approval of new courses in polytechnics has usually involved a review of supporting book-stock and periodicals. This in turn frequently created a need to extend both the range of current serials acquisitions and back-runs of key journals. The existence of excellent support from Boston Spa has not enabled the polytechnics to avoid the need to create reasonable retrospective stocks. In some subject areas, the provision of adequate serials related to new degree submissions caused significant diversion in spending patterns in the absence of special capital funds. The high cost of collection building was particularly felt in certain subject areas. The field of law, for example, requires the spending of tens of thousands of pounds to meet basic first degree requirements, and the maintenance of significant collections in the field of science and technology increasingly places pressure on library funding. Despite these problems, the polytechnics have endeavoured to create improved collections of serials and have been prepared to allocate 40 per cent of the book-fund for this purpose.

The balance of resources between those provided for teaching on the one hand and for research on the other has also continuously exercised the mind of the serials librarian. While it is beyond dispute that polytechnic involvement in research has been considerably less than in the universities, it is nevertheless the case that they are now introducing more higher degrees and research work into their programmes. This in turn is bringing greater pressure on library budgets and making it imperative for a higher element of selectivity and planning to be applied to stock building. Polytechnics located outside London have particularly difficult decisions to make in that they may not have access to other major research collections within reasonable travelling distance and are faced with the high cost of developing their own advanced stocks. London area polytechnics are generally better placed to take advantage of the major research collections conveniently at hand, but the ability to borrow or have access to research material housed elsewhere has not solved the problem of to what extent polytechnics should allocate funds to the building of expensive research collections. It may be necessary, when considering this question, for the librarian to differentiate between material required to support research activity having the full support of the institution and that conducted out of private interest. The distinctions can be very fine in some cases but it is clear that priority should be given to research having strong institutional backing. In any case, whenever a research proposal is submitted, some account should be taken of associated library costs and additional funds obtained for this purpose.

Another and related question to be faced is whether the library purchases serials purely in relation to current demands or with an eye to the future and the creation of major subject collections for the use of successive generations of students and researchers. The purchase of the periodical of substantial academic worth but low current usage may well be justified in relation to the long-term academic well-being of the institution. The library must also consider whether or not it is capable of maintaining expensive serial commitments designed to offer subject coverage agreed within terms of local or regional co-operation. The extent of a library's altruism can be influenced by declining purchasing power, although commitments of this kind should not be lightly dismissed. Indeed, sensible local co-operation acted as a protection against the ravages of inflation in the mid-seventies when discussions were held between groups of institutions with a view to maintaining area copies of important but expensive serial publications. The immediate availability of a journal on the premises provides the ideal solution, but its location in another library in the same area may provide an acceptable and cost-effective response to the needs of the academic user.

Recent increases in the annual rate of inflation have tended to underline the importance of an initial careful selection of serials. The average cost of a typical academic periodical, now over £30, is such as to induce caution in the mind of the librarian under pressure to add a title to stock. Once a subscription has been taken out there may well be a reluctance to cancel, particularly if bound sequences have been established. Factors such as price, relationship with existing stock, alternative availability and intrinsic worth must be investigated. In the early years of polytechnic development this degree of control was probably not fully exercised and minor retribution followed when the inflation of the mid-seventies played havoc with serial prices. Academic institutions reported over 30 per cent inflation in a single year and realized that if the trend continued periodicals and continuations would absorb an alarming proportion of funds. As a result, for the first time in their short history, polytechnic libraries began to examine seriously the true value and worth of their holdings and requested academic colleagues to consider how best to find cancellations representing 10–20 per cent of total holdings.

Experience at several polytechnics showed that the selection of an initial list of cancellations, perhaps to the value of 5 per cent, was not difficult. Academic staff were helpful once they realized that the alternative was a greatly reduced supply of book-stock and a freeze on new subscriptions. However, when a second wave of cancellation became inevitable, as a result of persistent inflation and static funding, cries of indignation began to be heard. It was at this point, for instance, that the difficulties created by the splintering of subjects around sites and courses became more apparent. It was clear that the needs of those who taught a subject as a minor option in a modular degree course had less interest in certain learned journals than fellow academics teaching in the same area in a single-subject honours course. One man's cancellation became another man's disaster. The librarian was often faced with conflicting advice and had the added difficulty of ensuring that all interests had been consulted before decisions were taken. There was a danger in this situation that months of consultation and analysis might lead to very limited results and targets not being achieved.

It became necessary, therefore, to establish certain criteria designed to guide these activities. Multiple copies were an obvious target for cutback, as were those resources which had been selected and accumulated in relation to courses now suffering a decline or which had undergone radical change. It was found that a substantially redesigned course always created a demand for new serials coverage without the reverse process of cancellations taking place.

Pressure on space and finance encourages librarians to reject the idea of the incremental growth of serials stock. While the Atkinson Report has suffered a fierce rejection by academic librarians, its basic premise that libraries cannot continue to grow unchecked has been accepted by librarians prepared to set up rolling programmes of stock-editing leading to the systematic relegation of material. The regular editing process, ideally conducted by subject librarians in consultation with academic staff, is more desirable than occasional panic exercises carried out when inflation or space problems became acute. While it is inevitable that a net growth in stock will occur, the rate of expansion can be checked by the use of such methods.

The centrality of periodicals in the search for current and specialist information not only raises questions of the purchase and storage but also of subsequent indexing, retrieval and exploitation. Phillpot and Houghton[2] point out that 'in certain areas of design, industrial design and fashion design the periodical is arguably the principal source of information'. With books virtually non-existent 'for both up to the minute information and for historical research material, the periodical may be the only extensive source'. Furthermore, given that browsing can be inefficient when the need for information is pressing, the question of systematic retrieval has to be faced. Printed indexes provide some answers but many fringe periodicals are not indexed and the publication of indexes often runs months behind requirements. This raises the question of local indexing and the time the librarian can usefully spend scanning serial publications. Hatfield Polytechnic attempted the task of providing an in-house index on cards for the benefit of industrial and academic users, with some success, but the investment of time and finance raised critical questions of cost effectiveness. Many librarians attempt some indexing on a modest scale where printed index coverage is known to be deficient, and such an example at Middlesex Polytechnic for Art and Design articles has proved to be very useful to both librarians and users.

Students involved in advanced work will be heavy users of serials but even at this stage need help with the tracing of material through printed index and abstract services or, increasingly, by means of on-line information retrieval. Recent developments in this field are providing quicker, more efficient ways of tracing required information, but users require considerable assistance if computer services are to be used effectively. It has been suggested that the librarian, acting as an information intermediary, should help the user to structure his enquiry and guide him through the difficulties of on-line retrieval. As Williams[3] has reported, the untutored user may well achieve little at great cost if help is not forthcoming. At the moment, the majority of retrieval exercises in polytechnics involve the use of extensive and expensive collections of printed indexes and abstracting services, but the signs are there that printed services having only modest use may be cancelled as costs increase and will be replaced by the provision of on-line information retrieval facilities.

Polytechnic librarians have given a great deal of thought to the display and exploitation of periodicals and the degree of commitment to subject librarianship has influenced their treatment of stock. Current issues are frequently located in a periodicals area near the main entrance of the library, but in other cases material is displayed on the appropriate subject floor where book-stock and bound and current periodicals are found together under the control of specialist subject teams. Both methods offer strengths and weaknesses. It is likely that a polytechnic strongly committed to subject librarianship, as at Hatfield, will prefer to bring subject collections of serials and monographs together in the one area, with subject specialist staff on hand to exploit the collection and to help readers with their enquiries. On the whole, this is an effective approach to the task of maximizing stock usage, but such is the extent of inter-disciplinary work in polytechnics that it can be argued that the creation of subject collections militates against this approach to study. Users can very easily fall into the habit of using only one area of the library, thus depriving themselves of access to a much wider range of material. The geographer operating in the main geographical collection may well be missing vital planning material located in the law and architectural areas. Adequate display, guiding, publicity and instruction can substantially overcome these problems.

It is crucially important that current journals are displayed attractively in order to arouse interest and their availability advertised in current awareness bulletins, contents page services and regularly-revised holdings lists. It is also vital for academic staff, with help from the librarian, to produce effective student reading lists. These should be revised regularly and made available to the library in advance of distribution to students. Co-operation between librarians and academic staff should extend to the selection of key articles which might be provided in quantity for selected groups of students once appropriate copyright clearance has been obtained.

Perhaps the more vital aspect of the exploitation of serials stock in polytechnics has been the provision of programmes of library instruction carried out by Subject or Tutor Librarians. It is difficult to monitor the impact of this work but it seems likely that interest in periodicals and continuations has increased as a result of this activity. Some polytechnics have developed their user-instruction programmes to a fairly advanced level. Initial basic instruction for the first-year student is often followed by more intensive subject-based teaching at a later stage in the course when the student is faced with his first major project. The student's search for up to date information leads him naturally to the periodical, and his activities are substantially helped by library courses designed to make him aware of sources and their use. Subject librarians often supplement this instruction by offering tutorial guidance to individual students and by distributing short guides to literature searching. Tape/Slide programmes have also been used to good effect. The combined impact of printed publicity, library instruction and the normal readers' advisory services undoubtedly guarantees substantial use of serial materials.

The future importance of serial publications in the academic library is beyond question, but the high cost of subscriptions, binding and storage is bound to raise questions concerning future approaches to stock selection and retention. The polytechnics have no long tradition of commitment to major stock development in this area, and it seems likely that advances in micro-publishing and computer services will change approaches to serials librarianship. It is not difficult to envisage a reduction in paper copy and the placing of greater reliance on on-line information retrieval, microfiche presentation and the electronic transmission of information at one time only available on the printed page. To that extent, it is possible to predict a change in the nature of services provided and the need to place a great deal of effort in user education to ensure that academics and students are aware of trends. This is not to say that the printed serial is becoming unimportant, but new technologies and services will change patterns of use and raise fresh questions about allocation of resources. Fortunately, the polytechnics are quite well placed to respond to this situation.

REFERENCES

1. McGregor, J. W. 'Serials staffing in academic libraries'. *The Serials Librarian* 1 no. 3 Spring 1977. 259–72.
2. Phillpot, C. and Houghton, B. 'Periodicals and serials', in P. Pacey (ed.) *Art library manual,* Bowker, 1977. Ch. 9.
3. Williams, P. W. and Curtis, J. M. *Short term experimental information network project – Final Report.* University of Manchester Institute of Science and Technology, 1975. 20–4

10

Industrial Libraries

B. G. Dutton

'If I may repeat a phrase made on a number of occasions by some of the public librarians: "Who the hell do these industrials think they are?" my answer is that we are the most important group of librarians in existence' (Doris Palmer, as 1977 Chairman of the Library Association Industrial Group.)[1]

WHAT IS AN INDUSTRIAL LIBRARY?

To judge the effectiveness of a present-day industrial library by the size of its materials collections, whether of serials, books or other, would be as imprecise as judging the size of an iceberg from a sighting above the water-line, for the industrial library is not primarily a collection of materials but an *information facility* designed to provide access to relevant and timely information to meet the needs of a mission-oriented clientele ranging from research workers to production managers, from sales staff to safety officers, so that each can make a more effective contribution to the well-being of the business to which all belong.

As such, it has a number of well-defined characteristics which set the environment for the functioning of the various serials processes and operations described in the first section of this book, and it is the purpose of this chapter to examine these characteristics and then to go on and show how they impact on serials processes and operations in a progressive industrial library.

CHARACTERISTICS OF THE INDUSTRIAL LIBRARY

Timeliness of Output

Of all the characteristics of the industrial library, timeliness in response to the satisfaction of users' needs is unquestionably the most important. This timeliness is of two sorts — the speedy acquisition of any document which the user has identified as needed, and the provision of new information whilst it is still new. It is this latter service which explains the predominant position of the serial in the industrial library, for no other type of document is so all-embracing, covering for example, research results, news items, statistical data, announcements, correspondence, and advertisements for products and services.

Mission-oriented

Industrial libraries do not exist to satisfy any legal or social requirement. They are set up by organizations specifically to meet the information needs of those organizations within defined financial limits, and if they fail to meet these twin criteria they risk dissolution.

As a consequence, they must be quickly responsive to changing requirements, and to this end they are completely mission-oriented. Thus, whereas traditionally, industrial libraries handled mainly scientific and technical information in a research and development context, the increasing need for industry to be keenly competitive to stay in business has led to a considerable widening of the library role to serve commercial and business information needs. These needs in turn are sufficiently distinctive to demand a reappraisal of procedures. Equally, subject interests are constantly changing, and this is reflected by appropriate changes in the make-up of the collections.

Non-self Sufficiency

The effectiveness of an industrial library does not depend on the quantity of materials held. As Davinson says,[2] 'every librarian likes to be able to make an immediate supply of material no matter how abstruse the request. However, the cost of providing the abstruse on demand is becoming prohibitive' — floorspace dedicated to storage of little-used materials, particularly if staffed, is inefficient in wealth generation. Even the largest industrial library is small enough to allow serials staff to be familiar with the time-usage patterns of most serials, and the key to effective working lies rather in the ability quickly to identify documentary sources of information to meet specific needs and the operation of efficient routes for subsequent acquisition of material required.

Thus when an operation is available through an external commercial service, this is the preferred choice with participation in a shared service coming second; internal procedures need particular justification.

Examples where a commercial service is often most cost-effective include the borrowing of lesser-used documents from the British Library and subscribing to commercial press-cuttings services. The fact that external services demand payment in hard cash as distinct from salary allocations is a stimulus to users to distinguish the 'nice to have' from the 'need to use'.

Accessibility

There is an inverse relationship between the distance that an industrial potential library user has to travel to visit his library and the extent of his personal use. Since it is rarely cheap to 're-invent the wheel', the organization needs its staff to extract maximum benefit from existing information and hence sets up the principal library centrally where, unfortunately, space is at a premium. Consequently, subsequent expansion is rarely possible and the Atkinson concept of the self-renewing library, regarded as novel by academic institutions, is both normal and practicable in the fields of commerce, technology and most science. However, as the industrial library moves from being a research service to become an organization resource, the more it becomes necessary to set up service points, also of limited size, in other departments to accommodate the desk-bound.

Traditional Emphasis on User Training

The desire of an industrial organization to exploit existing information also manifests itself in the high attention which has always been paid to the education of users into an understanding of serials and their use. In the past, methods were somewhat restricted by the lack of supportive resources, but as it becomes increasingly the norm for all kinds of libraries to concern themselves with the exploitation of their holdings as distinct from exercising an archival function, the picture is changing rapidly. Self-instructional packages (tape-slides, work manuals, etc.) are becoming increasingly available whilst courses on the exploitation of the serials literature are run by many local centres for industrial librarians.

Use of Professionally-unqualified Staff

In the industrial organization, it is not uncommon for the library to be both managed and run by staff without professional library qualifications. The manager (and any information scientists in the organization) will often have taken up their positions by transfer from other functions, whilst the processing of serials is considered to be just another junior clerical task requiring no great skill or knowledge. As a result, and again also to encourage use of the library, serials identification and handling systems require to be simple.

PROCESSES AND OPERATIONS

It is proposed in this section to draw attention to aspects of the processes and operations described in Part 1 which are peculiarly applicable to industrial libraries, relating these where appropriate to the characteristics just described. It is anticipated, however, that as economics and the computer exercise an increasing influence in these operations, differences between all kinds of libraries will lessen. Thus Urquhart's description[3] of the academic librarian of the future as a 'cost-conscious manager concerned to provide the maximum service using the minimum resources' accurately describes the present-day industrial librarian.

Selection

The subject interests of many industrial organizations are constantly changing to such an extent that active on-going monitoring is required not only to ensure adequate selection choice but also to avoid continuing subscriptions to serials no longer relevant. User participation is actively encouraged, both spontaneous and arising from distribution of publishers' notifications.

Staff of industrial firms make particularly high use of computer-generated SDI profiles of periodical article titles and/or abstracts to provide current awareness, and these items can provide a valuable supplementary indication of serials potentially suitable for purchase by the library. (Indeed, profile output can be embarrassing to the serials librarian since references can arrive well ahead of the journal issue itself, causing customer irritation as well as increased administrative effort.)

Acquisition — Borrowing

The British Library affords the quickest all-round source for borrowing serials and also, when all costs are taken into account, the cheapest, and it is encouraging to the time-conscious industrial librarian to note that there is on-going experimentation to maintain and even improve both the ordering and delivery systems.

Electronic ordering facilities are rapidly becoming available whilst full articles corresponding to bibliographic references received during on-line interrogation of some computerized data-bases can already be ordered from the British Library at the time of interrogation by the same means. For delivery, the success of a recent experimental van delivery service of documents is expected to lead to introduction of such a system over the UK as a whole. The latter service will also reduce staff packing effort necessary for document return.

Acquisition — Purchase

In selecting a supplier for purchase, special attention needs to be paid to the time factor involved in the transport of material of topical interest. In the case of certain weeklies, such as the *Economist,* a delay of even one day may be intolerable to an industrial manager, and in such circumstances a local newsagent may offer the best service.

In the UK, multiple copies often arrive more quickly if sent in individual wrappers rather than in bulk packages, although in cities bulk van deliveries may be feasible. For overseas journals, it may be sensible to have one copy sent by airfreight or airmail. If microform (or magnetic tape) format is ordered, it should be remembered that delay can occur at airports while customs officials confirm that VAT requirements have been met.

Use of standing orders for yearbooks, directories, etc., whilst convenient, may result in delivery delay as some publishers give priority to spot orders since these may lead to new business; if used for monographic series, on-going relevance must be monitored also. Commercial services exist which for a small premium will supply a copy of any published serial within a stated time-period.[4]

Controlled circulation journals whilst rarely containing much original article materials are often valued by the industrial user for their advertisement content. These may often be acquired at an advantageous rate by applying to the publisher in the name of a senior executive of the organization.

As public interest and involvement in the interactions between industry and society grow, the industrial serials librarian is likely to have to devote increasing effort to the identification, acquisition and monitoring of 'alternative' or 'underground' journals, particularly those published in his firm's geographical area or subject field — one directory[5] currently lists several hundred of these.

Display and Circulation of Current Issues

This is an area where different approaches are required to satisfy the respective needs of science and technology-oriented staff and those on the commercial side. The former are characteristically browsers, (and are encouraged to be so, despite attacks on the effectiveness of this approach,[6,7]) and like current journals to be displayed and by subject grouping, whereas the latter are more office-bound and prefer immediate circulation with just a few journals on display in alphabetical order for quicker access. (It is a further characteristic of the industrial library that several copies of news-type journals may be bought to ensure timely receipt of current information.)

Circulatee decisions are best developed on an individual title basis. In principle, circulatee order should be based on recipients' need rather than on hierarchical position. In practice this may not be achievable, but senior executives are time-conscious and will, on gentle prompting from the librarian, usually agree to copies being passed on quickly, perhaps marked for later attention, when they are absent. Alternatives to routine circulation range from provision of a facility for initialling copies of serials on display if subsequent circulation is required through to circulating one or more of several commercial publications made up of the contents pages of journals in a particular range of disciplines and catering specifically for this form of current awareness. The British Library Lending Division offers such a service on individual journals.

The Main Collection

From the viewpoint both of encouraging the user and of assisting the non-professional staff, the layout of the main collections and guides to location should be as simple as possible. For the journals, a simple alphabetic sequence is to be preferred to a subject grouping, whilst for directories, monographs, etc., a simple arrangement adapted to the particular collection is to be preferred over sophisticated classification or an over-enthusiastic use of symbology.

Certain types of serials (other than periodicals) play a particularly important role in the industrial library. These include the annual reports of other companies (sometimes accessible only through shareholders), stockbroker and bank reviews and directories. The last of these are relatively expensive and a small but up to date collection is to be preferred to a more diverse one of varying vintage. The British Library has recently acknowledged a responsibility to develop its resources in this area.[8]

Indexes to serials also should be of simple construction, avoiding title abbreviations if possible and stating clearly any conventions that are used.

Where journals are to be bound, speed of return is an important consideration in the choice of a binder. Some commercial services will make special arrangements for the quick return of items in high demand. Particular care should be demanded over the treatment of business journals containing advertisements mixed with text since it is only too easy, when advertisement pages are removed, to lose isolated snippets of news which will be needed in subsequent retrieval operations. The size of individual volumes should also be kept down since, irrespective of the easy availability on the premises of original journal copies, industrial users are avid photocopiers of single articles to form personalized reference collections for purposes of research, and spines crack easily when thick volumes are forced open on a platen.

Microformat can play a useful space-saving role for maintaining or acquiring older runs of journals, but caution should be exercised in its use of supplying recent serials since irrespective of improvements in microform technology, the majority of users have a subjective dislike of the medium and will react to its introduction by not reading material and particularly long articles in this form. In fact, the typical industrial library is not well suited to the provision of attractive microform reading/browsing conditions. Moreover, some reading is done out of office hours, and although truly portable fiche readers are now available which can be used at home, equipment is not yet available which permits easy reading (as distinct from quick reference look-up) on 'plane or train.

Disposal

Numerous attempts have been made to devise general formulae to assist in the disposal (and selection) processes for journals, based on bibliometric studies, such as citation counts, and are claimed to work well for large libraries, but for relatively small collections such as typify the industrial library, analysis of actual use (including the temporary withdrawal of material to secondary storage to identify reference activities) is probably the most reliable criterion. Caution is required even by this method for recently-commenced journals since use may grow considerably after two to four years as references are picked up to papers.

Because industrial libraries are characteristically mission-oriented, with changing goals, no special merit is placed on maintaining long, continuous runs of journals, especially in fields no longer germane. If interest reawakens, much of the older material will not be wanted again or can be re-acquired more usefully in microformat.

This approach is in marked contrast to that of academic libraries where, 'a new subscription is a commitment'; 'it is better not to place a subscription than to have to cancel one'.[9] This view is confirmed by White[10] but ignores the fact that many of the new journals, especially but by no means exclusively those in science and technology, are created as a medium for communication in new fields, the early exploitation of which can be critical to the success of the industrial firm.

The high standard of loans facilities afforded by the British Library also makes it attractive to dispose of older holdings in favour of borrowing from this source, especially since the BLLD will normally accept that material which it does not itself hold.

Budgets and Costs

The fortunes of an industrial library are closely related to those of its parent organization, and the industrial librarian, in justifying his budget, needs to demonstrate in terms understandable to his general manager the contribution which his various services are expected to make to the success of the business. Whilst this can be demanding it is a fairly simple process compared to the dialogue necessary between public library and local authority or between academic library and government, since all levels in the industrial organization share closely the same easily identified objectives.

Serials have always constituted the major part of the materials budget of the industrial library (Burkett[11] quotes 55 per cent as a typical figure) although this difference from other main types of library is steadily lessening as serials costs grow disproportionately.

The pre-payment of journal subscriptions over periods longer than a year, usually at a discount, may superficially appear to be an attractive way of saving money but in principle, in a thriving business, the capital thus taken up should be better employed invested in the main objectives of the business. On occasion, change of subject interests would also result in a commitment to irrelevant titles.

The high use made by staff of industrial firms of computer-generated current awareness (SDI) profiles and of on-line retrospective search based on periodicals contents poses a range of budgeting problems. Selective charging out of costs is desirable to measure true need (in fact early experience points to the industrial end-user being willing to prove his need with his money), but most computer data bases cover a range of periodicals orders of magnitude greater than the average industrial library will stock, and hence the subsequent acquisition of full texts by borrowing can be expensive both in direct cost and through introducing a demand for provision of translations, Japanese affording a special problem to industrial librarians. Particular discipline is required in operating those on-line services which supply primary articles from bibliographic citations by command at the time of search.

New cost elements likely to arise over the next two to three years are those associated with copyright (through changes in the Copyright Act) and lending generally (through any Public Lending Right Act). In both cases, the major concern to the industrial librarian is not the actual sums of money to be paid (despite current preoccupation with this aspect) but that the accounting may involve considerable administrative effort.

THE FUTURE

The decade of serials librarianship to 1990 is likely to be dominated by the consequences of a continuing rise in the cost of human labour relative to the costs of electronics hardware.

This will have a particular impact on industrial libraries in terms of the continued development of mechanized systems to keep down staffing requirements, and minimize the costs of ancillary human-based services.

There is not likely to be any major decline in the role of the paper-based serial in libraries as a whole. However, the progressive industrial library, at least in the advanced countries, will have developed a very different approach to serials handling. Before many of these developments can come to fruition on a large scale the question of adequate financial compensation to publishers will have to be resolved. Once this is achieved we shall see an on-going contraction in serials purchase concomitant with an expansion of serials availability by electronic transmission on demand until only those serials are purchased which serve a true browsing function. The rate at which new technology is actually applied to transmission of serials content will in part be influenced by the reluctance of public and academic libraries to pay any premium for timeliness. There will be an accelerating tendency for primary and secondary periodicals to be replaced by synopses and back-up material, with very little demand for the latter. This in turn will particularly benefit the industrial user by reducing electronic transmission costs and reading effort.

Money will be available to industrial libraries to support many other kinds of technical development in the serials field where these can be seen to improve the effective use of information, e.g. use of video- and audio-cassette journals, holograms, etc.

Increasing sophistication in the application of domestic telecommunications equipment — the TV set and the telephone — will lead to some industrial tasks being conducted from the home, and traditional on-the-spot library services will need to be supplemented to take account of this.

Thus the industrial serials librarian, although needing different skills, will still be very much in business!

REFERENCES

1. Woodworth, D. (ed). *Economics of serials management: proceedings of the 2nd Blackwell's Periodicals Conference.* Loughborough, Serials Group, 1977. 113.
2. Davinson, D. *The periodicals collection.* Revised and enlarged ed. London, André Deutsch, 1978. 166.
3. Woodworth, *op. cit.,* p. 4.
4. e.g. Alan Armstrong and Associates Ltd and other organizations listed at intervals in this firm's *Library and Information News.*
5. *Directory of alternative periodicals.* 3rd ed. Brighton, Smoothie Publications, 1974.
6. Mayes, P. (ed). *Periodicals administration in libraries.* London, Bingley, 1978. 45-6.
7. Urquhart, D. J. 'National lending/reference libraries or libraries of first resort'. *BLL Review* **4** no. 1 Jan. 1976. 7-10.
8. Hookway, Sir H., in response to a question at Aslib 52nd Annual Conference, Edinburgh, 1978.
9. Mayes, *op. cit.,* p. 41.
10. White, H.S., at Aslib Annual Conference, Edinburgh, 1978.
11. Burkett, J. *Industrial and related library and information services in the United Kingdom.* London, Library Association, 1972. 192.

11

Government Department Libraries

Geoffrey Hamilton

Serial publications are of great importance in government department libraries, and typically account for more than 75 per cent of the stock measured in shelfrun, and for an even higher proportion of departmental expenditure on the purchase of publications. The reason for this preponderance is that government departments need a constant supply of up to date information covering the whole range of matters in which they are involved, and in order to obtain it must receive a very large number of that class of publication — viz, serials — which has been developed over the past 300 years to communicate current information.

In spite of the importance of this material in departmental libraries, and the very considerable effort that is expended in handling it, hitherto little has been written about it. The 1974 consultants' report on central government departmental libraries[1] includes results of a sample survey of library users which showed that an average of 63 per cent of staff were officially receiving periodicals on circulation, and 17 per cent got personal copies of newspapers. The companion report on departmental libraries' reserve material[2] includes some statistical tables on holdings of pre-1946 serials, and an analysis of binding activity during 1973/74. The present paper enters upon largely uncharted territory, and concentrates upon the experience of one group of libraries in the belief that the problems encountered there are similar to those which arise in other departments.

The context of the following account is the network of libraries known as 'The Departments of Industry and Trade, Common Services: Libraries' (DITLS). This network has developed from the grouping of libraries that occurred after the formation of the Department of Trade and Industry (DTI) in 1970. Today DITLS comprises separate libraries for the Departments of Energy, Industry and Trade; libraries for the Monopolies and Mergers Commission and the Office of Fair Trading; the Statistics and Market Intelligence Library (SMIL); the Marine Library of the Department of Trade; a branch library of the Department of Industry serving several blocks of staff located in the Millbank area; and a legal library. All these are in central London, but the network also includes libraries in other parts of the United Kingdom; while the Department of Trade headquarters library also serves Diplomatic Service Commercial Officers in nearly 200 British Embassies, High Commissions and Consulates throughout the world. All told, the number of serials titles currently received in DITLS is over 25,000. In many cases several copies of a serial are acquired. The number of incoming items handled in a year is about one million.

Within these departments DITLS is responsible for supplying all publications needed in connection with official business, and no expenditure on publications can be incurred without library approval. In this respect the situation differs from that found in some other government departments, where only publications needed for library purposes are acquired on the librarian's authority, and the acquisition of other publications falls within the province of another official, such as the Clerk of Stationery. In general, most periodicals received by DITLS are needed for circulation to officials. Newspapers, weekly journals of comment and opinion, scientific and technical periodicals, trade journals, academic journals, specialist news services are all well represented amongst the items which circulate regularly. Although various services are available which use other means to bring information from serials to notice, there is no prospect that circulation of periodicals will ever be totally superseded. These alternative services include press summaries or press-cuttings services, provided by each department's Press Office, the weekly *Contents of Recent Economics Journals* produced by the Department of Trade Library, and the current awareness bulletins prepared by several other libraries. Experience with these shows that it is possible to reduce the circulation of periodicals, and so achieve some worthwhile economies by cutting the number of subscriptions to a title, but the interests within each Department are so wide ranging, and subject to such frequent changes, that it will never be possible for an intermediary to scan and select from all potentially useful serial publications.

A centralized Serials Acquisitions Section undertakes ordering of serials on behalf of most DITLS libraries, though some of them find it more convenient to order their own, particularly newsagents' items, or if their subject interests change frequently, and consequently periodicals that provide background information are needed for only relatively short periods. The many departmental offices which have no library are granted authority to make certain local purchases, subject to control by the library service. In all cases the Acquisitions Section handles invoices and subscriptions as they pass to the Common Services Accounts Branch, and prepares monthly analyses of expenditure broken down by libraries, for the information of the authorizing officer in each library (this is the Senior Librarian).

In the DITLS Serials Acquisitions Section, professional (as opposed to executive) and clerical staff are used. The duties in this section are almost entirely housekeeping, for example, no cataloguing, classification, scanning, indexing or abstracting is done. The basic professional grade (Assistant Librarian) has advantages over similarly-graded executive staff because library school training gives some basic knowledge of the difficulties of serials management and the problems of acquisition. This means Assistant Librarians can be effective very quickly, which is important because they are not normally kept on this work for more than 18 months. They are also capable of checking bibliographies and understanding things like alphabetization, and some are able to make a reasonable stab at translation and transliteration. Above the basic level, more experienced professionals provide continuity; experience and knowhow in such fields as evaluation of material, interpretation of need, knowledge of the right source (and alternatives) for any particular item, listing of serials for any particular need; and management ability.

Responsibility for selecting serials, and for decisions to terminate a regular supply, rests with each library. The need for a regular supply of a serial is assessed on the basis of information about its content and the interests of library users. Although the Library Service holds the purse strings, and the formal authorization of a librarian is a prerequisite to acquisition action, many selections are in effect made by library users. Sometimes the initiative is theirs, and the request for a supply is sparked off by publicity from a publisher or as a result of having seen the publication at a trade exhibition, or during a meeting with industry or officials from other departments. In other cases libraries or Serials Acquisitions Sections circulate descriptions or specimen issues of new serials to divisions likely to be interested in their contents.

For expensive items the endorsement of a statement of need by a Head of Branch (Assistant Secretary level) may be sought before an order is placed, or the supply may be arranged for a trial period — usually a year — and subscription renewal made dependent on a satisfactory assessment of the item's value. The Library Service has agreed a policy with senior management that restricts the number of daily papers and political/cultural weeklies circulated in a division.

Although many new serial subscriptions are for circulation to divisions, the place of serials in the stock of each library is constantly borne in mind. Directories and yearbooks are heavily represented in the reference collections of all libraries, although in many cases the need in one or more divisions for desk copies for ready reference is such that additional copies must also be provided. There is often a gradation in need for the very latest information, so that some economy can be effected by arranging a second distribution, under which some sections receive the immediate past issue of an annual, for instance *Who's Who* or *Statesman's Yearbook*, when the new one arrives. There are also some serials which, although certainly worth having for the sake of predictable items of departmental interest, do not publish material relevant to a particular division's work often enough to justify circulation. The library acquires such serials, and takes steps (such as reproduction of contents in a current awareness bulletin or analytical cataloguing) to bring relevant contents to the notice of interested parties. Where the relevant material in a serial overlaps the interest of two or more departments, the question of number of copies and their allocation is settled through discussion at the weekly Book Selection Meeting attended by all Senior Librarians.

An important factor in serial selection for government department libraries is the frequency with which new interests develop in the departments, are avidly pursued for periods of time which may be of very limited duration, and then are dropped. This accounts both for the extent to which selection involves the users and the relatively high proportion of new subscriptions which are placed for well-established titles. There is for each library a core of serials which have in all probability been regularly received since publication commenced, and are likely to stay in the acquisition programme for as long as they continue to be published. Others are acquired to meet a particular information need resulting from departmental involvement in a specific task.

Another typical feature of serials selection in government libraries is the emphasis on deciding the number of copies required, rather than a yes/no decision on acquiring a serial at all. This is because of the size of the departments served, the dispersal of officials with similar information needs over several locations (even within the same building, peculiarities of layout may result in as severe communication problems as are found in two separate but reasonably adjacent buildings), and the need for a number of officials to have simultaneous access to the same information source. The future development of 'electronic journals' might resolve these problems; so long as the simultaneous availability of serials in n locations can be achieved only through the provision of n copies, government department libraries will have to continue to handle multiple copies of many serial titles, which in a few extreme cases may be numbered in the hundreds rather than in tens.

The channels of supply used for acquiring serials comprise those which are also employed by other kinds of libraries, as well as some which are peculiar to government departments. Until recently practically all purchasing of any kind of publication for government departments was arranged through Her Majesty's Stationery Office, and there was no provision in departmental votes for expenditure on publications. The trend in recent years has been for departments to be authorized to purchase more categories of publications, and consequently for an increasing proportion of expenditure on publications to be borne by departments. There are a few special cases, chiefly annuals, where the total need for the Civil Service is for so many copies that HMSO is able to negotiate a significantly more favourable bulk purchasing discount than individual negotiations by departments could achieve. These special cases apart, departments are free to make their own arrangements for serials acquisition, and the supply of many items is arranged via newsagents, subscription agents or direct from publishers.

Some government departments, including those served by DITLS, have two other sources of supply through which significant numbers of serials are received. These are (a) exchanges and (b) supplies via Diplomatic Service overseas posts, which together account for many of the overseas statistical serials and trade directories acquired for the

Statistics and Market Intelligence Library. There are two kinds of exchange arrangements. The first is organized under the 1928 International Convention Relating to Economic Statistics, Article 9 of which provides for exchanges between contracting governments of single copies of any published economic statistics or statistical series. The other is an *ad valorem* exchange, under which a UK government department can arrange with an institution in another country to exchange publications of equivalent value. In both types of exchange HMSO accepts responsibility for supplying the UK publications, while the overseas publications involved are sent direct to DITLS. The main advantages of these arrangements are their elimination of foreign currency transactions, and their avoidance of normal distribution channels which may not be well developed. The disadvantages are the delays which often occur, the difficulties in taking effective hastening action, and the frequent changes in the names and organization of foreign government departments which can make it very difficult to be sure with whom the exchange is being made.

The use of the Diplomatic Service overseas posts as local agents for acquiring publications is a facility enjoyed only by a few Whitehall departments. DITLS is able to use posts because of the responsibility it has inherited from the Board of Trade Library for supplying the commercial officers in overseas posts with publications and information needed to support their work. Except for the few countries with which the United Kingdom does not have diplomatic relations, there is a world-wide network of posts. The value of this facility is therefore very great, and without it DITLS would be unable to maintain the quality of service that its users have come to expect. Many acquisition problems of foreign serials can be simply resolved on the spot, items which are not available through normal trade channels can be obtained, and bills can be settled locally in the local currency. (The sterling equivalent of all such bills is notified to DITLS through the Foreign and Commonwealth Office Accounts Branch, and the sums involved are then recovered from the DITLS vote for purchase of publications).

The need for several copies of the same serial title arises in the case of many foreign publications, as it does for serials of UK origin. Since only one copy can be obtained under exchange arrangements, any additional copies of exchange serials must come as a consequence of separate arrangements. If the serial is one in which key statistical information is first published, it may be necessary to make extra special arrangements for one copy (at least) to come via air mail. Foreign serials, not acquired through subscription agents, are one of two major classes of material not delivered direct to the libraries which need it. Experience has shown that it is preferable, because less confusing to staff in overseas posts, to give consistent instructions for all materials to be sent to the central Acquisitions Section. The consequential drawback, that for this material checking-in records must be maintained in at least two places, is judged to be an acceptable feature in the present recording system. The other case in which direct delivery is avoided is when a reduced subscription rate applies to multiple copies delivered to the same address.

The checking-in system for serials in all DITLS libraries is a manual one using Kardex records. Different varieties of Kardex cards cater for varying frequencies of publication. Each card also carries a statement of the circulation applicable. The size of most of the departments served, and the frequency with which changes in the allocation of accommodation, personnel and business within divisions occur, makes it impossible for the libraries to keep abreast of such alterations. The circulation system that has been evolved in DITLS makes use of Division (in some cases Branch) Liaison Officers, whose responsibilities include the maintenance of detailed circulation records for serials needed in their division or branch, and the circulation of those serials when received from the library. Generally speaking, when a serial has finished its circulation it returns to a library, and is stored there. Retention policies vary, between and within libraries. Because the main concern of most government department libraries is with up to date information, the great majority of serials, in DITLS at least, are held for limited periods only, on a range from six months to 15 years. A few periodicals and annuals are of sufficient continuing importance as information sources to justify permanent retention. It is also DITLS policy to retain permanent, archival copies of all publications, serial and monographic, issued by the departments served.

Bibliographic control of serials is achieved, in DITLS, through the Kardex records in each library, through the compilation and regular revision of periodicals holdings lists for most libraries, and through the inclusion in the library catalogues of entries for all serials which are permanently retained, as well as for most directories and yearbooks whether or not they are held permanently. There are comparatively few serial entries in the INTERLIB COM-fiche catalogue covering all DITLS libraries, because only entries for serials which have been acquired or have needed revised entries since April 1976 are included. It is therefore also necessary to refer to the card catalogues for each library or, in the case of SMIL, to the visible index entries maintained there, in separate sequences for its collections of directories and statistical serials.

Although serial publications as a whole present sufficient problems to satisfy all but the most masochistic of librarians, it should not be forgotten that the reason for their being acquired at all is for the sake of their contents. Fortunately, the most effective way of exploiting many periodicals is simply by circulating them to people who have an interest in the fields they cover. The circulation of surrogates, in the form of contents lists or lists of selected articles, is a refinement, while the preparation of analytical entries and their incorporation in library catalogues or in separate indexes is a means of providing for the retrieval of articles when, in the librarian's judgement, the expenditure involved is justified. All of these practices are in use in DITLS. A centralized cataloguing service faces particular difficulties in undertaking analytical cataloguing since the reason for selection of an item for this treatment is not always readily apparent to a librarian unfamiliar with the interests of the users of a particular library. The subject indexing of analytical entries by a centralized cataloguing service, therefore, does not always sufficiently reflect a local focus of interest, and some libraries find it necessary to make local arrangements for recording significant periodical articles, supplementing both the established library catalogues and published indexes and abstracts.

Entries in the DITLS catalogues are prepared to AACR standards, and the INTERLIB co-operative cataloguing system for government libraries accepts the MARC format. However, the particular needs of the users of SMIL's collections of statistical serials and directories have led to a decision to maintain that library's visible indexes in an arrangement which reflects the user's approach. This is almost invariably for an information source for a particular country or regional grouping of countries, containing data on a particular industrial product, economic activity or social feature. Therefore the index entries are arranged first under country of coverage, with subject subdivision according to a consistent classification. For SMIL's users a strictly bibliographical basis for record organization would be a tiresome irrelevance. A grouping of entries under country headings is also a feature of the Kardex records for serials checking-in, in SMIL and other libraries. There are two main advantages in this practice. First, it is easier for the clerical staff, who initially handle incoming material, to associate particular items with a certain country than to assign to the correct segment of an alphabetical file titles which are in non-Roman scripts or other foreign language titles which begin with articles or modified characters. Second, by concentrating in one area of the Kardex all publications from a given country, it is easier to recognize what is happening when changes in titles or series numbering occur, and for one or two members of staff to build up a considerable expertise in that country's publications.

The extremely wide range of interests within any Department, whose officials are constantly involved in interdepartmental discussions on matters peripheral to its major concerns, and the way in which new topics of interest come and go, means that any thought of self-sufficient libraries can be speedily dismissed. The resources of any DITLS library are available on equal terms to all the departments served, but even so it is necessary to make extensive use of inter-library lending for serials, drawing particularly upon the resources of the British Library Lending Division, other government libraries, and public corporations. The urgency of need in certain cases makes the delays of inter-library lending unacceptable, and hence it is frequently necessary to purchase a single issue of a serial not regularly received. Another form of co-operation within DITLS is the acquisition of a single copy of expensive items, for circulation to two or more departments. There is co-operation also on the disposal of back runs of certain serials, for example statistical publications from SMIL go to the British Library and Warwick University Library. Informal co-operation on acquisition of expensive serial publications of interest to the business community is achieved through regular meetings between representatives of SMIL, the City Business Library and the Science Reference Library.

The increasing availability of serials in microform has made it possible to achieve considerable savings of space through substituting, for example, microfilms of *The Financial Times* and *The Times* for bound volumes. Some statistics, for instance foreign trade figures from the Organization for Economic Co-operation and Development (which appear much sooner on fiches than in paper form) and French monthly trade statistics (which are no longer available in a paper edition), and legal material, e.g. the *Official Journal of the European Communities*, are held in microfiche form, and new items are steadily being added to the libraries' microform collections. There is an active in-house programme of microfiching, particularly in SMIL, through which serials whose physical format makes them unfit to withstand normal library usage, and those foreign government serials which are produced in such limited editions that the quantity required cannot be got, are made available for library use. SMIL and several other DITLS libraries have copying machines to handle hard copy reproduction and fiche to fiche duplication.

A particular problem associated with government departments is their liability to undergo frequent changes in organizational structure. These changes may be accompanied by the emergence of new departments, but in other cases there is simply a transfer of functions between existing departments, with consequential changes in the arrangements for supplying publications and library services. In addition, accommodation moves are continually going on, in which staff and their work are shifting between buildings or within the same building. All of these changes pose problems for government librarians, and can sometimes throw up several months' work simply to amend circulation records and issue revised delivery instructions to suppliers. The development of DITLS on a common service basis can be seen as an attempt to mitigate the consequences of organizational changes within the departments served. However, no pattern of library service organization can be completely immune to the effects of structural change in the departments served.

Automation of serials handling is a tempting prospect, though so far little has been introduced into government department libraries. Several DITLS libraries make use of departmental data processing facilities to store details of large circulations, and to print out supplies of addressed labels. The Central Management Library of the Civil Service Department has gone further with its Label/Report System for printing addresses for distribution lists and for recording management information, including who receives each publication and the costs of supplying it.[3] Development of a computer-based union list of serials in government libraries and the investigation of automated systems for serials ordering, circulation and control are matters which the INTERLIB 1 Sub-committee on Enhancements has recommended should be included in future INTERLIB activities. The problems are so pressing in some departments that action at departmental level is a possibility.

The importance of serial publications in government departments is a consequence of their continuing pre-eminence as sources for the latest information on the matters which concern those departments. Information has to be bought, but it is an essential input to government.

Therefore, adequate funding has to be allocated for the procurement of this essential commodity. The challenges that serials pose in government libraries are many and varied; but the basic problem to be resolved is always that of securing a quick and reliable supply as economically as possible. In some departments the librarian is helped in this by having access to unconventional supply channels. When the material has been acquired, the familiar problem arises of how can it most effectively be exploited? Circulation of surrogates (contents lists, analytical entries in accessions lists) is a partial solution, but for many users nothing can replace the circulation of complete issues. The emphasis on currency of information means that it is only for a minority of serials that a permanent file is retained; the implementation of limited retention policies minimizes the storage space problem for many govenment libraries. In all serials activities the guiding principle is that what is done should result in the best possible service to the library's users.

REFERENCES

1. P-E Consulting Group. *Civil Service Department study of central government departmental libraries: final report.* London, Civil Service Department, 1974.
2. P-E Consulting Group. *Civil Service Department study of departmental libraries' reserve material: final report.* London, Civil Service Department, 1975.
3. Hume, S. 'ADP—Automated distribution of papers'. *Management Services in Government,* **32** no. 2 May 1977.101–05.

12

Learned Society Libraries

Feona J. Hamilton

INTRODUCTION

Learned — characterized by or associated with learning: ERUDITE', pronounces tersely my copy of Webster's. 'Society' has several explanations, including this one: 'a voluntary association of individuals for common ends; *esp:* an organized group working together or periodically meeting because of common interests, beliefs or profession.' Using these definitions as a basis, this chapter on serials in learned society libraries will deal with both learned societies and professional associations.

In the areas of science and technology alone, there are hundreds of learned societies and professional associations, and at least as many again in the humanities. Most issue at least an annual volume, and probably a periodical as well. This amounts to a vast output of printed material to be stored and yet be easily accessible to the would-be user. As an example, it is estimated that some 500,000 items were published during 1979 in the field of chemistry alone.

PUBLISHING PROGRAMMES

Royal Society

The most famous of these learned societies must surely be the Royal

Society of London. Founded in 1660 by a group of natural philosophers, it was to be a meeting place for discussion among friends on scientific topics. Religion was specifically excluded from these discussions. At first, the group met at the home of John Wilkins, but as they became more firmly established and began to hold regular meetings with regular demonstrations, they needed a permanent base. In order to disseminate their findings and the results of their experiments to other members, they began to publish papers almost from the beginning. The *Philosophical Transactions of the Royal Society* were first published in 1665 and have continued to the present day. As time passed, numbers grew, and so did the amount of written work. The *Philosophical Transactions* were split into *Series A (Mathematical and Physical Sciences)* and *Series B (Biological Sciences)* in 1887. These both contain papers normally exceeding 24 pages containing results or methods of critical importance.

The *Proceedings of the Royal Society* also appear in *Series A* and *Series B*, and cover the same topics within each series as the *Transactions.* They have been published since 1854 and were divided in 1905. These appear more frequently than the *Transactions* — six parts or more per year rather than two parts — but consist of papers not normally exceeding 24 pages.

Two more titles have appeared more recently. Since 1938, the Royal Society has published its *Notes and Records*. This concentrates on the history of science, the history of the Society itself, and on the lives and scientific achievements of its past Fellows. In 1932, there appeared the *Obituary Notices of Fellows of the Royal Society,* renamed in 1955 *Biographical Memoirs of Fellows of the Royal Society.* It is acknowledged to be an authoritative record of some of the most important developments in science and the men responsible for them.

Zoological Society

The number of titles issued by the Royal Society is not so unusual as may at first be thought. The Zoological Society of London issues even more serial publications. Founded in 1826, the Society began publishing in 1831 with the *Proceedings of the Committee of Science and Correspondence of the Zoological Society of London.* This contained abstracts of the most interesting communications received by the Society, and was circulated each month. In 1833 a new journal was published — the *Transactions* contained longer papers, and the *Proceedings* the shorter. In 1965 the latter was renamed the *Journal of Zoology*, under which title it continues to be published.

The next publication from the Zoological Society was the *Record of Zoological Literature*, subsequently renamed *Zoological Record*. The first volume appeared in 1865. It took the form of an abstracts journal, listing papers and books published in one year, and including, at first, comments on their merits by the recorders. This latter practice was subsequently dropped, as it met with some criticism, and the second part contained instead a subject and a geographical index. The growth of zoological literature has meant a considerable expansion in the size of the *Zoological Record*, which now appears in numerous sections, according to species (e.g. Pisces, Aves, Mammalia). In order to facilitate production, and to enable the *Record* to appear as quickly as possible after the year in which the listed papers and books appeared, a computerized system has recently been adopted.

A relative newcomer to the Zoological Society's list of publications are the *Symposia of the Zoological Society of London*. The symposia themselves began in 1959, and generally consist of a two-day meeting on a particular subject within the field of zoology. The papers given at these meetings are subsequently published in a single volume, and those attending are frequently world authorities on their subject, with the *Symposia* containing papers by many famous names.

The *International Zoo Yearbook* appeared in the same year, and contains papers and other items concerned specifically with animal conservation, mainly in zoological gardens and parks throughout the world, where such work is mostly carried out.

Library Association

The flood of such publications from learned societies is equally matched by the professional associations. The Library Association itself provides a good example. Its publications include those issued from the Headquarters building in Ridgmount Street, London, plus all the titles emanating from the Branches, Groups and Sections. The main titles with what might be termed national coverage are: *Library Association Record*, issued free to all members, and containing mostly news items, some short articles, letters and Headquarters announcements; the *Journal of Librarianship*, containing longer and more scholarly articles;

British Humanities Index, British Technology Index, Library and Information Science Abstracts, all in the indexing and abstracting field; and *RADIALS (Research and Development – Information and Library Science) Bulletin,* a journal listing research and progress and giving a short résumé of each project. The *Students' Handbook* and the *Yearbook* are both issued annually.

ACQUISITION AND MAINTENANCE

Planning and Design of Serials Area

One of the main problems facing any learned society or professional association library will be that of insufficient space. Added to this are the problems of obtaining and maintaining the correct conditions for storing older material. All such material will need to be logically arranged and housed in the most suitable storage system.

Most learned societies and professional associations are housed in buildings which were not originally built for the purpose for which they are now used. It is unusual for the library to be modern or specifically designed as a library although, of course, there are exceptions to that rule. The Zoological Society of London has an excellently designed library, opened during the last decade. It is inside a building of a considerably older date, but which was nonetheless originally designed as office and library accommodation. The new library has taken the place of the old meeting-room, which had housed some of the library stock previously, as had several smaller rooms, now converted into offices.

It can be very useful to have several small rooms available for the use of the library. Certainly, one of the first things that should be ensured is that the library of any learned society or professional association has at least one room suitable for the storage of older material. Such a room, since it should be infrequently visited, could be fitted with mobile shelving, which would greatly increase the number of volumes which could be housed there. Correct temperature and humidity levels will also be more easily maintained in such an environment. In this room would be kept the complete run of the institution's publications, in the original format, and any other rare or archival material which the library may have in its keeping. Such early volumes will give the publishing history of the learned society or professional association, sometimes stretching back some hundreds of years. These volumes will frequently have been printed on handmade paper and bound in leather. These will deteriorate if left on shelves on open access. This will happen partly through use, careless handling — or, indeed, any kind of handling, if it becomes excessive — and partly through being exposed to dust, temperature changes, possibly direct sunlight, and so on.

Obtaining Serials

Apart from its own publications, the learned society or professional association library will attempt to cover those serial publications appearing in its own field both in this country and overseas. This will lead to more space being needed, plus the usual budgetary problems associated with the soaring prices of serial publications. Journals, particularly, will have the added problems associated with the storing of numbers of loose parts, generally too small to stand by themselves.

Most learned societies and professional associations maintain contact with their opposite numbers overseas as well as in the home country. This means that a considerable proportion of the material received will be in foreign languages. It is helpful, therefore, if the librarian is also something of a linguist, or at least has an aptitude for languages, which will enable him or her to recognize rapidly the subject matter of foreign language periodicals and serials. Many journals provide an English language abstract.

Naturally, the serial publications which the library should hold will not all be from other learned societies and professional associations. Commercial publishers, academic institutions, and the publishers of more popular magazines also issue material which should certainly be available to library users. These can be discovered by scanning those journals already received, encouraging publishers to send publicity material and catalogues (more difficult to stop than to start!) and through personal contact, always a fruitful source of information.

Format

The space problem may be solved in a number of ways. Mobile shelving may be installed, operated either manually or electrically, or the format in which the material is stored may itself be changed. Thus, some scientific titles are now available in microform. This generally takes the shape of microfiche, and a complete journal part will consist of only two or three fiches at the most, as the standard fiche contains 60 or 98 frames. There is also a 'super' fiche containing 208 frames. Fiches can be easily stored in the specially manufactured storage units, which often consist of drawers similar to those used for manufactured storage units, which often consist of drawers similar to those used for catalogue cards, only larger. This is because the average fiche will measure 105 mm × 148 mm, against the standard catalogue card's 75 mm × 125 mm. Many of these storage units are manufactured in a wide colour range and heavy duty plastic, which can considerably enhance the interior decoration of the library. When planning to use microform, it is as well to bear in mind that, although the fiches themselves may take up little space, it will be necessary to provide the wherewithal to read them. This will mean not only microform readers, but tables or desks on which to place them and chairs for those using them. All taking up space!

Cost

The financial considerations connected with obtaining the serial publications for the learned society or professional association library are not so daunting as they may at first seem, although they are certainly formidable enough. As an indication of the nature of the problem, the average price of periodicals in the fields of science and technology for 1978 was £61.15, for medicine it was £38.52, and for humanities and social sciencies it was £17.65. These figures are based on an international survey, which, in view of the previously mentioned international coverage necessary for the learned society or professional association library, gives a truer picture than British figures alone. Since the institution of which the library is a part is almost certainly publishing its own material (see above), some of the serials may be acquired on an exchange basis. When such a programme is initiated it is important to make sure that the exchange is a fair one. This should be assessed not only with regard to the physical make-up (number of pages, frequency, and so on) but also by comparing the actual content of the publications. Are the papers of the same intellectual level as that produced by the home institution? Is the percentage of pages devoted to papers, news, announcements, the same as in the publication to be exchanged? Actual price is much more difficult to assess, as this will vary according to currency fluctuations.

Finally, of course, it may be a useful goodwill gesture to exchange publications which will give a slight bias in favour of the overseas institution. Similarly, one may be fortunate enough to find oneself on the receiving end of such an arrangement. There are many overseas institutions who are willing to donate some of their publications: not usually their proceedings or annual volumes, but a useful flow of items can quite easily be built up. The disadvantage of relying too heavily on donations is in maintaining a complete run.

Storage

The problems connected with dealing with loose parts can be solved in several ways. Journals may be purchased in microform (see above). This will certainly take up less space, and pages are less likely to be missed or lost. Binding in hardback form is not as popular as it was, because the cost has become so prohibitive. There is also the disadvantage of having considerable periods of time when an entire year's volume of a particular serial is not available for use. Even with a home bindery on the premises there is sure to be some delay. There are now many different kinds of storage boxes and shelf dividers on the market, some of which are manufactured in standard sizes (usually A3 or A4) to take one volume per box or division. Also useful for combined storage and display are periodical shelving systems, consisting of the usual horizontal shelves, covered by a diagonally slanted front shelf on which the current issue may be displayed. These last are not suitable, however, for long runs. Generally speaking, a section devoted to current periodical titles will be in the main part of the library, with those volumes of, say, five years or more ago, stored in mobile stacks.

Records

Recording of serial publications must be done with great accuracy. It is all too easy to 'lose' a journal part or a volume. This can lead to unnecessary expense, since a duplicate number will have to be ordered. Many library equipment and library stationery suppliers produce ready-printed forms for recording the receipt of serial publications. Occasionally a local stationer will be prepared to print forms to one's own specifications. These can be filed either in narrow drawers, which work on the 'visible index' system, or in sheaf catalogues — an old fashioned but extremely effective method. There should also be a visible index available for library users, giving location, title, publisher and holdings. The publisher is particularly important, as there are frequently two journals with the same title. This seems to be a particular tendency among science and technology publishers. Whether serials are classified or not will be a matter of choice, since for a relatively small number of serials (say a hundred or so) it is not really necessary to do more than shelve them in alphabetical order of title. This not only makes for faster and easier shelving, but also for ease of access for the user. Checking for missing parts should be done regularly — preferably twice a year. This is because overseas publications particularly become out of print in a relatively short time, and it may be difficult, if not impossible, to obtain them. Diplomatic wording of a letter requesting missing parts is necessary, particularly to those institutions which are donating their publications. However, it is worth taking the trouble in order to maintain good relations.

Archive Function

This last comment leads to my final consideration — how long should serial publications be retained by the library. Naturally, this decision will depend largely on the amount of space available. Solutions such as obtaining journals on microfiche, mentioned above, will help the librarian to maintain within the collection items which will be of historical interest — sometimes within a relatively short time. Certainly, these libraries should fulfil an archival function, as they will frequently possess one of the very few copies of some serials in the country. Sometimes this will be because of the narrow subject range in which the learned society or professional association is involved, and sometimes because of the international coverage of its subject interests. To adapt a well-known axiom — when in no doubt, do *not* throw it out!

Conclusion

Following all these regulations will obviously not be possible for all librarians, but the framework of tasks and ideas written here is nonetheless a very basic one, drawn from personal experience. Maybe better ways of performing various of the more monotonous tasks will already be in existence. Readers of this chapter will notice that all references to mechanized systems have been omitted. This is deliberate: the majority of learned societies and professional associations have libraries which are too small to make the installation of computerized or other mechanized systems worth while.

BIBLIOGRAPHY

Library Association Record **80** no. 5 May 1978 226-7.

Russell, C. A., (ed.) *Science and religious belief: a selection of recent historical studies.* London, University of London Press/Open University Press, 1973.

Taylor, L. J., (comp.) *A librarian's handbook.* London, Library Association, 1976 [1977].

Woodworth, D. *Guide to current British journals.* 2nd ed. London, Library Association, 1973.

Zuckerman, *Prof. Lord. et al. The Zoological Society of London, 1827-1976 and beyond.* London, Academic Press, 1976.

13

Local Schemes of Co-operation

D. W. Bromley

The history of local schemes of co-operation between libraries in industry, academic and public sectors is well documented.[1,2,3,4,5] Since the initial foundation of SINTO (Sheffield Interchange Organization)[6] by Joe Lamb, City Librarian of Sheffield, in 1933 over 30 schemes of local co-operation now cover most of the larger urban areas of the country as well as some of the more rural parts. One of the primary purposes of the local schemes in their formative years was to improve access to periodical holdings in local areas by creating formal interloan facilities between specialist libraries. Bearing in mind the traditional secrecy maintained between industrial companies in the era before the Second World War, the success of Joe Lamb in encouraging a free exchange of periodicals and information between companies, including those in close commercial competition, is all the more remarkable. It is a tribute to his vision that SINTO preceded the establishment of the Yorkshire Regional Library Service by two years, and similar schemes in other parts of the country by nearly 20 years when, in 1951, CICRIS (West London Commercial and Technical Library Service) was established in Acton, followed by groups in most of the other parts of the country.

The earlier schemes were established by and centred in local public libraries but at a later date there was a tendency for the responsibility to be shared, e.g. in SEAL (South East Area Libraries Information Service, Lewisham), or for the headquarters to be set up in an academic library such as ANSLICS (Aberdeen and North of Scotland Library and Information Service). Almost all of the schemes of co-operation concentrated in the 1950s and early 1960s in developing facilities for the exchange of periodicals to a very large extent. Monographs and other exchanges were less important while co-operative training, publications, exchange of information, staff exchanges, publicity, which would become important at a later stage, were much less evident. The dominant principles of the co-operative schemes were free exchange of non-confidential published materials in book, periodical and report form, and access to the know-how of specialists. A co-ordinating centre, or group of centres, was at the heart of all the successful co-operative schemes.

The schemes are variously financed. Some are entirely supported by their parent organizations, others levy nominal subscriptions to contribute to overheads and some raise sufficient additional income to be financially independent in part. Groups such as BRASTACS (Bradford Scientific, Technical and Commercial Services), CIS (Cornwall Information Service) and HULTIS (Humberside Libraries Technical Inter-loan Service) are among the minority of groups charging no membership and subscription. The majority levy annual subscriptions in the range £10–£25 which provides a separate income to finance publications, offers a modest degree of independence from their parent organizations, and in some cases supports their own clerical staffs. LADSIRLAC (Liverpool and District Scientific, Industrial and Research Library Advisory Council) charges variable subscriptions rising to £100 a year depending on the volume of service offered to members. A new concept has been adopted by HERTIS (Hertfordshire County Council Technical Information Services) who have abandoned subscriptions in favour of charges on a cost-recovery basis for services other than lending and quick reference which the local authority is statutorily required to provide under the Public Libraries and Museums Act 1964. Photocopies and loans are charged at British Library Lending Division rates, information work is charged at £5 per hour and on-line services operate on a cost-recovery basis.

A number of co-operative schemes have developed publication programmes and in many cases they are available to non-members by subscription. HERTIS, LADSIRLAC, NANTIS (Nottingham and Nottinghamshire Technical Information Service) and SINTO all have well-established news bulletins containing relevant bibliographic topics as well as local domestic information. Others have issued directories of members, including CICRIS and WESLINK (West Midlands Library and Information Network). HATRICS (Hampshire Technical Research Industrial Commercial Service) and CADIG (Coventry and District Information Group) are amongst groups that have established reputations for publishing bibliographies and reading lists. LADSIRLAC is one of the few organizations still issuing a monthly index to recent technical periodical literature, although several other schemes including NANTIS offered such services for many years.

The early development of local union lists of periodicals was common in almost all of the local co-operative schemes. For many years SINTO maintained a union list on cards in the City Library Headquarters until 1967 when the first printed list was published, maintained and kept up to date by supplements and cumulations maintained on punched cards. Later, the data was transferred to computer records. At Aberdeen, ANSLICS has similarly transferred its index card records to a DEC 20 computer. HERTIS and HULTIS are among the schemes publishing a union list of periodicals available to members and non-members.

Local co-operation between libraries in a restricted geographic area was seen to be particularly advantageous in providing fast and immediate access to periodicals and other specialized material at a time when inter-library loan facilities were more efficiently developed to facilitate the exchange of monographs and books rather than periodicals. In many cases the concentration of specialist firms in a particular geographic area (for instance the steel industry in Sheffield or the hosiery industry in Nottingham) enabled special librarians to draw on each other's resources and to develop informal co-operative arrangements which increased their efficiency and reduced their operational costs at the same time. Co-operation revealed extensive resources where information could be pooled. The remarkable depth and diversity of periodical resources in an area was often discovered only after special libraries had recorded and notified their individual holdings.

Local access to material saved considerable time and cost in obtaining loans at a time when the alternative was a laborious and time-consuming option of obtaining loans through the regional library bureau, from the Science Museum for those libraries granted special loan facilities, or the alternative of approaching other specialist libraries directly.

Development of the National Lending Library at Boston Spa had a slow but dramatic effect on the priorities and policies of local co-operative schemes. Gradually it became obvious that local schemes of co-operation had no need to compete with the range and comprehensiveness of periodical loan services offered from the new national service. As a result the emphasis within the co-operative schemes on periodical inter-lending services waned and the local co-operative schemes have in recent years been much more involved in co-operative training, publicity, publishing of bibliographical guides and directories to local resources. In the recent past there has been evidence that the policy imposed by the Treasury during the period of economic restraint, of increasing the proportion of cost raised by direct charges has in some cases caused a revival of interest in local periodical inter-lending arrangements, although it is almost certain that in future such practices will be limited to satisfying very urgent requests only. Present transport and manpower costs, even for messengers and drivers, will inhibit frequent local direct exchanges if the full cost-effect of such arrangements is calculated.

The trends identified by the influence of the British Library services have resulted in a reduction in the number of union lists of periodicals published, but the increasing availability of sophisticated and flexible computers has introduced a new element into the scene. This is typified in Sheffield where, following the publication of the Sheffield University Research Project on local co-operation,[7] the Sheffield Libraries Co-ordinating Committee was established to formalize and extend existing co-operation from the university, polytechnic and public library. The Co-ordinating Committee set up working parties comprising professional librarians from all levels within the constituent member libraries to deal with specialist topics such as resources, information services, automation, research and development, training and periodical provision. The periodicals working party agreed to rationalize all periodical records into a single file maintained on the university computer. The file now contains all holdings for the three main constituent members and is being extended to incorporate all SINTO member periodical records, and ultimately the periodical holdings of other colleges of further education outside of the main groups. From this computer file a COM microfiche union list of periodicals is published, issued three times a year to coincide with the beginning of each academic term and is made available to staff and users in the constituent member libraries. Facilities also exist to furnish individual libraries co-operating in the project with their own domestic records and also to print out subject lists on demand. The lists of individual libraries' holdings can be published in computer printout in full form, in COM microfiche, or 16 mm cassette form to provide domestic lists of records. The ease and flexibility of production has revolutionized the listing and identification of periodicals within the local area, and this may well influence and alter the patterns of use and inter-lending in Sheffield which in the past were well established. Not least of the problems encountered before the project could materialize was that of obtaining agreement on periodicals cataloguing rules. Local variations had to be abandoned by the participants in favour of strict adherence to the *Anglo-American cataloguing rules,* before work could begin, with the result that complete re-cataloguing had to be undertaken.

The increasing number of periodicals published and the need to rationalize periodical filing policies in all libraries is possibly the second most significant factor after inter-library loan facilities in encouraging local co-operation in limited geographic areas. Except in the most piecemeal fashion, serious rationalization of holdings cannot be effected without accurate records of the holdings of individual libraries as a first step towards identifying gaps in provision, as well as the extent of redundant duplicate back files which can be pruned without reducing the effectiveness of local resources. In this respect the availability of an up to date union list of periodicals is essential before such rationalization can be accomplished, and it is possibly in part the lack of such records that has limited the extent to which individual libraries have felt it possible to take part in file rationalization exercises. Increasing pressure on space, together with the effect of ideas such as that envisaged in the concept of the self-renewing library, will renew interest in reducing unnecessary duplication and retention of little-used or unused files in individual libraries. It is perhaps surprising that little consideration seems to have been given to the establishment of local joint reserve collections, providing an intermediate store within close access to the contributing members in an area where costs are lower than in most of the high-rental buildings occupied by most large central and academic libraries. It is possible that joint activity of this kind might be more common in local co-operative groups in the United Kingdom in the future, comparable to the Hampshire Interlibrary Center in the USA. On the other hand the relatively small size of the country may be such as to make it more practical for little-used periodical files to be preserved centrally in the British Library Lending Division where they are more generally available, than to establish a chain of local intermediate stores.

Co-operation in storage and retention of files can also be matched by local consultation in decisions on periodicals selection and the length of files. Co-operative selection is practical only to a limited extent and is probably successful only if agreement can be reached on broad areas of individual specialization which reflect the primary activities of the member libraries. Such arrangements will enable consultation on the selection of new titles to be limited to the more highly specialist series and titles of marginal interest. The limitation on most co-operative selection plans is the high hidden cost of time and manpower required to administer such schemes together with the natural reluctance of most libraries to commit limited purchase budgets to co-operative arrangements which result in the acquisition of material which may be regarded at best as only of marginal interest to the users of the purchasing library. In general, there is evidence that public libraries are more able and willing to commit funds to such co-operative projects than academic and special libraries, and many schemes set up in the flush of early enthusiasm fail for want of complete commitment from all participants.

The concern for better information facilities to smaller firms is a recurrent theme in the declared objectives of many of the co-operative groups. Recognizing the ability of the larger industrial information services to achieve a large measure of self sufficiency, co-operative groups such as LINK (Lambeth Information Network), LIST (Library and Information Services in Teesside) and NANTIS specifically aim to improve and strengthen the provision of information services to the smaller commercial and industrial companies in their areas. For this reason their membership requirements are less exacting in terms of the existence of established formal library or information services, and they include more members joining the co-operative group in order to secure better information services than can normally be expected from local public library reference services. In some cases the co-operative group has in effect become a trade name for the more intensive information services provided by the local authority and has succeeded in encouraging local commercial and industrial companies to use services which, operating under the auspices of the public library, might be scorned.

A new factor likely to have a dramatic influence on the level of local co-operation in the provision of periodicals and related bibliographical services is the phenomenally fast growth in the availability and use of on-line computer terminals. HERTIS was the first co-operative scheme[8] to recognize the potential value when it installed an on-line service and made it available to its members in 1975. Since then several public libraries have installed equipment and made it available to small firms and organizations in their area through their local co-operative groups on a subsidized or full cost-recovery basis. Most of the large firms with established library and information units already have, or soon will have, such facilities, but the potential for corporate use of on-line terminals will enable co-operative schemes to make the otherwise high capital cost of acquiring and operating terminals available to many smaller local companies.

The growth in the number of co-operative schemes led to the establishment of SCOCLIS (Standing Conference of Co-operative Library and Information Services) in 1964 with the object of providing a forum for discussion and exchange of information between the co-operative schemes, provide a body which could co-ordinate the activities of the various schemes which now exceed 30 in number, and also provide a focus to represent matters of common interest to government and central agencies.

Activities have included the submission of evidence to government committees of enquiry, co-operating with the Science Reference Library on matters affecting regional patent deposit libraries and organizing a co-operative indexing project for newly-registered private companies. A publications programme includes a news bulletin — *SCOCLIS News*[9] issued three times a year, a *Directory of Members*[10] and a microfiche edition of samples of members' publications.

The need to establish a co-ordinating body such as SCOCLIS indicates the extent to which local co-operation has grown in recent years. The network of co-operative schemes is now one of the outstanding features of library organization in the UK, and the schemes each contribute in their own differing ways to improving local information exchange, indirectly contributing to the economic prosperity of their own local communities.

REFERENCES

1. Atkins, J. L. 'Local technical information co-operative schemes'. *Aslib Proceedings* 21 no. 11 Nov. 1969. 444-53.

2. Atkins, J.L. 'Library services to industry', in H.A. Whatley (ed.) *British librarianship and information Science, 1966-70.* Library Association, 1972. 497-503.
3. Chesshyre, H. 'Local co-operation — a positive force'. *Aslib Proceedings.* **18** no. 4 April 1966. 92-107.
4. Peck, T. P. 'LADSIRLAC, SINTO, HERTIS and all that'. *Special Libraries* **65** no. 4 April 1974. 196-200.
5. Smith, N. E. 'Current developments in some local co-operative library schemes in the UK'. *Journal of Documentation* **34** no. 2 June 1978. 110-18.
6. Bebbington, J. 'Twenty-seven years of co-operation with industry'. *Librarian and Book World* **49** no. 2 Feb. 1960. 21-26.
7. *Local library co-operation:* final report on a project funded by the Department of Education and Science, by T.D. Wilson and W.A.J. Marsterson, University of Sheffield Postgraduate School of Librarianship and Information Science, 1974.
8. Woodrow, M. 'Indexes on-line'. *Assistant Librarian* **69** no. 9 Sept. 1976. 146-9.
9. *SCOCLIS News.* Published three times a year, SCOCLIS, Central Library, Sheffield, S1 1XZ.
10. *SCOCLIS Directory of Members,* 1979. SCOCLIS, Central Library, Sheffield, S1 1XZ.

14

Regional Schemes And Networks

Jean Plaister

The Regional Library Systems which were set up between 1928 and 1937 following the publication of the Kenyon Report in 1927 were voluntary associations of libraries based on geographical groupings for the purposes of co-operation and interlending. They were formally recognized in Section 3 of the Public Libraries and Museums Act 1964, but many years later the implementation of this Section is still awaited, although, now that the effect of local government boundary changes has been assimilated there is pressure on the Minister to do so.

This is not to imply that membership of the Regional Library System is limited to public libraries. Although public libraries dominated the regions in the South-east until 1969 because the bureaux were housed in the National Central Library, non-public libraries have always been participating members of other regions.

Traditionally, the Regions have been involved in the compilation of lists of serial holdings held within their areas, but as in all matters relating to the Regions, the practice has varied and there has been no common standard or practice.

As a general rule, the Regions have tended to separate 'periodicals' from other types of serials although the line of demarcation has never been a clear one.

Annual reports, directories and almanacs have tended to be regarded as monographs and recorded as such in the regional union catalogue or produced as separate lists, for example, Miss S. Smith's catalogue of directories and almanacs held in Scottish libraries.

Some Regions have produced printed lists for sale whilst others have maintained manual catalogues at Headquarters so that the Regional Library Bureau can act as a referral centre for periodical locations. Some have produced full lists, others specialist ones. With the increasingly high cost of publishing there appears to be a tendency to produce specialist lists such as the union list of periodical holdings in the medical libraries participating in the Yorkshire and Humberside Joint Library Services, or to maintain union lists at Headquarters for referral purposes, making no attempt to publish.

The North Western Regional Library System produced its last union list in 1967 and has recently decided to abandon the idea of a revised printed list for the present and to keep an up to date one at the Bureau. The West Midlands Region also maintains a manual catalogue at its headquarters.

In the days of the London Union Catalogue and the South Eastern Regional Library System the union list was produced by the London and Home Counties Branch of the Library Association. The first edition of *LULOP* (London Union List of Periodicals) published in 1946 recorded the holdings of all municipal and county branch libraries in the Metropolitan Police District with the addition of the holdings of boroughs such as Watford in Hertfordshire and Dartford in Kent which were just outside the boundaries of the Metropolitan District. Subsequent editions widened the scope of *LULOP* and the last edition published by the London and Home Counties Branch in 1969 included all the significant public library collections in London and the Home Counties.

The London and Home Counties Branch having decided not to publish further editions of *LULOP* the mantle fell upon LASER, the Region responsible for London and the Home Counties. This was not quite so onerous a task as might be supposed as the former London Union Catalogue and South Eastern Regional Library System (which amalgamated to form LASER) had maintained updated files between the publication of new editions of *LULOP* and manual lists of the holdings of libraries outside the scope of *LULOP.*

LASER decided to collect afresh in detail the serial holdings of its members and began by collecting the periodical holdings of the public libraries within the Region. Other types of serials such as directories, yearbooks, etc., will be added at a later date as will the holdings of other members of the Region such as the Polytechnics.

These public library holdings number some 17,500 titles and between 40,000 and 50,000 locations, and there is considerable pressure on LASER to publish a list of holdings which would supplement the referral system at present being provided by the LASER Headquarters.

THE ROLE OF REGIONAL SCHEMES

What then is the role of the Region at present? With the establishment first of the National Lending Library for Science and Technology and then of the British Library Lending Division, it was felt by some that regional lists of serials and even the Regions themselves would be unnecessary. The *Report on the future pattern of interlending* produced in 1977 by the National Committee on Regional Library Co-operation drew attention to the fact that although there were some areas where it was important to ensure that the activities of Lending Division and the Regions do not duplicate each other, in many fields activities are complementary, and in others they are unique to each organization.

The Working Party identified four types of interlending:
(a) informal — library to library based on personal knowledge of library resources and the use of published bibliographies and directories of resources,
(b) direct — library to library using ISBN and BNB serial number lists with locations produced by the Regions and subject specialization schemes developed by the Regions,
(c) regional — requests channelled through a regional centre,
(d) British Library Lending Division — loans from and via the Lending Division.

It was felt that these four types needed to co-exist, but that close co-operation was required to avoid unnecessary duplication.

The Lending Division has extensive holdings of:

Serials
Report literature
Conference proceedings
Official publications

147

The Working Party agreed that there was little point in an extensive regional involvement with most of this material. However, serials, particularly in urban areas, are used extensively for reference purposes, and additional means of access to the holdings of neighbouring libraries are necessary, whether these be organized locally or for a larger area.[1]

In practice, there is a continuing demand for information on holdings and pressure for the publication of lists. The information provided from lists of serial holdings is used for a number of purposes as LASER has found from counting and analysing the requests received by telephone, telex and post.

All too frequently these days is the request for information on other holdings of a particular serial in the area, which will enable a library to decide whether or not it should continue subscribing to that serial.

Another use is for reference to a file of a particular serial. In the humanities access to a long run may be an essential part of a project.

Details will also be found in regional lists of the holdings of 'popular' serials and material produced in this country and abroad for ethnic minority groups resident in this country. This latter material is not generally held by the British Library Lending Division but may satisfy a very real social and educational need.

In addition to these uses there is of course the request to obtain a photocopy or go to read an article in a particular serial, while communication between libraries within a particular Region has been improved by the development since 1975 of transport schemes for inter-library loans. These may be organized by the Region for its members or by a Region in co-operation with the British Library. The LASER Transport Scheme serves at present its own members and has a contract with the British Library to carry traffic to Lending Division users in Greater London. This Scheme serves over 750 organizations and carries some 12,000 items per week.

Regional locations, particularly in public libraries, may also be used to supplement the holdings of an academic institution and students will be sent to libraries with good collections in specific subjects. This has proved to be the case where libraries have collected serials as a part of an allocation under a subject specialization scheme. There was an obligation on libraries participating in the London Union Catalogue Metropolitan Special Collections Scheme to purchase serials within their subjects in addition to monographs. When the scheme was revised in 1974 and became the LASER Subject Specialization Scheme the purchase of serials became optional and it will be interesting to see what effect this will have on the resources of the Region in the future.

THE FUTURE ROLE

What is the role of the Region and the regional list likely to be in the future?

It has been suggested that the regional list flourishes best in an urban area and it is certainly the case that schemes have been actively encouraged in Birmingham, London and Manchester.

It is also suggested that a 'local' list as distinct from a 'regional' list may be a more effective tool. How 'local', however, should coverage be to provide an adequate selection of material and how many libraries should be involved if any attempt is to be made to provide comprehensive subject coverage? Experience with subject specialization schemes generally indicates that coverage must be regional rather than local.

Again, which libraries should be included in a regional list? Should it be limited to the members of a particular Regional Bureau or should its coverage be wider and cover the holdings of libraries within the area who would find no profit in being conventional members of a Region, but yet have much to provide in terms of serial resources?

Many questions need to be answered. As with so many British institutions regional lists of serials were established to meet a particular need. They have become an important source of reference in some areas but there has been little standardization of design or format and the relationship of their holdings to the resources of the British Library Lending Division have not been thought through nor has their relationship to the UK National Serials Data Centre or to a national network been discussed in any great detail.

The *Report on the future pattern of interlending* dealt briefly with the situation. Discussing the division of responsibilities between the Lending Division and the regional systems it said that the Lending Division has extensive holdings of serials, report literature, conference proceedings and official publications and agreed that there was little point in an extensive regional involvement with most of this material. It added the following, however: 'serials, particularly in urban areas, are used extensively for reference purposes, and additional means of access to the holdings of neighbouring libraries are necessary, whether these be organised locally or for a larger area.'

The Working Party Report calls for studies to be carried out into standard reporting and recording systems for many types of material, and a welcome development in the serials field is the setting up of a British Standards Committee to formulate a standard for serials holdings statements. The adoption of a standard which could be used for lists of serials in individual institutions through to regional and national lists of locations would be an important step towards the development of a national network and would encourage the use of automation techniques.

This standard will, it is hoped, provide, as does the draft version of a similar American standard, the means to record in considerable detail the holdings of an individual institution, the branch and site holdings of institutions which are traditionally recorded in a regional list through to the national list which with its wider geographical coverage will only be able to record holdings under the name of the institution or library system.

THE USE OF AUTOMATION

Although the use of standards both for holdings and for bibliographic citation are as appropriate to manual files as to machine-readable ones, they are essential if there is to be meaningful exchange or amalgamation of machine-readable data, and it is interesting to speculate whether we should have had such an abundance of standards but for the advent of library automation.

This is not to denigrate the use of library automation to create serials files but rather to welcome this means of maintaining up to date records of holdings.

Automation is likely in fact to provide the method for the future of maintaining and possibly publishing regional union lists of serials holdings.

The cost of publishing a general regional list by conventional printing methods is probably prohibitive unless the venture is heavily subsidized. It has been estimated that the LASER list of some 17,500 titles with between 40,000 and 50,000 locations would run to two volumes of 500 pages each and although there is considerable pressure for publication, the relative shortness of the print run would appear to make conventional editing and printing quite uneconomic.

We must, therefore, look towards other methods of publication and of maintaining up to date files. The answer appears to lie in the maintenance of files in machine-readable form which can be updated at regular intervals and either accessed on-line or produced at a relatively low cost by COM on fiche or film.

The cost, however, of generating the initial data base for a file is considerable and the ability to use bibliographic records created elsewhere has much to recommend it. As yet little has been accomplished co-operatively in this country. The British Library Bibliographic Services Division is producing machine-readable records for new serial titles and changes of titles as is the Library of Congress. The British Library through the UK National Serials Data Centre is participating in the International Serials Data System (ISDS), but the size of the file generated to date by the ISDS International Centre in Paris is such that it offers very little to the potential creator of a machine-readable file. The file will grow, of course, but how long can individual organizations afford to wait?

Can we not learn from North America where a co-operative scheme called CONSER[2] has been established to create a data base of bibliographic records of serial publications which can be used to create local, regional and national lists of serials holdings? Beginning in 1975, it is anticipated that the completed file will contain between 200,000 and 300,000 titles. The bibliographic information will be verified as far as this is possible by the Library of Congress and the National Library of Canada, and these two bodies will take over the responsibility for maintaining the file when the project to create the initial data base is complete.

The project is managed by the Council on Library Resources which has contracted the Ohio College Library Center (OCLC) to operate it using the OCLC on-line cataloguing system. It is interesting to note that a 'regional' union catalogue — the Minnesota Union List of Serials (MULS) — was used as the data base for the initial base file.

Machine-readable union catalogues of serials are being created in Britain by various organizations. BLCMP (Library Services) Ltd has a union catalogue of the serials holdings in the libraries within its membership. It uses the MASS format which was developed jointly by

BLCMP and the Loughborough University of Technology.[3] Although there are discrepancies between MASS as used by BLCMP (Library Services) Ltd, and the Library of Congress MARC format for serials due to the need felt by BLCMP to maintain a compatible format for monographs and serials, BLCMP MASS is compatible with the MARC exchange format as used for monograph records.

The University of London, Library Resources Co-ordinating Committee (LRCC) is creating a machine-readable union catalogue of the serials holdings of its constituent colleges. LRCC utilized the records, with some modification, in the BLCMP (Library Services) Ltd union catalogue of serials, but will be limiting the use of its own records at present to its member colleges.

Although not totally compatible in format the BLCMP and LRCC serial files must surely form the basis for retrospective file conversion in Britain. If the files of the British Library Reference Division and the British Library Lending Division were added we would indeed have a data base comparable with that of CONSER.

LASER believing that the only method of maintaining an up to date union catalogue of serials is in machine-readable form has been discussing with BLCMP (Library Services) Ltd the creation of a data base for its file.

Ideally one would like to see a situation for serials similar to that which exists for monographs, where the ISBN (International Standard Book Number) provides the access key to the bibliographic information on the MARC data bases. A selective record service for serials would provide both the Region and the local library with a ready made file to which could be added detailed holdings and housekeeping information at the regional and local level as appropriate.

There are problems, however. It will be many years before unique numbers in the form of ISSN can be added to all current serials titles let alone the retrospective ones. There are problems of compatibility of physical format and of the operation of copyright and royalty agreements for the re-use of records. There appears, however, to be no reason why with good will and co-operation these difficulties should not be overcome.

Work is in progress to reach agreement on a standard bibliographic format for serials and for a standard for serials holdings. If there can be general acceptance of these standards by librarians in libraries of all kinds the way looks fair for further co-operation.

This brings us back to the role of Regional schemes and networks in relation to serials.

If the future regions, whether they be the traditional regional bureaux or regional groupings set up for this purpose, can create machine-readable union catalogues of serials either by exchanging bibliographic data with other co-operatives and/or by drawing on the resources of national and international data bases there are new and expanded roles for library co-operation and the sharing of resources:

(a) the creation of individual library lists of serials for internal use by the production of sub-sets of the regional file (this is already being suggested within LASER where individual branch locations are recorded in the union catalogue);

(b) the rationalization of holdings and the planned purchase of titles on a co-operative basis;

(c) the publication and sale of general and specialist lists of serials with locations on microfilm or microfiche with supplements to keep them up to date, thus providing readers with a directory of resources;

(d) the feeding of this information into a national network for the wider use of resources and the supplementing of the services of the British Library.

Automation and the growth of networks facilitates multiplicity of functions ranging from output or on-line access for reference purposes to selection and acquisition control. This multiplicity of functions is likely to make the regional approach to serial listing and control economic and necessary to further developments at all levels.

REFERENCES

1. *Report of the Working Party on the future pattern of interlending.* National Committee on Regional Library Co-operation, 1977, 5pp.
2. Anable, R. 'CONSER: An Update', *Journal of library automation,* vol. 8 (1) March 1975, pp. 26-30.
3. Birmingham Libraries Co-operative Mechanisation Project. *BLCMP MASS manual: input procedures for serials cataloguing.* Birmingham: BLCMP, 1973, 134pp. (MASS Working Paper No. 2).

Part 3

WIDER ISSUES

15

Inter-lending and Co-operation

K. G. E. Harris

In the past serials have been among the great mysteries of librarianship, with their own priesthood, rituals and relics. Devotees of the cult today are rapidly being proselytized by the subject specialist faithful. The fundamental truth is that librarians have consistently overstated the importance of serials, and nowhere more than in library co-operation. In any case, that importance has declined and is continuing to decline with new methods of information transfer, as evidenced in any issue of the *BLLD Announcements Bulletin*. That 'serials remain the most important means of rapidly demonstrating to the learned community new knowledge in all fields of study, particularly in the natural sciences and technology', as the staff of the Library of Congress had it in 1964,[1] would tend now to be disputed by those many scientists who are claiming that literature is often already out of date by the time it is published in any form.

The reducing importance of serials is only beginning to be appreciated by librarians and is not yet a major factor in rejection, and consequently in inter-lending policy. One feels that the day of declining use with research workers more and more interested in reports and in unpublished literature is coming. That it is not yet is apparent, if one can judge from British Library Lending Division statistics and suggestions that increased access, which we certainly have, is leading to increased demand.[2] This situation may not be permanent, and one is aware of the problems of learned societies, of the growing importance of microforms, of publication on request, and of all the other trends which have been identified, in particular, in the current research undertaken by Professor Meadows and his team at Leicester University.[3] There is indeed strong evidence that the rate of growth of new periodical titles is slowing down. Nancy Johnson has produced figures for legal periodicals which suggest that there was an 8.9 per cent annual increase in titles of library-worthy publications in the years 1907 to 1977.[4] However, the overall growth of serials titles is now reduced to 4 per cent and may be declining to 2 or 3 per cent.[5] That periodical circulation figures are holding in libraries could well be due to the massive increases in inter-lending and the corresponding greater ease of access. It may not be too perverse, in fact, to imagine that the British Library Lending Division with its widespread lending and photocopying activities is actually helping to save the learned periodical from disaster.

Inter-lending patterns have undoubtedly changed because librarians are having to cut back on purchases for a variety of reasons. Libraries have never been self-sufficient, to the extent that one feels that the Joint Committee on the Union List of Serials must have had its tongue in its cheek when it considered that no library had even assembled as many as half the serial titles in existence.[6] Undoubtedly inflation has been a major factor in reducing purchases, with the average United Kingdom price per title rising from £6.45 in 1965 to £30.11 in 1976,[7] and, in the United States by 12.2 per cent in 1978 over 1977.[8] Library budgets have just not kept pace. That cost has been a major factor is shown in three interesting studies undertaken at the Universities of Glasgow, Hull and Illinois.[9] The fear of the serials budget taking over the whole revenue allocation has become real.

Another major factor which is becoming more and more appreciated is the very low use of serials in relation to their cost. Many studies indicate this. As an example, the National Library of Medicine discovered that 88 per cent of the serials titles in its collections were used less than once a year,[10] and this is quite characteristic. The trend is shown conclusively in the British Library's own research which reveals that 5,000 titles (or about 10 per cent of intake) account for 80 per cent of demand and that 8,500 titles (about 17 per cent of intake) account for 90 per cent of demand.[11] A lot of serials are bought by libraries never to be consulted. This is supported by Hull University's finding that there is no significant increase in inter-library loans after the cancellation of a large number of titles,[12] and by John Urquhart's perceptive comment based on the research into relegation of stock at Newcastle University that 'low borrowing use generally predicts no current use'.[13]

People keep saying that librarians when considering cancellations do not take into account availability through inter-lending,[14] and it is not mentioned as a factor, for instance, in Glasgow University's cancellation policy, possibly because a very high proportion of the materials no longer taken could not be requested on inter-library loan.[15] Despite this, although admittedly in a special library context, Bernard Houghton's research showed that in the most-stretched favourable conditions, only for 51 per cent of periodical holdings is it likely to be more economic to buy rather than to borrow.[16] In fact there are strong suggestions that special libraries do use national inter-lending as a factor in selection as opposed to the rather less cost-conscious public and academic libraries. Maurice Line estimates that industrial libraries in the United Kingdom obtain about 20 per cent of their users' needs through inter-lending,[17] and such a high proportion can only be arrived at in conjunction with a conscious selection policy. However, while it can be argued that national inter-lending affects selection policy relatively little, this is certainly not the case with local inter-lending. That Newcastle University Library when considering cancellations should consult Newcastle Polytechnic Library to examine the degree of overlap, and whether the Polytechnic would be willing to take up some of the subscriptions, should be an example of quite normal practice. It is almost inevitable that holdings in another local library will increase user satisfaction over inter-lending from outside the locality, despite Stuart's rider that local conditions may vary to the extent that they affect satisfaction time.[18]

The truth is that the first real impetus to effective serials inter-lending was given through local arrangements and was largely pioneered, as so many useful developments have been pioneered, with the help of special librarians. By modern standards the SINTO (Sheffield Interchange Organization) operation is not large and has declined from 2,482 loans in 1967–8 to 1,087 loans and 300 photocopies in 1977–8. Another network, TALIC (Tyneside Association of Libraries for Industry and Commerce), has remained fairly static at about 3,600 loans per annum.[19] These loans are mostly of serials, but represent quite modest activities. The proliferation of small local groups following the SINTO example was to meet a real local need felt particularly by special librarians and able to be supported by a prestigious and imaginative public library service. Much of the work done was, and remains, informal and cannot be properly recorded statistically. This sort of inter-lending machinery became the norm in urban areas after the war and up to the inauguration in 1961 of the National Lending Library for Science and Technology, and still has a useful though relatively minor part to play. The SINTO-type operation still retains the advantages of speed, relative informality and close personal contact.

As inter-lending between mainly small libraries in limited urban communities developed, there were found to be problems of availability and a corresponding interest in creating union catalogues. That this was normal pre-Urquhart thinking is shown by the parallel obsession with union catalogues for books which affected the regional bureaux. The local or regional catalogue did have a part to play in those days of more scattered and less comprehensive collections and of more difficult communication. Coupled with *Ulrich,* the *World list of scientific periodicals* and the *British union-catalogue of periodicals,* with its sometimes less than reliable information on holdings, the local union catalogues provided a bibliographic back-up service. An inter-lending service appropriate to the period was established, and parts of it still exist usefully, in the case of modern serials lists, reinforced by the need to use the computer.

Meanwhile there was a considerable amount of informal inter-lending, varying from the sort of agreement whereby Newcastle upon Tyne City Libraries presented runs of mathematics periodicals to the local university library, on condition that access continued to be granted to its readers, to the quite informal telephone arrangement. It is in Newcastle that the idea of informal inter-lending has been developed through the concept of areas of excellence in different libraries to the pitch where an approach can be made directly to the library specializing in a subject without the intervention of formal machinery or local union lists.[20] That the system is not comprehensive is immaterial. It need only be for material relevant locally because of the national lending services.

That local library co-operation can be fruitful is shown by the fact that serials provision overlaps surprisingly little. When, for example, the Periodicals Bank of the Associated Colleges of the Midwest was created, it was found that of the total holdings of the ten libraries joining the scheme only 730, or just under 10 per cent of the 7,411 subscriptions, were held in common.[21] And these were similar libraries in institutions teaching, by and large, to the same curricula. Most studies seem to suggest that this sort of situation is not unusual. It is an interesting exercise to examine titles listed in the *British union-catalogue of periodicals* and its supplements to confirm a quite surprising lack of overlap.

Despite attempts at union lists and rationalization, it is still often difficult in both local and regional inter-lending to find out what is available where, and then trying to achieve a loan. Organization tends to be haphazard and costly, particularly where transport or postage is involved. The multiplicity of sources of material coupled with the multiplicity of supply points makes successful operation difficult. Yet a refinement of this system was the solution suggested by librarians when the National Lending Library was being considered. As Maurice Line points out in an interview with Dennis Barker it 'doesn't work very well' because catalogues are expensive and inaccurate, because librarians are not good at reporting, because of factors of scale, and because of refusals to lend. Some proof can be found in the average supplying time by co-operatives in the United States of three weeks, let alone Italy where 'it is dreadful'. The British Library solution takes five days on average.[22]

The concept of periodicals banks as opposed to using the stocks of individual libraries is now widely accepted, although in the United States it is still possible to recommend a series of banks as opposed to a centralized service.[23] This is despite the fact that this approach has been largely exploded by the success of the British Library Lending Division. However, even in the United States a 'National Periodicals Center' is now being planned, holding all subject areas except clinical medicine, with an initial collection of 36,000 titles rising eventually to 60,000 titles, and using photocopying facilities extensively.[24]

The concept of a National Periodicals Center shows how great has been the influence of the British Library Lending Division. Beginning, as far as serials are concerned, with the National Lending Library for Science and Technology in 1961, its production-line methods and effective use of the postal service soon gave it a pre-eminent position in inter-lending. Its original aim was to supply research scientists with all the significant literature in whatever language the literature was originally published,[25] and this was organized through a collection of serials and a translation service. Extension of activity into the social sciences and into books was inevitable, simply because the National Lending Library system soon proved itself so superior to all other forms of inter-lending. The British Museum and the succeeding British Library Reference Division have always been opposed to providing a really national service, and even in their present planning Thomas has a point when he writes: 'The new (Somers Town) building is a huge white elephant which will service the needs of dilettante scholars who happen to live in London'.[26] The regional systems have never been particularly strong on periodicals, possibly because of their strong public library bias.[27] Local networks have always lacked comprehensive coverage.

The growth of the National Lending Library and its successor the British Library Lending Division has been phenomenal. Between 1963 and 1976 it doubled the number of periodicals taken, from 26,470 to 50,780.[28] The total British inter-lending position today is that 56 per cent of its loans are still of serials, of which 57 per cent are to academic libraries, 38 per cent to special and other libraries, and 4 per cent to public libraries.[29]

The National Lending Library development coincided with another revolution: the popularization of photocopying. Photocopying had been with us for some time, but its mass use can possibly be traced to the end of the Xerox patent and the introduction of cheap equipment with improved technology. Photocopying has many advantages over its rivals. Microfilming is manifestly uneconomic.[30] Facsimile transmission is in its infancy. Libraries tend to prefer copy to be as near to normal print as possible and not to need intermediary machinery.[31] Photocopies can be kept by the user with all the advantages of permanent retention. Photocopying improves use because it permits the original to remain in its home library and so to minimize the possibility of loss or damage.

The extent of the photocopying revolution should not be underestimated. It is believed, for example, that 114,000,000 items were photocopied in United States libraries in 1976.[32] While photocopying of this magnitude has made reliance on national collections easier and assisted information transfer, as Maurice Line has pointed out[33] it has also caused problems. The effect on publication and the copyright implications are matters of considerable dispute. Publishers would claim that photocopying has seriously affected small circulation journals on specialized scientific subjects and the like;[34] a view which they hold tenaciously. However, what research has been done suggests that mass photocopying actually has little connection with journal sales.[35] Woodward's suggestion that it would appear 'that the bulk of interlibrary lending involves journals that would never be purchased by the recipient library'[36] seems on the surface to contradict the actual experience of the British Library Lending Division. In fact, there appears to be considerable evidence that the most popular journals and ones to which libraries must subscribe are those from which the vast bulk of photocopying is done.[37] There would seem to be little or no threat to the small journal.

The question of copyright is equally controversial and has led to discussion and legislation in a number of countries. The seriousness of the problem is not to be underestimated, but it is probable that the major abuse of copyright in photocopying takes place in schools and offices rather than in libraries. To a great extent copyright problems in photocopying journal articles is an emotive issue very like public lending right, in which new legal controls may hurt existing services at great cost without providing any real benefit to copyright holders. The dangers of reducing photocopying cannot be ignored. As Maurice Line has pointed out, 'more restrictive copyright regulations would of course reduce availability of serials because items would have to be lent rather than photocopied'.[38]

Considerable progress has been made in international co-operation on serials, with the International Serials Data System, born in 1972, developing along interesting lines.[39] Centres have been set up in a number of countries, with an international centre in Paris. The concept of an international data base is not new but, in this case, with the establishment of ISSN and with real co-operation on an automated data base, interesting work is being done. Outside the ISDS, international lending is increasing, with ideas for facilitating loans being put forward. Many are on the lines discussed by Maurice Line: 'A library would send an interloan request first to its national centre, which would explore national resources. In the event of failure, it would send a request to a regional (supranational) library, from which there might be an 80 or 90 per cent chance of satisfaction. If this supranational library could not supply, it would forward the request to the international library'.[40] In this way international loans could become an extension of internal loans.

Whatever plans are under discussion, international lending is progressing, and particularly with more and more overseas libraries coming to rely on the British Library Lending Division. In fact, some Americans seem to be doubting the need to set up a rival system in the United States. As long ago as 1976, Illinois University Library reported 1,070 titles to its Center for Research Libraries, to be advised that CRL owned 29 of the titles and would subscribe to 144 more, but that Boston Spa already possessed 615 of the titles.[41] What is more, the British

Library Lending Division can be expected to beat the estimated average supply time of between one and two months for international requests.[42] These are reasons why the British Library Lending Division is already acting as the most important international agency, with about half of its overseas loans going to Western Europe and about 20 per cent to the United States of which about a third are for US journals.[43] For serials, the photocopying statistics are probably more useful than the overall loan statistics and show an increase from 9,700 requests in 1967 to 393,000 requests in 1977-8.[44] In fact, the growing international role of the British Library would seem to qualify Maurice Line's statement that 'it cannot be stressed too strongly that effective international lending is impossible without efficient lending systems within each country'[45] as far as serials are concerned. With books it is a different matter. That, of course, is once the problems he has listed about repayment of costs, customs regulations, censorship and copyright are overcome.[46]

A final area of international co-operation which is less important in Britain but more elsewhere is the exchange of serials. It is used as the method of building up foreign serials collections in many Communist and underdeveloped countries. Vilma Alberani gives the reasons for the popularity of exchanges as avoiding price increases, coping with political considerations, assuring the rapid diffusion of the results of research, and honouring international agreements.[47] The scale can be massive as, for example, in the case of the Lenin State Library in Russia which receives 60 per cent of its foreign books, 88 per cent of its serials and 82 per cent of its periodicals by exchange. And in the case of developing countries, exchange may be the only way of obtaining serials.[48] However, while many British libraries participate in exchange arrangements they are frequently sceptical of their value, particularly when they examine some of the gratuitous candidates sent to them in efforts to begin exchange agreements.

Serials have been the target for many scare stories in the past with efforts to blame inter-lending for publishers' financial problems. Co-operation between libraries on serials is claimed to be helping towards the death of specialist publications, to photocopying and copyright practices which deny a fair living to publishers (who may or may not be paying their authors), to endangering the dissemination of research findings. Yet despite a massive increase in co-operation in the past decade and beyond, none of this seems to have happened. The number of titles increases significantly every year, to the extent that one can argue that there are far too many publications. If only some of the complaints made were true! One must argue that inter-library co-operation in serials is good for the dissemination of ideas, good for library budgets, and good for healthy publishing.

REFERENCES

1. Library of Congress. General Reference and Bibliography Division. *Union lists of serials: a bibliography.* Washington, Library of Congress, 1964.
2. Welsh, W. J. 'Libraries and the new technology' in *Academic libraries by the year 2000.* Bowker, 1977. 187.
3. See, for example, *Trends in scholarly publishing.* British Library, 1976. (Report no. 5299HC).
4. Johnson, N. P. 'Legal periodical use survey', *Law Library Journal* 71 no. 1 Feb. 1978. 177.
5. Wootton, C. B. *Trends in size, growth and cost of the literature since 1955.* British Library, 1977. 81. (Report no. 5323HC).
6. Joint Committee on the Union List of Serials. *Final report.* Washington, Council on Library Resources, 1966.
7. Wootton, C. B. *op. cit.* 53.
8. Brown, N. B. 'Price indexes: U.S. periodicals and serial services'. *Library Journal* July 1978. 1356-61.
9. Rodger, E. 'Pruning periodical subscriptions at Glasgow University Library'. *Aslib Proceedings* 30 no. 4 April 1978. 145-53; Brennan, M. M. 'Periodical cancellations: what happened at Hull'. *BLL review* 5 no. 2 April 1977. 67-73; Swartz, L. J. 'Serials cancellations and reinstatements at the University of Illinois Library'. *Serials Librarian* 2 no. 2 Winter 1977. 171-80.
10. Gore, D. 'How to cut subscription costs'. *Management problems in serials work.* Greenwood Press, 1973. 107.
11. Line, M. B. 'UAP and inter-library lending'. *IFLA Journal* 4 1978. 119.
12. Loveridge, E. 'Selection, acquisition and recording'. *Periodicals administration in libraries.* Bingley, 1978. 41. The British Library Lending Division estimates that 3 per cent of periodical requests are for titles previously taken by libraries. Woodward, A. M. 'Replacement of periodical subscriptions by British Library Lending Division services'., *Interlending Review* 6 no. 2 April 1978. 41.
13. Urquhart, J. 'Relegation'. *Periodicals administration in libraries.* Bingley, 1978 120.
14. See, for example, Swartz, L. J. *op. cit.,* p. 176; Woodward, A. M. *op. cit.,* p. 42.
15. Of the serials cancelled nearly half were abstracts, directories, year books or duplicates. Rodger, E. *op. cit.*
16. Houghton, B. *Rationalisation of serial holdings and the use of the British*

Library, Lending Division. Liverpool Polytechnic, 1975. 47. See also Williams, G. *Library cost models: owning versus borrowing serial publications.* Washington, National Science Foundation, 1968.

17. Line, M. B. 'UAP and inter-library lending', *op. cit.,* p. 118.

18. Stuart, M. 'Some effect on library users of the delays in supplying publications', *Aslib Proceedings* **29** no. 1 Jan. 1977. 41.

19. Statistics supplied by Sheffield Interchange Organisation and Tyneside Association of Libraries for Industry and Commerce (now superseded by Network).

20. Harris, K. G. E. 'Co-operation: the Newcastle experience'. *Library Association Record* **75** no. 8 August 1973. 148.

21. Blair, S. 'The costs of providing access to periodical literature in academic libraries'. *Catholic Library World* **49** no. 2 Sept. 1977. 71.

22. *The Guardian,* 25 Nov. 1978, 17.

23. See, for example, Gellatly, P. 'Debits and a few credits: can serials prices be controlled?' *Illinois Libraries* **60** no. 2 Feb. 1978. 101.

24. Gwinn, N. E. 'A national periodicals center'. *Library Journal* 1 Nov. 1978. 2166-69; *American Libraries,* Oct. 1978, p. 511.

25. Lucht, I. and Blair, S. 'The ACM Periodical Bank and the British National Lending Library'. *Management problems in serials work,* Greenwood Press, 1973. 4.

26. Thomas, P. A. 'Micropublishing and libraries in the future'. *Aslib Proceedings* **30** no. 5 May 1978. 167.

27. Periodicals are appreciably less important in public libraries with expenditure ranging from only 0.5 per cent to 12 per cent of the bookfund and with an average of only 227 titles per library authority. Oldham, C. M. and Davinson, D. E. *The usage of periodicals in public libraries.* Leeds Polytechnic, Department of Librarianship, 1975. 27; Luckham, B. 'Periodical purchase and readership'. *Research in Librarianship* **4** 1972-3. 141.

28. Wootton, C. B. *op. cit.,* p. 17.

29. This is a useful commentary on libraries' use of serials. Line, M. B. and Steemson, R. J. 'Interlibrary lending in the United Kingdom'. *Interlending Review* **6** no. 2 April 1978. 32-3.

30. Wootton, C. B. 'The economics of microfilming serials at the BLLD'. *BLL Review* **5** no. 1 Jan. 1977. 28-9.

31. *Trends in scholarly publishing.* British Library, 1976. 49. (Report no. 5299HC).

32. *Information Hotline* May 1978. 10.

33. Line, M. B. 'Universal availability of publications'. *UNESCO Bulletin for Libraries* **31** May 1977. 118.

34. Tongeren, E. van. 'Documentation notes'. *Journal of Documentation* **32** no. 3 Sept. 1976. 198-206.

35. Line, M. B. and Wood, D. N. 'The effect of a large-scale photocopying service on journal sales'. *Journal of Documentation* **31** no. 4 Dec. 1975. 234-45.

36. Woodward, A. M. *op. cit.,* p. 42.

37. Line, M. B. and Wood, D. N. *loc. cit.*
38. Line, M. B. 'Access to resources through the British Library Lending Division'. *Aslib Proceedings* 27 no. 1 Jan. 1975. 14.
39. For up to date accounts see Bradley, I. 'The International Serials Data System in 1978'. *Canadian Library Journal* June 1978. 167–71; Rosenbaum, M. 'ISDS register of serial publications'. *UNESCO Bulletin for Libraries* 32 no. 3 May-June 1978. 151–3.
40. Line, M. B. 'Principles of international lending and photocopying'. *International Library Review* 9 1977. 376.
41. Swartz, L. J. *op. cit.,* p. 176.
42. 'International lending statistics'. *IFLA Journal* 3 no. 2 1977. 121.
43. Davey, J. S. and Line, M. B. 'International activities of the British Library Lending Division'. *State Librarian* March 1977. 2 (Information supplied by M. B. Line).
44. 'The performance of the British Library Lending Division international photocopy service'. *Interlending Review* 6 no. 3 July 1978. 94.
45. Line, M. B. 'Principles of international lending and photocopying'. *op. cit.,* p. 371.
46. Line, M. B.'Universal availability of publications'. *op. cit.,* p. 117–8.
47. 'Associazione Italiana Biblioteche'. *Bolletino d'informazione.* N.S. Anno XVII (4), Ottobre-Dicembre 1977. 322.
48. Allardyce, A. 'UAP and the exchange of publications'. *IFLA Journal* 4 no. 2 1978. 122 and 124.

16

Abstracting and Indexing Services

Stella Keenan

INTRODUCTION

Definition

Abstracting and indexing services (also known as secondary or accessing services) can be defined as continuing bibliographic services produced by various types of organizations and containing abstracts and/or references to primary literature which enable a user to locate the original text. The literature may consist of books, monographs, primary journals, reports, government documents, patents, conference papers, preprints, etc., and the information provided by the secondary service may consist of tables of contents or bibliographic references arranged under an alphabetic or classified subject arrangement. A secondary service may cover a very narrow specialized area and a small number of primary documents, or it may cover a very broad area and a large number of documents. The size of the subject area covered does not necessarily determine the number of primary documents scanned. A very specialized area made up of a combination of subjects may necessitate covering a great many primary sources in order to cover the subject area adequately.

Secondary services may be issued as printed bulletins and journals, on cards, in microform, or on machine-readable tape.

Purpose

The basic function of an abstracting and indexing service is to save the time of the user. The growth of the primary literature, which is reflected by the growth of secondary services (see Table 16.1) has made it a physical impossibility for any person to keep abreast of information in a particular subject area. Abstracting and indexing services fulfil two major functions:

1. Current awareness — providing the user with rapid and current information on documents in a particular field of interest.
2. Archival function — providing the user with a retrospective collection that allows for an exhaustive search for information over a period of time.

In addition, abstracting services in particular can save reading time. It has been stated that 'at best, abstracts can save about nine-tenths of the time needed to read the original documents. Alternatively, they can broaden the scope of reading by a factor of 10'.[1] Abstracting and indexing services can also facilitate selection of documents and can overcome the language barrier.

Growth

The growth of secondary services are, of course, related to the growth of the primary literature. The National Federation of Abstracting and Indexing Services has published statistics of its member services since 1958. Table 16.1 is extracted from the latest tables issued by the Federation in 1979.[2] It shows the discipline- and mission-based services that are members of the Federation and have been publishing a service since 1957.

Parallel with the development of the secondary services has been the establishment of organizations set up to co-ordinate the activities of the services. In addition to NFAIS in the United States, there is the Paris-based International Council of Scientific Unions Abstracting Board (ICSU-AB).

TYPES OF ABSTRACTING AND INDEXING SERVICES

Abstracting and indexing services may be produced by different kinds of organization such as:

Table 16.1 National Federation of Abstracting and Indexing Services: member service statistics

	Type	1957	1967	1977	1978	Estimate 1979	per cent increase 1957-77
American Meteorological Society	P	5,000	9,000	7,200	7,200	7,200	44
American Petroleum Institute[a]	P	11,615	29,151	66,000	76,778	79,000	468
American Psychological Association	D	9,074	17,202	27,004	26,292	29,000	198
American Society of Metals	P	8,219	23,800	33,351	31,758	33,000	306
American Theological Library Association Indexes[b]	D	1,100	3,241	8,051	10,200	10,500	632
BioSciences Information Service	D	40,061	125,026	250,148	262,000	275,000	524
Chemical Abstracts Service	D	102,525	269,293	478,225	498,559	527,000	366
Engineering Index, Inc.	D	26,797	51,670	97,380	98,215	110,000	263
Medical Documentation Service[c]	P	1,500	1,692	2,500	2,500	2,500	66
Sociological Abstracts Inc.[d]	D	1,015	9,460	13,800	15,890	13,800	1,260
Subtotal		206,906	539,535	983,659	1,029,392	1,087,000	375
Defence Documentation Center	P	21,015	52,972	27,732	26,941	30,000	32
Department of Agriculture[e]	P	98,409	102,198	126,000	178,000	170,000	28
Department of Energy[f]	P	14,042	47,055	160,000	165,000	170,000	1,039
National Library of Medicine[g]	D	104,517	165,000	259,980	251,828	250,000	149
National Oceanic and Atmospheric Admin.	P	876	1,224	2,646	2,750	2,750	202
Subtotal		238,859	368,449	576,358	624,519	622,750	141
INSPEC	D/P	16,452	71,032	165,399	181,330	195,000	905
National Library of Australia	D/P	2,500	4,000	13,000	11,960	12,500	420
Subtotal		18,952	75,032	178,399	193,290	207,500	841
TOTAL		464,717	983,016	1,738,416	1,847,201	1,917,250	274

P = Project-oriented service
D = Discipline-based service

Notes

a   Coverage of world-wide literature, excluding patents, until 1961, when patent coverage began. Augmented patent coverage in co-operative effort with Derwent Services began in 1972. The Petroleum Energy Business News Index began in 1975.

b   Figures are for journal articles only; a substantial number of book review citations are not included. Figures for the years 1957–1967 are estimates.

c   Figures for the years 1957–1967 are estimates.

d   Figures from 1967 on include items from Language and Language Behavior Abstracts.

e   Figures represent indexing citations published in Bibliography of Agriculture. Since 1970, B of A produced by commercial publisher from data on CAIN (cataloging and indexing) tapes purchased from NAL. Starting with January 1978 this figure represents citations of AGRICOLA Sale Tapes prepared by USDA/TIS.

f   The large increase in 1976 over 1975 is due to the increased scope of interest of ERDA beyond that of the AEC. The 1976 and forward figures are for the ERDA Energy Information Data Base from which a number of abstract journals and other information products are produced.

g   The indexing backlog was eliminated in 1972. The total of 225,000 articles for 1975 also includes 11,000 Special list items which appeared in Special Bibliographies and the MEDLARS data base but not in *Index Medicus*. The 1976 figure also includes about 12,000 Special List items. The 1978 figure includes 19.265 Special List items.

Source National Federation of Abstracting and Indexing Services. Member Service Statistics, February 1979.

(a) professional organizations;
(b) industrial companies;
(c) government departments;
(d) national libraries;
(e) not-for-profit organizations;
(f) commercial organizations;
(g) research associations;
(h) trade associations;

Secondary services were divided into two groups by Robert Heller and Associates in 1963 in a report which presented a national plan for the abstracting and indexing services in the United States.[3] This report was prepared for the National Federation of Abstracting and Indexing Services, and the division was restated by Federation members in 1973.[4] The division is into discipline-oriented services and project- or mission-oriented services.

Discipline-oriented Services

These services aim to provide comprehensive coverage of a given field of knowledge by capturing the literature at the time of its primary publication, adequately abstracting and indexing it, making the information available as quickly, broadly, and conveniently as possible, and storing it for later use. There are a limited number of comprehensive discipline-oriented services as these are directly related to the basic division of knowledge into generic classes (e.g. chemistry, biology, physics, mathematics, engineering, geology, and psychology). These services should be maintained at an adequate level regardless of economic fluctuation, major catastrophes or other considerations. Discipline-oriented services require resources to enable them to maintain their service at the level described above.

Project- or Mission-oriented Services

These services' aim is to serve an identified user group that has a specific identified area of interest usually defined in terms of a task rather than a traditional discipline. Usually such groups are either inter- or intra-disciplinary. For example, the *Abstract Bulletin* of the American Petroleum Institute draws on the literature of chemistry, mathematics, physics, and other fields of science and engineering to serve the oil industry. The literature covers shifts as the industry changes its interest and as new technology develops. Project- and mission-oriented services may be developed by technical societies, trade associations, commercial enterprises, government agencies, etc. In contrast to the discipline-oriented services, project- and mission-oreinted services are likely to be less permanent. They should be directly related to the requirements of a segment of the user community, established in response to particular demands and changed or discontinued as warranted.

Project-oriented services should make maximum use of the discipline-oriented services to reduce duplication of intellectual effort in the preparation of the project-oriented service. It is not suggested that duplication of material between discipline- and project-oriented services should be eliminated, but rather that the intellectual effort of preparing data bases be shared. As project-oriented services should be established only in response to an identified user demand, these services are expected to be commercially viable and should require no subsidy unless an initial seed funding is required to launch a particular service. When a project-oriented service is not able to sustain itself through direct support from users, then that service is no longer required by the user community it was created to serve. Such a service should be modified in light of known user requirements or discontinued.

TYPES OF ABSTRACTS

An abstract has been defined as an abbreviated, accurate representation of a document usually without added interpretation or criticism.[5] It should not be confused with an annotation which is a brief note usually only a sentence or two long which describes the content of a document or with a summary or synopsis which usually occurs within a document and is written by the author to restate the main points of the document. An abstract is usually between one-tenth to one-twentieth the length of the primary document, though this figure should be regarded as a rough guide. Abstracts are usually indicative or informative. In certain cases they may be critical, biased or slanted, if this is required by the user community to be served.

Abstracts may be *indicative* indicating the scope of the article and summarizing the subject content, or *informative* giving information about the factual contents, e.g. data, methods, conclusions. Although these distinctions between indicative and informative abstracts are easy to state, in fact many services actually produce a mixture of indicative and informative abstract. Articles that depend on illustration, statistical tables, etc. cannot be abstracted informatively.

The American National Standards Institute first published a standard for writing abstracts in 1970.[5] This states and defines that the content particularly of scientific and technical abstracts, should cover the purpose, methods, results, conclusions, collateral and other information. While this statement will be easy to apply to scientific and technical literature it is more difficult to apply to the literature of the social sciences and the humanities.

The biased or slanted abstract may be produced to meet the needs of a particular user community. For example, the service produced for the research staff of an industrial company may stress the use of a particular product, chemical compound or other substance of interest to the staff.

An indexing service which has become increasingly important is the citation index, which was first developed for the information community by the Institute of Scientific Information in the early sixties. This index provides access to the primary literature in science, technology, the social sciences and the humanities in terms of the citations provided by the authors of the primary documents scanned. There is no intellectual abstracting and indexing as provided by the conventional services, but the citation indexes provide a very valuable secondary service of great importance in the information world. Mention should also be made of the critical abstract that will try to assess the value or quality of the original document; it has been argued for many years that improved critical abstracting services could identify the 'best or most useful' material, though it is also argued that there are very few abstractors capable of preparing adequate critical abstracts.

SOURCE OF ABSTRACTS AND INDEXES

Indexing and abstracting may be undertaken by staff appointed by the producer of the service. Staff members may be appointed as full-time abstractors and indexers or they may be expected to spend a portion of their time on this activity. An alternative to having staff-prepared abstracts and indexes is to use 'volunteer' abstractors who are not on the staff and are geographically removed from the producer's location. The relative merits of these two types of abstract and index preparation have to be decided by the producers of the secondary service, taking such factors as economics, subject specialization, language capability, speed and control into consideration.

As some primary documents contain author abstracts, the producers may decide to use these for the secondary publication, taking into account such factors as speed, expense, author ability as an abstractor, need for slanted abstracting, etc.

One of the main considerations must be the degree of standardization and control that the service producer wishes to exert over the secondary publication. Reference has already been made to the ANSI standard[5] which provides general non-mandatory guidelines for writing abstracts. However, most secondary services publishers will produce their own rules and instructions. A summary of these is given in *Abstracting concepts and methods*, by Borko and Bernier[1] and a more detailed survey with many examples was reported by Borko and Chatman in 1963.[6]

At the time of writing (mid–1979) it is regrettable to report that there is no single, authoritative standard for the bibliographic description that forms an integral part of abstracting and indexing services. There have been several attempts to remedy this situation. Since the Borko and Chatman study which identified the wide diversity of style in a number of major services, several attempts have been made bilaterally, nationally, and internationally. On a bilateral (or trilateral) basis, Chemical Abstracts, BioSciences Information Services of Biological Abstracts Inc., and Engineering Index Inc., produced a joint bibliographic guide in 1977.[7] This agreement developed from overlap studies undertaken jointly by the three services in the early 1970s.

Two sets of recommendations for the form of bibliographic citations have recently been issued by the British Standards Institution, namely BS 1629:1976, *Recommendations — bibliographical references* and BS 5606:1978, *Citing publications by bibliographical references*. The former is particularly suitable for secondary services, while the latter is essentially an abridged version of the former.

On an international level, Unesco's UNISIST programme has produced, in association with ICSU-AB, a manual[8] for converting bibliographic data relating to a variety of primary source material into a common machine format. An office situated within the British Library's Research and Development Department maintains and promotes the manual.

The CA/BA/EI agreement represents one type of *de facto* standardization — that is, that by the virtue of the size of established services, their practices are copied by smaller services and become standards in their own right. The national standards organizations and intergovernmental organizations such as Unesco have to develop standard recommendations and guidelines through committee procedure; *de facto* standards are also developed at the international level with the subject-based international systems such as the International Nuclear Information System (INIS). INIS is regarded as the prototype for these subject-based systems, and the agricultural information system AGRIS (International Information System for the Agricultural Sciences and Technology) uses the same rules, style and conventions as the INIS service.

MACHINE-READABLE ABSTRACTING AND INDEXING SERVICES

The attempt to cover the rapidly increasing primary literature has resulted in greatly increased costs for the secondary publishers. At a time when the cost of everything from paper to ink to labour costs is rising sharply in the world, the cost of producing a service increasing at even a low annual rate is considerable. The mechanization of the major abstracting and indexing services started in the late 1950s and early 1960s. Martha Williams has estimated that fewer than 20 bibliographic files were available to the public for information retrieval purposes in 1965.[9] By 1976 there were over 300 publicly available services available in machine-readable form. As these services became available in this form, they began to be called *data bases,* and they contained the bibliographic information contained in the printed secondary services. By 1977 it was estimated that there were 422 bibliographic data bases available in Europe.[10]

The most important bonus to be provided by the advent of machine-readable files is the provision of a vastly increased amount of natural language text for searching. The development of the KWIC index allowed titles to be manipulated for manual use, but this had been limited to the title words, possibly 'enriched' by the service producer. Titles, abstracts and, if in the file, full text can now be searched. Increased sophistication in search strategy, the use of Boolean logic and right- and left-hand truncation all play their part in exploiting the powerful tool of natural language available in the machine-readable form of the abstracting and indexing service.

As the major services have shifted from manual to mechanized production systems, two radical changes have occurred in the production process. This is the idea of 'single input — multiple output'. As an example of 'single input — multiple output', an item may be selected by INSPEC for inclusion in *Physics Abstracts*. This same article will also be listed in *Current Papers in Physics*, and, if it contains engineering information, it will be included in both the abstracting journal and the current papers publication for engineering. In addition, the reference will be included in the machine-readable file. The basic concept of 'single input — multiple output' is that the bibliographic and intellectual analysis (abstracting, indexing, categorizing, etc.) is keyboarded once and checked for accuracy. The record can then be used over and over again as required. This production concept is the basis of mechanized bibliographic services being produced today.

The basic idea of 'single input — multiple output' means entering information into the file once only, checking the record to ensure absolute accuracy and tagging for later retrieval all the useful information elements in the record. This multiple use of the record allows not only manipulation within the main published product for entry under more than one heading or for index generation, but also its re-use in subsets of the main file. Pre-packaging allows large discipline-based services to produce specialized smaller and cheaper information services aimed at a particular interest or speciality. Re-packaging also allows rapid response to a national priority interest such as the environment in the late sixties and early seventies and the energy crisis in the mid-seventies. Re-packaging may also be a co-operative arrangement under which two or more services may generate subsets which are merged to form a new information product. An example of this is HEAPS (Health and Environmental Pollutants) produced jointly by Chemical Abstracts Service and the National Library of Medicine.

The development of abstracting and indexing services in machine readable form allowed the service producers to keep pace with the literature growth and generate the printed publications from the machine file. The machine file in its turn provided the information handling world with a new commodity. Retrieval capability increased as any element that had been appropriately tagged for searching could be retrieved. It became possible to search for items by very precise data, language, country, document type parameters, etc. The power of negative searching could be used to screen out material in certain languages, from particular countries, etc. In addition, some data-base producers provided more information access points in the machine file than was economically feasible in the printed product. The deep indexing of the National Library of Medicine provided 15–30 index points in the machine file with far fewer appearing in the printed *Index Medicus.*

Utilization

The utilization of the machine-readable file presented a challenge to the information community in the late fifties and early sixties. The library literature of this period began to discuss the 'information retailer' or the 'information middleman'. Information Documentation Centres (IDCs) were established to acquire by lease or licence the machine-based bibliographic files and offer a search service to the user.

Other users of machine-readable bibliographic services were large companies, government departments and other organizations such as universities who had computer facilities available to make use of the machine-readable files.

Batch-mode Use

The early use made of machine-readable files was in *batch-mode*. As in manual searches, it is necessary to discuss the search request with the user so that the information need is identified. A search statement must then be prepared making use of Boolean logic (AND, OR, NOT); the searchable items available in the file together with the software can then be used to search the machine-readable file.

The search statements are recorded on a search tape which is run against each tape as it is received at the service centre. The searching is done by a serial record-by-record scan to obtain matches between the search tape and a particular issue of an abstracting and indexing service in machine-readable form. As many search statements or profiles can be matched at one pass, this method of searching for recent information can be used to provide a current information or SDI service. Retrospective searching is more difficult in batch-mode as searches begin to involve lengthy computer runs.

Disadvantages of batch searching, especially from the users' point of view, are that it denies the user direct access and does not allow the user to interact with the computer. There is also the time delay that the user experiences in waiting for the search results. There may be a delay of days or even weeks before the search results are available.

On-line Services

On-line services provide a search capability from a number of machine-readable files that are stored on a computer which is usually remote from the user's location. On-line provides the user with direct access to the data base and it provides an instant response. Searchers' statements can be modified during the search process as on-line provides the capability of *interacting* with the stored file. J. L. Hall has summed up the batch and on-line search methods as follows:

> Batch searching also involves another constraint in that it requires a rigid and pre-established query formulation with little or no opportunity for the searcher to revise the formulation in the middle of the search. This is in complete contrast to the on-line situation in which the searcher can very rapidly test the validity of a search formulation using an on-line inverted index thus avoiding the constraints involved in the computer batch or searching of lengthy serial files.[11]

The development of on-line retrieval services was pioneered by the National Library of Medicine, who commissioned System Development Corporation to design the ELHILL software that is used in the NLM's MEDLINE system and NASA who used Lockheed to develop the RECON software for the NASA and European Space Agency's on-line retrieval system. The latter has been available in the UK since the mid-seventies as the DIALTECH service available from the Technology Reports Centre.

Both Lockheed and System Development Corporation have developed commercial on-line services — the Lockheed service is known as DIALOG and System Development Corporation have developed ORBIT. The British Library set up BLAISE (British Library Automated Information Service) in 1977, choosing the ELHILL software for the system. This system allows for on-line and off-line retrieval of records from the MEDLARS files such as MEDLINE, TOXLINE etc., and the UK and Library of Congress MARC files.

It is obviously not possible in the scope of this chapter to discuss in detail the characteristics and relative advantages and disadvantages of manual, batch-mode and on-line retrieval from abstracting and indexing services. The user community to be served, the type of library (public, academic, special, etc.) and the availability of financial and staff resources have to be considered. Suffice it to say that on-line services are becoming an established service in many companies, government departments, academic institutions and professional organizations, while public library authorities are also beginning to explore the provision of on-line information services based on bibliographic files.

LIBRARY CONSIDERATIONS

Selection and Acquisition

The individual library will need to make decisions about the abstracting and indexing services in terms of the needs of its users.

As librarians have to decide which secondary services to purchase, they should apply the basic criteria that they would use for other reference tools, modifying these to fit the particular nature of abstracting and indexing services. An examination of the introductory *front matter* of the service may provide answers to some of the questions that should be asked as selection decisions are made. Selection criteria should cover the following points:

Purpose and Scope

What is the purpose and level of the service? Who forms the intended user group? What is the stated subject coverage? How old is the service? What is the extent of retrospective coverage? How many items are covered annually? What types of primary material are covered? How many periodicals are covered either fully or selectively?

Indexes

How can information be retrieved on a subject? Is the arrangement *alphabetical* by subject or *systematic* according to a thesaurus such as *Medical subject headings?*

Library Considerations

Is there an index by document type — patents, books, bibliographies, conference proceedings, reports, theses, patents, formulae, chemical substances, etc.?

Is there an index by organization — either author's affiliation or place where work was done?

Form and Layout

What is the physical form of the service? Is it issued as a journal or on cards, in microform, on computer tape or as a computer printout?

What is the physical appearance of the service?

Authority and Accuracy

Who prepares the abstracts and indexes? Who publishes the service? How is the service edited? Is there an advisory committee?

Frequency and Currency

How frequently is the service issued? Are there any cumulations? What is the time-lag between the appearance of the primary document and its inclusion in a service?

Style

What type of abstract is used — informative, indicative, critical? Is the abstract of optimum length? What style of bibliographic reference is used?

Does the entry contain journal abbreviations, translation of foreign language titles, language indication of primary document, etc.?

Objectivity

Is there any apparent bias in the service? Is there any difference between English and American terminology in use? Have there been any changes over a period of years in coverage or terminology? Is the subject coverage slanted to a particular user interest?

Relationship with Comparable Works

How does the service compare with others in the same field? How does the coverage correspond to the primary documents in the library's own collection? How does the price compare with similar services?

Directories

There are many directories which give information on abstracting and indexing services. These range from general lists covering all subjects to special directories that cover services in a particular form such as machine-readable or services that cover a particular subject area.

Ulrich's international periodicals directory, published by the R. R. Bowker Company, lists abstracting and indexing services in one section. In addition, this directory lists under the title of the primary journal, the major abstracting and indexing services that cover the title listed. A directory of abstracting and indexing services available in the UK was published by the British Library in 1978.[12] This covers all subject areas and gives details such as coverage, number of items per year and format (printed, machine-readable, etc.). Aslib and EUSIDIC have published three editions of *Data bases in Europe* with the latest edition appearing in 1977. This covers bibliographic data bases and factual data banks. More recently, A. Tomberg has published the *EUSIDIC database guide*;[13] this directory is an international guide with a European emphasis. It lists every data base reported as potentially available to the public, regardless of geographic origin, in 1978. The number of unique entries is:

Bibliographic files	533
Data bases	568
	1,101

This is not intended to be a comprehensive list of directories, but merely identifies some of the more recent ones available at the time of writing.

Cost Considerations

Librarians and information workers faced with decisions concerning the provision of abstracting and indexing services must weigh the relative aspects in terms of the requirements of their users. It is not possible in this chapter to develop in detail the decision factors as each person must make his/her own assessment in terms of the parent organization and the users.

The decision to start or continue the provision of the printed abstracting and indexing service should consider the following:

(a) the rising cost of the annual subscriptions to published services;
(b) staff time in processing each issue as it is received;
(c) staff time in performing literature searches; and
(d) storage, binding and preservation costs.

In evaluating the machine-readable abstracting and indexing service, the information worker should consider the following:

(a) cost of external service provision;
(b) staff time and training costs;
(c) equipment costs; and
(d) service costs which may include payments for communication, information documentation, training costs, list of references, etc.

Information services may also need to consider the additional requests that might be generated by the use of external abstracting and indexing services. It is to be expected that libraries and information centres, when the original decision to purchase a given abstracting and indexing service is made, will select those which best reflect the primary journals already in their collection.

As external services are used, the user may start to demand copies of original documents that are not contained in the library collection. This may increase the number of interlibrary loan requests or even lead to a re-evaluation and reassessment of the library collection. Access to the original documents must be considered together with a discussion of the provision of abstracting and indexing services.

Document Access

Abstracting and indexing services are not complete in themselves. It has already been noted that they are sometimes called secondary services, as their function is to cover the primary literature to provide access to information that goes far beyond the capability of any one person to locate and read, or the capacity of any one library collection.

Any consideration of abstracting and indexing services must include a discussion of document access and document availability. The process of information transfer is not completed until the person with the information need has stated the question, the appropriate information tools have been used, and an answer has been obtained. If in the process of answering the question the user is given a list of references to be consulted, the enquirer must know how to obtain the original document.

In the UK users are especially fortunate in having the British Library Lending Division as a source of primary material. Other countries are not as fortunate, a fact which makes BLLD one of the principal sources of primary documents for many other countries, both developed and developing. Unesco has been examining this problem and has established a programme of UAP — Universal Availability of Publications.

SUMMARY AND FUTURE OUTLOOK

Decisions concerning the provision of abstracting and indexing services must, of course, be based on the requirements of the users and the environment in which the library service functions. The purpose of the library service will determine the type of abstracting and indexing services to be provided, the form in which these services should be made available, and the degree of external services (batch-mode, custom or group SDI or on-line services) to be provided.

Special libraries probably have the best-defined user community with clear objectives to determine the function of the library service to be provided. They will make use of external service points such as research and trade associations to provide specialized services in areas of interest. Special libraries must scan the literature for different types of information — scientific and technical, business and economic, trade development, etc. They need to maintain internal abstracting and indexing services to provide detailed information on commodities and research topics that relate to company concerns.

Internally generated reports, technical and business, will need to be controlled through an internal indexing and possibly abstracting system. With more emphasis on the journal, report and patent literature and much less use of the monograph literature, special libraries are very concerned with making the optimum use of abstracting and indexing services.

Academic libraries have to consider the role of the secondary services as they provide the literature and information support services required for the educational curriculum of the parent institution. Scientifically and technically oriented universities were among the first to make use of machine-based services in the early 1970s. In the late 1970s colleges and polytechnics became increasingly interested in using the services in this form. The increased availability of social science and humanities data bases in machine-readable form is making educational institutions in these subject areas take a new and positive look at the capabilities of computerized services.

School libraries need access to secondary services to guide students to the literature that they need to extend their lecture notes and text books. The *British Technology Index* and the *British Humanities Index* should be staple reference services in school libraries, especially at the secondary school level of O- and A-level examinations where students should start their preparation for university educational methods.

In looking to the future, schools can be expected to make increasing use of microprocessors and minicomputers. At home, there is the advent of teletext information systems that can be made available through the domestic television set. Systems such as the Post Office's Prestel (originally Viewdata) system and the broadcast services of the BBC (Ceefax) and the IBA (Oracle) have the potential of changing the information habits of future generations with a subsequent impact on the provision of library and information services in schools.

Public libraries are also watching and assessing with some concern the impact of new technology on traditional information service provision. 1978 saw the establishment and the beginnings of experimentation with the provision of on-line information services in public libraries. At this time over 15 per cent of UK public library authorities were planning to use either teletext or bibliographic services in on-line mode in the foreseeable future.[14] The British Library Research and Development Department is supporting research in some public library systems and is also supporting the Library Association and Aslib in research into the use of the teletext systems. The implications of these activities and the continuing debate on the economics of the provision of special services in public libraries must be of current concern and importance.

In attempting to look into the crystal ball of the future of abstracting and indexing services, one would probably see two crossed lines. These lines represent the graphical representation of the rising costs of people, paper, print and post. The second line represents the falling (we hope) costs of computing, communication systems, etc., and the two lines are expected to cross and redistribute the economic structure of the information industry in the next five to ten years. How to balance the rising costs of the one and the falling costs of the other, is the main problem facing the librarian and the information worker today.

Abstracting and indexing services in some form are essential information tools. Writing in 1975 one of the first textbooks for on-line information services,[11] J. L. Hall quotes Dr Samuel Johnson who more than two hundred years earlier said: 'Knowledge is of two kinds. We know a subject ourselves or we know where we can find information upon it.'

REFERENCES

1. Borko, H. and Bernier, C. L. *Abstracting concepts and methods.* London and New York, Academic Press, 1975. 6–7.
2. National Federation of Abstracting and Indexing Services. *Member service statistics,* February 1979.
3. National Federation of Science Abstracting and Indexing Services. *A national plan for science abstracting and indexing service,* 15 March 1963. Washington, D.C., NFSAIS, 1963.
4. National Federation of Abstracting and Indexing Services. *History and issues, 1958–73.* Philadelphia, Pa., NFAIS, 1973.
5. Weil, B. H. 'Standards for writing abstracts'. *Journal of the American Society for Information Science.* 21 no. 5 1970.351–357.
6. Borko, H. and Chatman, S. 'Criteria for acceptable abstracts: a survey of abstractors' instructions'. *American Documentation* 14 no. 2 April 1963. 149–160.
7. American Chemical Society. *Bibliographic guide for editors and authors.* Washington, D.C., 1974.
8. UNISIST/ICSU-AB Working Group on Bibliographic Descriptions. *Reference manual for machine-readable bibliographic descriptions.* Paris, Unesco, 1974.
9. Williams, M. E. 'Data bases — a history of developments and trends from 1966 through 1975'. *Journal of the American Society for Information Science* 28 no. 2 March 1977. 71–8.
10. Tomberg, A. *Data bases in Europe: a directory to machine readable data bases and data banks in Europe.* 3rd ed. Aslib/EUSIDIC, 1977 (European user services; 1).
11. Hall, J. L. *On-line information retrieval.* London, Aslib, 1977.
12. Burgess, G. *et al. Inventory of abstracting and indexing services published in the UK.* London, British Library, 1978.
13. Tomberg, A. *EUSIDIC database guide.* Oxford, Learned Information, 1978.
14. Keenan, S. 'On-line information services in public libraries'. in *Study School and National Conference, Brighton, 1978, Proceedings.* London, Library Association, 1979. 169–74.

17

Bibliographic Standards

Ross Bourne

A short answer to the question of whether bibliographic standards are necessary might be that by their very nature serials are capable — more so than monographs — of being recorded in a variety of ways, and that standardization promotes consistent treatment. For example, take a not unlikely situation in which Journal 'a' becomes Journal 'b', followed by Journal 'c' and perhaps Journal 'd', over a period of, say, 10 years; the character of the original journal, not to mention its numbering, has been retained throughout these various title manifestations. To all intents and purposes, this is the same journal. Which is the most useful form in which that journal can be recorded: 'a'? 'd'? or 'a', 'b', 'c' and 'd' successively, with references to and from earlier titles? All of these solutions have been adopted by catalogues and bibliographies at one time or another, and a cataloguing code will favour one of them, while users, it is hoped, will know the correct convention to apply when they approach a particular file of serial records. But as all serials cataloguers know, a simple 'a', 'b', 'c', 'd' progression of titles is the least of their problems: a complex but not unusual family tree is presented in Fig. 17.1.

Consistency within a single serials file is one thing. Standardization, however, assumes consistency amongst a number of files, not only at local level but also at national and international levels. Just as I need the English language, with all its rules of grammatical construction, in order

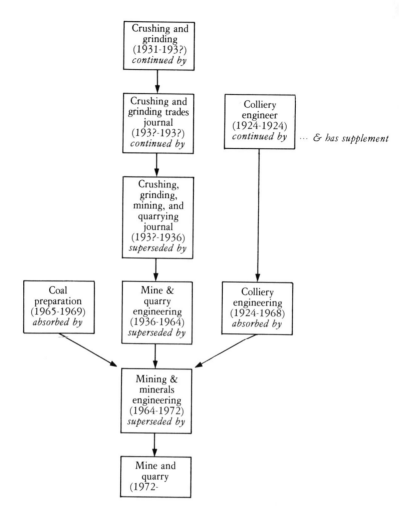

Crushing and
grinding
(1931-193?)
continued by

Crushing and
grinding trades
journal
(193?-193?)
continued by

Colliery
engineer
(1924-1924)
continued by   ... *& has supplement*

Crushing,
grinding,
mining, and
quarrying
journal
(193?-1936)
superseded by

Coal
preparation
(1965-1969)
absorbed by

Mine &
quarry
engineering
(1936-1964)
superseded by

Colliery
engineering
(1924-1968)
absorbed by

Mining &
minerals
engineering
(1964-1972)
superseded by

Mine and
quarry
(1972-

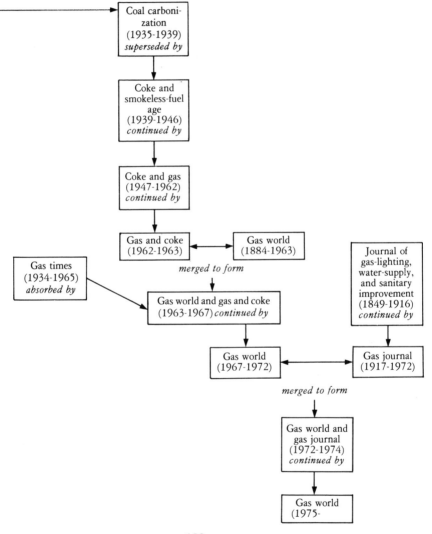

to communicate, so a catalogue record constructed according to consistent rules is essential if that record is to be used to maximum advantage outside the library for which it was originally created. This chapter, then, deals with those bibliographic standards for use at national and international levels which are actually being applied or are in the course of preparation. But librarians in small environments may well ask whether they need worry about international standards. Their clientele may be less demanding, their collections are small, their cataloguing minimal, and what they do not stock themselves is probably obtainable from the British Library Lending Division at Boston Spa. The answer lies in the possibilities becoming available through recent communications technology, such as on-line interrogation of information services like INSPEC and MEDLINE, and the Post Office's Prestel viewdata service, which will permit access to information by means of the combination of television set and telephone. The point being made is that the librarian of a small library need not feel isolated from the resources of larger and more affluent libraries. The new technology does facilitate access to more information than has hitherto been feasible, and although it is not cheap, it is likely to become cheaper as computer storage becomes more miniaturized. But if the librarian is to rely upon external sources to provide him with information which he cannot afford to acquire himself, then that information must be available in a form which is neither inconsistent nor unduly localized. A standard bibliographic description is as relevant to a small branch of a public library as it is to a national bibliographic agency or to an international file of records, although that is not to say that the *degree* of detail must be identical.

CATALOGUING

This section is confined to the *Anglo-American cataloguing rules* (AACR). The 1967 edition[1] drew a distinction between serials and other works of mixed authorship (a distinction which must have seemed curious to users of catalogues in which monograph and serial records co-existed) and on the whole was biased towards printed monographs. A revision of AACR was published towards the end of 1978,[2] and like the earlier edition is a joint undertaking of the national libraries and national library associations of Canada, the United Kingdom, and the United States. Unlike its 1967 predecessor, however, it exists in a single text, and applies the general-to-specific principle much more consistently, so that *all* forms of library material, including serials, are handled in a similar fashion, with particular exceptions peculiar to particular forms of material being dealt with in separate chapters. So in Chapter 12 on the description of serials, reference back to Chapter 1, the general chapter, is necessary, while in the chapters on choice and form of headings, Chapters 21 to 24, there is *no* separate treatment of serials. Since serials are regarded as works of mixed authorship, the appropriate rule for mixed authorship can therefore be invoked, in effect providing for entry under title in most cases. The exception to this rule — also applicable to monographs — is the situation when a serial represents the collective, usually administrative, thought of an organization, say its rules, or a list of its members, or the minutes of its meetings; in such a case, main access is by the name of that organization. On the other hand, when an organization publishes or sponsors a journal but allows its membership to express their own views, that is not regarded as constituting the collective thought of the organization, and access by title rather than by corporate body is therefore required. To take a revered example, *Philosophical Transactions of the Royal Society* is entered as such, rather than under the name of the Royal Society, since it consists of individual and independent contributions by its members. On the other hand, the annual report and accounts of, say, the National Coal Board is clearly the collective responsibility of the Board, and is entered under the name of the Board. This change from AACR1 rationalizes the preference of many serials librarians for title entry, which after all is what many distinguished bibliographies such as the *British union-catalogue of periodicals,* the *World list of scientific periodicals* and the University of Cambridge's *Current serials* apply successfully already. However, it could be argued that the concept of the main entry is becoming irrelevant, since computer access need not depend upon a particular entry point. Indeed, AACR2, unlike AACR1, has the rules for bibliographic description preceding those for choice and form of heading, thereby seeming to attach less significance to the latter.

The new code enshrines most of the prescriptions of the first standard edition of ISBD(S),[3] which is based on the assumption that a serial record can be produced by reference to just one issue. Like the ISBD(S), serial description is divided into eight areas:

Area 1:   Title and statement of responsibility
Area 2:   Edition

Area 3:   Numeric and/or alphabetic, chronological, or other designation
Area 4:   Publication, distribution, etc.
Area 5:   Physical description
Area 6:   Series
Area 7:   Note
Area 8:   Standard number and terms of availability

Again like ISBD(S), areas and elements are demarcated by punctuation and spacing, so that a record can be scanned by a computer, or one in an unfamiliar language be correctly read, because of each element's distinguishing punctuation. For example, other title information such as a subtitle is always preceded by a space, colon, space, as is the name of a publisher; the context determines which element it is which follows.

IDENTIFICATION AND CITATION

In this section, a number of systems designed to facilitate the identification and citation of serials are described. These include the symbolic, in which numbers or letters are used to form a unique identifier for a serial, and the verbal, namely title abbreviations, the traditional shorthand by which scholars and scientists refer to their sources. These methods of identification and citation have developed because of the problems of controlling large numbers of homonymous serial titles, not to mention the difficulties brought about by frequently changing titles. A joint Unesco-ICSU-AB (= International Council of Scientific Unions Abstracting Board) feasibility study on the improvement of international scientific communication recognized these problems; the UNISIST report published in 1971 recommended that: 'An international registry of scientific periodicals should be established as a basis of a system for the normalization of the citations of the journal literature of science and technology ...'[4]

Shortly after the publication of the UNISIST report, the French Government, with the assistance of Unesco, set up the International Centre of the International Serials Data System (ISDS). Marie Rosenbaum, the International Centre's Director, has described the working of the system in a recent article.[5] Briefly, it is a decentralized system in which national and regional centres report the serial output of their countries to the International Centre in a MARC-type format. In turn, the International Centre publishes these records on COM microfiche and on computer exchange tape. The serial records created by the various ISDS centres constitute a brief bibliographic description, of which the most important features are: the key-title, a unique title derived from the title of the serial; the standard abbreviation of the key-title (of which more later); and an equally unique control number, the International Standard Serial Number (ISSN). The uniqueness of a title is determined solely by its wording. Hence, if that title changes, the key-title and its associated ISSN also change. Each record contains links, in the form of ISSN, to related records such as former and later titles, editions in other languages, etc., so in theory a family history similar to that displayed in Fig. 17.1 can be constructed. A key-title's uniqueness is achieved by ensuring that when a title is shared by two or more serials, it is qualified in some suitable fashion. Therefore, generic titles such as *Bulletin* or *Newsletter* are qualified by the name of the body whose bulletin or newsletter they are, while common yet non-generic titles such as *Choice, Focus, Contact,* etc. are qualified by the place of publication or start date or both. But the purpose of ISDS is not only to identify a publication and provide a standard citation for it in the form of an ISSN, key-title and abbreviated title, but also to make available a brief bibliographic record, capable of use within mechanized systems for the purposes of union listings, local catalogues, housekeeping operations, even subscription agents' files. ISDS, whose Centres number over 40 and are situated in East, West and Third World alike, is a manifestation of universal bibliographic control. Its rapid growth would have seemed impossible less than 10 years ago, but in these days of increased international contact amongst librarians it has become an accepted feature and has demonstrated that international bibliographic standards can be applied by librarians with very different traditions.

To the individual librarian, however, the chief output of ISDS is the ISSN which is appearing on a growing number of journals and other serial publications and whose assignment in the United Kingdom is the responsibility of the UK National Serials Data Centre, part of the Bibliographic Services Division of the British Library. The ISSN is an eight-digit number (including a check digit), preceded by the initials ISSN and split into two parts, separated by a hyphen, for convenient reading; ISO 3297 describes the system in more detail.[6] For example, each issue of *Journal of Library Automation* bears the number ISSN 0022-2240, and will continue to bear that number until such time as the title changes. Unlike the International Standard Book Number, however, the ISSN has no internal significance: the number is purely arbitrary, with no publisher, linguistic or national components. Therefore, a journal which retains its title but shifts its country of publication and changes its publisher, will retain its ISSN.

ISDS — in spite of its origins in the UNISIST recommendation which refers to 'scientific journals' — covers all types of serial publications at all levels, from comics to advanced scholarship. The ISSN, however, is not the only serial numbering system in use, having been preceded almost 20 years earlier by the CODEN system. CODEN was devised by Charles Bishop of the University of Buffalo for much the same purpose. It is now operated by the Chemical Abstracts Service, but unlike ISSN the orientation is more overtly scientific and technical. A CODEN consists, basically, of four letters, assigned mnemonically from the name of the journal itself, to which a fifth letter is added if the mnemonic is not unique; a sixth letter or number acts as a check digit, to ensure the correct citation of the basic code. The CODEN for the aforementioned *Journal of Library Automation* is JLAUAY. In the United Kingdom, CODEN are available from UKCIS at the University of Nottingham. In a sense, of course, ISSN and CODEN are rivals; in practice, both are frequently cited on the same publication. A 1973 article by Batik gives more information about the assigning and application of CODEN.[7]

Reference was made earlier to abbreviated titles, which of course have been in use for citation purposes considerably longer than either ISSN or CODEN. ISO 4[8] sets out guidelines by which title words can be abbreviated (for example, abbreviation is limited to words of more than five letters), while ISO 833[9] consists of a list — emanating originally from the National Clearinghouse for Periodical Title Word Abbreviations in the United States — of words abbreviated according to the ISO 4 principles. Basically, words with both a common root and a common meaning, in whatever language, share the identical abbreviation, thus 'phys.' may represent 'physical', 'physicist' and 'physics', not to mention the French 'physique' and the German 'physisch'. But 'physiology', a departure in meaning from the original root, becomes 'physiol.', while 'physician' remains unabbreviated so as not to be confused with either. Until its recent withdrawal ISO 833 was supplemented by further lists compiled by the ISDS International Centre, and ISO 4 itself is in process of revision. Whether these internationally agreed abbreviations will actually be used is another matter, of course, since many well established abstracting and indexing services already employ their own house abbreviations, and would presumably justify them on the grounds that their subscribers were accustomed to them. However, the currency of abbreviations formulated by ISO principles may well be increased by their use, which is mandatory, in ISDS records.

Each of these different forms of citation is being used in current moves to standardize not just the citation of serial titles but also their contents. An ISO Sub-committee is presently meeting with a view to developing the Biblid or Bibliographic Identification of Serial Publications (previously known as the Bibliographic Strip), which will seek to provide a standard citation for volumes and issues, articles, and individual pages. A similar form of citation is already in use in the United States for the purpose of facilitating the collection of copyright fees arising from the photocopying of articles. This need arose from the new United States Copyright Law which came into effect on 1 January, 1978, and which led to the setting-up of the Copyright Clearance Center Inc. as the agency which would collect copyright fees on behalf of publishers. The code consists of ISSN, date of issue, pagination of the article's first page, and the photocopying fee set by the publisher, plus an indication of whether an author royalty is also payable.

Although the provisions of the Copyright Law do not apply in the United Kingdom, a number of British serials with United States distribution are already bearing the recommended code.

INFORMATION TRANSFER

For information transfer, read MARC. MARC, or MAchine Readable Cataloguing, originated in the Library of Congress as a means of automating the printing of the Library's catalogue cards, and consists of a framework or format by which individual bibliographic elements are separately coded with a view to their subsequent computer processing. The production of catalogue cards is still a major function of MARC, at least in the United States, but the system has since adapted itself to the greater range of possibilities which are now available from computer and systems technology. The uses of automation are more fully described in Chapter 18, but at this stage it is necessary to recognize how the MARC format has influenced bibliographic control. Firstly, it is in the broadest sense a standard, although variations exist both at local and national level. Secondly, the MARC format provides a discipline by which the cataloguer is forced to identify pieces of bibliographic information and assign a particular coding to them. Thirdly, because of that, MARC is altering our views on how catalogues are used and accessed. In a conventional catalogue or listing, there are practical limitations on the number of access points which are provided; MARC coding enables more elements of a catalogue entry to be used for access than is usually feasible or economic, although it should be said that this depends upon the form of output. If MARC is used merely to automate catalogue card production, then little is gained; but recent computer technology enables a whole record to be searched for, say, key words in the title, or a bibliographic history of a serial to be constructed from ISSN present in the linking fields. MARC coding facilitates this type of search, unthinkable in pre-automation days.

LOCAL STANDARDS

Standardization at the local level almost seems a contradiction in terms. However, there is one area where it has recently been recognized that local standardization will improve overall access to serials. This is, the consistent presentation of holdings statements, or the recording of which issues of a serial are actually held by a library. Within a catalogue or listing which records the holdings of just one collection, this is perhaps not too important; but where a number of libraries are reporting their holdings to a central agency, the ways in which they report what they have can be as many as the reporting libraries themselves. Translated into regional and national terms, it becomes obvious that unless the central agency can lay down a standard, it will find itself hard put to control the different types of holdings statements which will emanate from the notifying libraries. As far as the user is concerned, it is self-evident that he will be better served by a holdings statement which is standard throughout the various libraries and union lists which he may use. At the time of writing, both the American National Standards Institute and the British Standards Institution have standards for serial holdings statements in the course of preparation. In addition to the presentation of the actual statement, these are both likely to include elements giving the date of the report, which will enable the user to see how old or recent the holdings information is, and a code to represent the completeness of the particular library's run. The latter code avoids the problems of setting out a long, involved statement for a run in which numbers of issues are absent, by indicating that the run is incomplete within a certain percentage range. Thus, a brief statement like 'Vol. 1, 1964–' is possible, with the code acting as a warning that, say, up to 10 per cent of the published run is missing. The combination of the date of report, the coverage code and a brief statement should enable the user to assess the likely usefulness of the library's run and the librarian to reduce the amount of space which the statement takes up.

This chapter on bibliographic standards answers, I hope, the question of whether they are necessary at all. The more that libraries rely upon one another, the more necessary it is that they speak the same language. Likewise, users are becoming more mobile. If the librarian exists to serve the user, then it becomes even more important that he should receive a similar quality of service wherever he goes.

REFERENCES

1. *Anglo-American cataloguing rules.* British text. London, Library Association, 1967.
2. *Anglo-American cataloguing rules.* 2nd ed. London, Library Association, 1978.
3. International Federation of Library Associations and Institutions. *ISBD(S): International Standard Bibliographic Description for serials.* 1st standard ed. London, IFLA International Office for UBC, 1977.
4. Unesco and ICSU. *UNISIST: study report on the feasibility of a world science information system.* Paris, Unesco, 1971. 94.
5. Rosenbaum, M. 'The International Serials Data System (ISDS)'. *International Forum on Information and Documentation* 2 no. 2 April 1977. 22–4.
6. International Organization for Standardization. *Documentation-International standard serial numbering (ISSN).* Geneva, ISO, 1975.
7. Batik, A.L. 'The CODEN system'. *Journal of Chemical Documentation* 13 no. 3 Aug 1973. 111–13.
8. International Organization for Standardization. *Documentation – International code for the abbreviation of titles of periodicals.* Geneva, ISO, 1972.
9. International Organization for Standardization. *Documentation – International list of periodical title word abbreviations.* Geneva, ISO, 1974. (N.B. this standard has now been withdrawn pending the revision of ISO 4 and the expected assumption of responsibility for maintaining standard abbreviations by the ISDS International Centre).

18

The Use Of Computers

P. A. Thomas

INTRODUCTION

Serials control has traditionally figured as a major problem area of library activity, of especial interest to both librarian and library user not only because of the increasing importance of serials as an information resource, but also because of the unruly nature of the material and the effort involved in acquisition and access.

The catalogue of woes is familiar to all concerned: the proliferation of new titles; changes in title; fatalities; changes in publisher and publication patterns; special issues and separately published supplements, indexes and title pages; missing issues and irregular arrivals included. There is also the sheer volume of titles.

Coping with all this variety represents a major labour-intensive cost element in all library budgets, and a complex, repetitive and troublesome workload for librarians: ideal candidates for computer-aided systems. Some librarians still say that the very factors that make computer applications desirable here also make it too difficult to accomplish and that effective manual systems are not only possible but may be preferable.[1,2] Nevertheless, there is an impressive and rapidly growing record of success.

The literature on this aspect of library automation is already extensive enough to generate reviews, state-of-the-art reports, and specialized bibliographies.[3-11] Institutes, workshops, symposia and clinics, conference proceedings, systems manuals and project reports, newsletters and ephemera on the subject present a microcosm of the total media problem. So much is happening, and so quickly, nationally and internationally, that as Paul Fasana says: 'it is virtually impossible to keep abreast of current happenings; it is almost like burying your head in the sand to interpret or find a logic in many of these events.'[12]

He goes on to discuss three areas of computer-related activity that he sees as important to 'conventional' libraries: standards, standards setting projects and code-revision activities. The whole area of computer-based serials control is becoming even more relevant to all librarians: partly through the pressures for standardization he mentions; partly through the opportunities and equally the increased need for co-operative resource sharing that technological advances are introducing; and because the activity of designing computer systems can provoke a new thoughtfulness about the purposes and procedures of our existing systems, and encourage understanding and improved practices.

SUMMARY OF DEVELOPMENTS

From the experimental systems of the early 1960s; through the proliferating local systems of the following decade, employing both off-line and later on-line technologies; to the initiation of powerful co-operative systems and library networks in the 1970s, librarians have demonstrated the potential benefits of computerization and their determination to achieve them.

Veaner's three major practical reasons for automating put it succinctly: 'to do something less expensively, more accurately, or more rapidly ... [or] which can no longer be done effectively in the manual system because of increased complexity or overwhelming volume ... [or] which cannot be performed in the manual system ...'.[13]

Filing and re-filing chores can be reduced, the number of forms decreased, and records may be located from any number of different access points, making more information more readily accessible than in the forced single-sequencing of manual files. The important daily task of check-in or receipt of serials parts can be eased, automatic prompting of claims for missing issues and notification of binding schedule dates are becoming standard requirements in systems design.[14-17] Indeed, the principle of making the maximum use of the first recording of bibliographic information throughout the sequence of processing activities generally, reduces duplication of effort and contributes to the development of integrated systems. Clerical effort can be released for more productive activities, and growing work volumes accommodated without corresponding growth in staff numbers.[18]

Most important of all, improved services to users, and to librarians as users of their own files, can be achieved. Information that was previously only available, if at all, through the mediation of library staff may be made readily available to users and to scattered work stations through the facility with which various listings can be generated, and now through on-line information retrieval via computer terminals.

With finite limits to the resources allocated to libraries, with rising subscription levels, with people costs increasing more swiftly than machine costs, unit processing costs must inevitably increase unless aided by machine processes. Nevertheless, the need for effective and efficient acquisition and control procedures must be the prime factor in automation decisions.

'Almost anything can be automated if enough economic resources can be invested in the development and maintenance of the system.'[19] The strategy of getting the most for one's money must be based on an awareness of just where the computer can be most useful. The choice is no longer simply between manual and computer systems. It must include an informed consideration of the wide variety of computer options available to achieve the required levels of operational performance, and the degree of involvement in other people's systems.

Up to the mid-1960s the computerized serials applications introduced into libraries used the available off-line technology to produce various types of listings, catalogues, holdings lists etc. and some control functions.[20] Some concentrated on piecemeal, independent projects for specific areas of activity such as acquisitions and accounts or inventory control; some, more rarely, began combining functions within a broad overall plan in a move towards a more integrated systems design.[21-23]

Records of current transactions were assembled into groups ready for processing and sent in a batch for keyboarding into machine-readable form. These records, existing machine-readable files, and programs were fed into the computer for processing (usually overnight), and outputs of printed lists, cards and forms were produced, as well as an updated machine-readable master file ready for the next cycle of operations: off-line batch processing.

Lists of holdings, catalogues, subject listings;[24] serial titles grouped by Departmental library, vendor, language or keyword;[25,26] predictive and non-predictive check-in routines and subscription renewals[27] were all attempted, and the resulting systems widely reported in the literature. Union lists stimulating user access and the elimination of unintentional duplication of holdings supported the movement towards greater sharing of resources.[28,29]

From the mid-1960s,[30,31] the technology allowed immediate entry of individual transactions to a computer-held file via on-line terminals connected directly to the computer with no waiting for batches of records to be assembled and without the intervention of punched cards, paper tape or magnetic tape.[32,33] Two categories of on-line applications have developed: conversational remote-job entry systems (CRJE) and interactive systems. In CRJE, inputs are fed to the computer via a printed or visual-display-type terminal, verified on the spot and accepted with instructions for later batch mode off-line processing. Outputs may be either via the terminal, or by the familiar forms of computer printout. Truly interactive systems involve staff entering information and commands at a terminal and getting in return second-by-second feedback from the computer accomplishing editing, verification, error correction, record entry and manipulation, file updating and information retrieval and display tasks on-line, and entering requests for any off-line printouts required as well.

Many existing, if partial, computer-based serials systems are successfully based on the production of various off-line listings, and this will continue to be a useful facility. The second edition of the Aslib *Directory of operational computer applications in UK library and information units*[26] notes 67 list applications compared with one check-in and five periodicals circulation systems. For full control and more significant impact on work processes and on user services, the development of on-line and remote access systems is of vital importance.

On-line systems, intelligent terminals, visual display units, mini-computers, large disc stores, advanced programming techniques and linkage to long-distance communications lines have all contributed to the creation of elegant systems which are far easier to use and much more effective than their manual counterparts.

They can also provide facilities which manual systems cannot: the automatic collection and analysis of operational statistics for management; powerful and sophisticated information retrieval techniques; ease of file management and updating; and automatic prompting for action, presenting relevant records and listings that remove the arduous file scanning and search tasks of manual systems.

All types of library are represented in the published project descriptions and systems presentations, and the particularly strongly-developed interest evidenced in early applications in university and medical libraries has continued — with the incorporation of an on-line option in the PHILSOM network,[34] the UCLA on-line serials system,[35] (Fayollat's excellent series of articles[36-38] on the latter includes a rare comparison of on-line and batch operations and a cost analysis) and the University of London Union List of Serials,[39] to name but a few.

The proliferation of machine-readable serials files,[40] standards and formats for serials records, and the movement towards formalized interlibrary co-operation and networking (both enabled by and dependent on the technological advances of computing and telecommunications industries) contribute to a confusing variety of options for the librarian. The aim must still be to achieve a good fit between users' needs and library services at an acceptable cost to funders.[41]

SYSTEMS DESIGN AND IMPLEMENTATION

Designing a computer-based system is obviously not undertaken in a vacuum. Traditional serials functions must be accommodated. Most importantly, discussions with staff involved in all areas of activity should form a major part of the programme right from the beginning. Not only do they know more about the detailed needs of the particular system, but the ultimate success of any new procedures introduced will depend on their acceptance and co-operation.

A major management criterion for the design of an effective system will be the increased efficiency of operations, more work accomplished by the same number of staff or the same amount of work by a lesser number of staff. Inevitably there will be fears of redundancy, of changing job contents and skill requirements, and of the effects of change and innovation generally.

The sooner information is shared, and positive participation in systems design and implementation invited as an ongoing process, the better the chances are of developing effective systems.

On organizational and operational levels the design of a fully integrated system, a concept highly valued by the data-processing specialist, promises more potential benefits.[42,43] The total needs are considered first and in detail, and attention directed to opportunities for relating activities to information content and availability from its first appearance right through the sequences of processing and control routines. The realities of systems development are such that it must often be achieved step by step through the development of interrelated subsystems, but at least it should be within a detailed overall framework of the total system concept. The human factors or social systems aspects should form an integral part of the process at every level of design, as some have ruefully endorsed in hindsight rather than in practice.

The ideal system would be one in which serial information would be captured as early in the process as possible, and added to as necessary throughout the following sequence of procedures. An on-line facility and good retrieval software would enable consultation and manipulation of the records at any stage, and the computer would be programmed to cope with file maintenance, the production of standard outputs such as orders, claims and lists as requested, and the automatic collection and analysis of operational statistics for management. Conversational type protocols at inexperienced- and experienced-user levels can lead staff through the sequences of required operations.

If complicated and less certain of success, library procedures involved in the acquisition and control of serials literature are at least basically similar to those for monographs. Practices for both differ widely within different libraries, and even between different parts or branches of a large library system. However, the differing procedures and activities are directed to one end: the acquisition, processing, use and maintenance of library materials.

Most libraries are involved in all or most of 18 common procedures within these four functional subsystems: Select, Order, Receive; Accession, Classify, Catalogue, Label, Shelve; Locate, List, Lend, Reserve, Recall, Inter-library loan, Photocopy; Bind, Replace, and Discard.

This functional commonality was observed in detailed analyses of many different types of library over a period of some years.[44] Although originally concerned with monographic materials, the model proved readily adaptable to serials handling activities. The complexity lies in the reiteration of tasks, and the sets of related transactions necessary to obtain not merely a particular title, but each and every part, issue, supplement, index and separately-published title page necessary to each volume's completion, and each desired subscription renewal whatever changes in title, publisher, source or publishing policies. With the addition of Claim to the list of procedures, because of its overwhelming importance in serials acquisitions, including subscription renewals in the definition of the Order procedure, and Check-in as a synonym for Receive, the model can provide a helpful framework for the design and analysis and evaluation of serials systems. There are obviously local differences in the set of procedures followed, and some variation in sequencing. Not all libraries accession, classify or lend individual journal issues for example, and variations in forms and information used are even more marked, but the underlying functions are common.

Basically the systems design task comprises the sequencing of the stages of procedural activity, the consideration of on-line and off-line components, and the definition of the various records (i.e. information contents and formats, and especially consensus definition of the elements of administrative/processing information) required for each task, and their generation or derivation from a standard bibliographic record such as that available in the various MARC files.

The computer routines needed pose by now fairly standard problems, however they may be solved in detail; the creation/use of a machine-readable file of serials data; the retrieval and display of records; the input of new records; the amendment and deletion of records or parts of records, and the output of records in the various formats and sequences required.

The major problem areas involved in applying these principles revolve around the content of the record, software specification, and finally implementation within the library, with communication between library staff, and library staff and computer personnel a key factor in all three.

STANDARDS AND FORMATS

The common link between all library procedures is the need for and manipulation of elements of bibliographic information together with various combinations of elements of administrative or processing information. The amount of information and the combination of elements needed to accomplish the various procedures varies. The number, size, shape and colour of all the forms on which these elements are transcribed and re-transcribed, filed and re-filed display almost unlimited variety. However, there is again a strong underlying commonality of function. Information and forms, whether embedded in manual or computerized systems, are used to accomplish the procedures involved in acquiring, processing, using and maintaining library materials.

Local differences are more often based on historical precedent than on a functional assessment of needs. Recognition of this factor is crucial to the design of a particular system; it is even more important in the context of joint or group projects, of regional and national networks, and in international co-operation.

It is difficult enough to standardize consistently the contents and formats of serials records for an individual library. The task is further complicated by the proliferation of national and international standards and standard setting activities:[45] the various MARC formats,[46-49] the International Standard Bibliographic Description for Serials, ISBD(S),[50] AACR,[51] the National Serials Data Program in the USA, the International Serials Data System of Unesco, the ANSI standard format for serials holdings information,[52] and the CONSER (CONversion of SERials) project.[53,54] These formats are aimed at defining the categories of bibliographic information necessary for the description and identification of serials and fixing their order in the bibliographic record.[55] Specific formats may have additional functions or emphasize varying aspects of definition. The result is limited variety and relative compatibility rather than the standardization and clarity once optimistically envisaged, and the need for computer programs to handle translation or reformatting between the generally available file and the individual system.

The whole problem of record content for computer-based serials control systems is further complicated by the need to include elements of non-bibliographic information. The processing functions of the system have very different needs from those fulfilled by formats designed for the exchange of bibliographic information or the production of a national bibliography. Order numbers, vendors' names and addresses, dates of ordering and receipt, booksellers reports are vital elements of information in the processing sequence.

National and international bibliographic formats have concentrated on the identification of serials, and have for the most part incorporated the traditional catalogue entry approach to bibliographic records: full bibliographic description and minimal local information, location implying classification numbers and holdings information for example. Elements of non-bibliographic information needed for what is often termed 'housekeeping routines' are ignored.

Local and regional formats have of necessity made more explicit accommodation for non-bibliographic information,[56,57] although most elements needed for individual systems have been added on an *ad hoc* basis from previous manual system practice and as perceived necessary. There are no broad consensus agreements as yet as a basis for national or international practice. Much existing work has limited applicability because of its specifically localized design. Many use a simple fixed field format, and individually adapted MARC-based records. The bibliographic area at least has been well documented, even if consistency and compatibility are only relative. No overall study of the functions and possible formats of non-bibliographic information has been undertaken, although the BNB Research Fund recently sponsored work on elements of information needed for monograph ordering,[58] there is an American draft standard order format, and the Ohio College Library Center (OCLC) network service plans include a full serials control facility for use by all their numerous and scattered subscribers.[59]

The work in America on a Standard Account Number and a Standard Order format,[60,61] the initiation of a computerized ordering system for publishers and booksellers,[62] and the computerized periodicals records of some of the larger subscription agencies all illustrate the importance of links not only with other librarians, but also with suppliers and publishers.

THE PERFECT FUTURE?

Planning and designing computer-aided serials systems, especially on-line systems, should present an opportunity to re-think objectives, practices and procedures, and standards of performance; and to look at the benefits to be derived from working more closely with other systems and previously-separated operations.

Traditionally it has been assumed that differing procedures have developed in response to variations in the local environment, and that these local variations should be accommodated to the fullest extent possible. Certainly there are various parent organization relationships that may require specific conformities in the information provided from one library. Similarly individual objectives, and more particularly, priorities in objectives and in resource allocation and service emphases, are important for an individual library's adjustment and flexibility within its environment.

Shared use of facilities, and particularly of centrally-produced serials data bases, however, requires a more disciplined approach to individual requirements. Variations can be accommodated, the range of options is wide, but their usefulness and the cost of providing them should be clearly demonstrated.

Mini-computers and networks are rapidly gaining acceptance as compatible and complementary tools, their combination offering acceptable solutions to many library problems.[19]

It may well be for instance that essentially local functions will be done more efficiently, reliably and less expensively on local mini-computers, drawing standard records from and contributing to a network-held bibliographic data base.

Effective use of the communications and computer resources now available may depend on balancing functions least subject to local variation and most dependent on large authoritative files with the local needs of small files with heavy transaction loads and frequent updating needs. Too many service demands on a single centrally held file could otherwise mean bad response times and excessive telecommunication costs; while the automation of existing systems or parts of systems, with all the duplication of information and processing routines, is expensive and isolationist.

However the mechanics are solved, the system needs from the library viewpoint revolve around an authoritative and comprehensive bibliographic data base, with effective and powerful retrieval software, that can be used with either centrally or locally held in-process files, with the minimum duplication of elements of bibliographic information. (Hence the increasing importance of the ISSN or other system linking numbers.)[62,63]

The rapidly developing facility for systems interconnection offers potential efficiencies that will depend on a willingness and an ability to standardize on record contents and formats, and to enlarge our conception of system boundaries. Librarians, booksellers, publishers, information brokers, authors and users become ever more closely related in the provision and use of information. It will not be enough for records to work in the context of the local system alone if future systems are to gain full benefit from the technological advances, and the growing trend for regional and national networking links.

The ultimate goals, not only of standardization as James emphasises it, but of the whole process of designing and operating serials systems, and the context for evaluating the impact of computers and networking, must be viewed in terms of 'increased efficiency, reduced processing costs, facilitation of information exchange and (above all) a greater degree of co-operation at all levels between the various components of the information services community'.[5]

REFERENCES

1. Huibert, P. 'Serials processing: manual control versus automation'. *Library Resources and Technical Services* 21 no. 4 Fall 1977. 345-53.
2. Blagden, J. 'Computer or manual systems'. *Library Association Record* 79 no. 2 Feb. 1977. 79.
3. Patrinostro, F. E. *A survey of automated activities in the libraries of the United States.* Tempe, Arizona, The LARC Association, 1971.
4. Pan, E. *Library serials control systems: a literature review and bibliography.* Washington, D.C., ERIC Clearing House on Library and Information Sciences, ASIS, Dec. 1970. (ED 044538).
5. James, J. R. 'Serials 75-review and trends'. *Library Resources and Technical Services* 20 no. 3 Summer 1976. 259-69.
6. Brodman, E. and Johnson, M. F. 'Medical serials control systems by computer — a state-of-the-art review'. *Bulletin of the Medical Library Association* 64 no. 1 Jan. 1976. 12-19.
7. Massil, S. W. 'Mechanisation of serials records: a literature review'. *Program* 4 no. 4 Oct. 1970. 156-68.
8. Pitkin, G. M. *Serials automation in the US: a bibliographic history.* New York, Scarecrow Press, 1976.
9. MacCafferty, M. *An annotated bibliography of automation in libraries and information systems 1972-1975.* London, Aslib, 1976.
10. Tedd, L. A. *An introduction to computer-based library systems.* London, Heyden, 1977.
11. Tinker, L. *An annotated bibliography of library automation, 1968-1972.* London, Aslib, 1973.
12. Fasana, P. 'Serials data control: current problems and prospects'. *Journal of Library Automation* 9 no. 1 March 1976. 319-33.
13. Veaner, A. B. 'Major decision points in library automation'. *College and Research Libraries* 31 no. 5 Sept. 1970. 299-312.
14. IBM. Corporation. *Library automation: computerized serials control.* New York, IBM, 1971.
15. Kimber, R. T. *Automation in libraries.* 2nd ed. Oxford, Pergamon Press, 1974.

16. Burns, R. W. *The design and testing of a computerized method of handling library periodicals. Final Report.* Project No. 4215. US Department of Health, Education and Welfare: Office of Education: Bureau of Research, Dec. 1970.

17. Grosch, A. N. 'Serial arrival prediction coding: a serial predictive model for use by system designers'. *Information Processing and Management* 12 no. 2 1976. 141–6.

18. Kilgour, F. G. 'New concepts in librarianship', in Edelhoff, G. and Lehmann, K.-D. *On-line library and network systems: symposium held at Dortmund University, March 22-24, 1976.* Frankfurt on Main, Vittorio Klostermann, 1977. 54–93.

19. Martin, S. K. 'Trends in library networks'. Paper given at the 88th Meeting of the Association of Research Libraries and Cooperative Systems, May 6th-7th, Seattle, Washington, ARL, 1976.

20. Stewart, B. W. 'Automated serials systems in perspective', in Salman, S. R. (ed.). *Library automation: a state of the art review, Papers presented at the Preconference Institute on Library Automation, San Francisco, California, 22-24 June 1967.* Chicago, American Library Association, 1969.131–7.

21. Vdovin, G. *et al. Final Report – Serials computer project.* San Diego, University Library and Computer Center, University of California, San Diego, 1964.

22. Pizer, I. H., Franz, D. R. and Brodman, E. 'Mechanisation of library procedures in the medium-sized medical library'. *Bulletin of the Medical Library Association* 51 no. 3 July 1963. 313–38.

23. The LARC Association. *Computerized Serials Systems Series. Vol. 1, issue 1; Vol. 1, issue 5,* 1975. (The series aimed at providing systems documentation to promote understanding through clear narrative description and extensive illustrative materials, one issue per system, and covered University of California, San Diego; Purdue University; University of Louisville; and Mankato State College before being discontinued. The first issue includes a list of 135 computerized library serials systems in the States.)

24. Evans, A. J. *et al. Periodicals data automation project.* Loughborough, University of Technology, 1969.

25. Evans, A. J. and Wall, R. A. 'Serials mechanisation: the current position in the UK'. *Program* 5 no. 4 Oct. 1971. 220–7.

26. Wilson, C. J. W. *Directory of operational computer applications in UK library and information units.* 2nd ed. London, Aslib, 1977.

27. Crismond, L. F. and Fatzer, S. B. 'Automated serials check-in and binding procedures at the San Francisco Public Library', in North, J. B. (ed.). *Proceedings of the American Society for Information Science, 32nd annual meeting.* Westport, Conn., Greenwood Publishing Co., 1969. 13–20.

28. Birmingham Libraries Co-operative Mechanization Project and Loughborough University of Technology Library. *MASS (MARC-based Automated Serials System). Working Paper No. 1.* Birmingham, BLCMP, Dec. 1970.

29. Norris, J. A. and Joerger, R. E. 'University of Florida Libraries automated union serials list', in North, J. B., (ed.). *Proceedings of the American Society for Information Science 33rd annual meeting*. Washington, D. C. ASIS, 1970. 73-7.
30. Wainwright, J. *Computer provision in British libraries*. Aslib Occasional Publication No. 16, London, Aslib, 1975.
31. Willmering, W. J. 'On-line centralized serials control'. *The Serials Librarian* 1 no. 3 Spring 1977. 243-9.
32. Duchesne, R. M. 'The use of computers in British libraries and information services: an analysis'. *Program* 8 no. 4 Oct. 1974. 183-90.
33. Markuson, B. E. *et al. Guidelines for library automation*. Santa Monica, California, System Development Corporation, 1972.
34. Johnson, M. F. 'A design for a mini-computer based serials control network'. *Special Libraries* 67 no. 8 August 1976. 386-90.
35. Bosseau, D. L. 'Case study of the computer assisted serials system at the University of California, San Diego', in *Proceedings of the LARC Institute on Automated Serials Systems*. H. W. Axford, (ed.). Tempe, Arizona, the LARC Association, 1973.
36. Fayollat, J. 'On-line serials control system in a large biomedical library: I. Description of the system'. *Journal of the American Society for Information Science* 23 no. 5 Sept.-Oct. 1972. 318-22.
37. Fayollat, J. 'On-line serials control system in a large biomedical library: II. Evaluation of Retrieval features'. *Journal of the American Society for Information Science* 23 no. 6 Nov.-Dec. 1972. 353-8.
38. Fayollat, J. 'On-line serials control system in a large biomedical library: III. Comparison of on-line and batch operations and cost analysis'. *Journal of the American Society for Information Science* 24 no. 2 March-April 1973. 80-6.
39. Rodgers, L. and Wainwright, J. 'The University of London Union List of Serials Project'. *Education Libraries Bulletin* 19 2 Summer 1976. 25-31.
40. Bourne, R. 'Building a serials file'. *Program* 12 no. 2 April 1978. 78-86.
41. De Varennes, R. 'Computerised serials system at Laval University Library: from off-line to on-line, some memories and accomplishments', in *Automation in libraries*. Ottawa, Canadian Library Association, 1970. 129-47.
42. Hayes, R. M. 'The concept of an on-line total library system'. *Library Technology Reports. Data Processing* May 1965 13pp.
43. Bosseau, D. L. 'The University of California at San Diego serials system — Revisited'. *Program* 4 no. 1 Jan. 1970. 1-29.
44. Thomas, P.A. *A procedural model for the use of bibliographic records in libraries*. Aslib Occasional Publication No. 4, London, Aslib, 1970.
45. Daniels, M. K. 'Automated serials control: national and international considerations'. *Journal of Library Automation* 8 no. 2 June 1975. 127-46.
46. MARC Development Office. *Serials: a MARC format*. 2nd ed. Washington, D.C., Library of Congress, 1974.

47. Canadian MARC office. *Canadian MARC communication format: serials.* Ottawa, National Library of Canada, 1974.

48. British Standards Institution. *Data elements essential to the interchange of serials records.* BS 5332. London, BSI, 1976.

49. Bramall, P. J. D. The present national and international state of MARC, in Irvine, R. (ed.). *Proceedings of the second SCONUL seminar: Practical MARC cataloguing.* London, SCONUL, 1976. 72-82.

50. International Federation of Library Associations and Institutions. *ISBD(S): International Standard Bibliographic Description for serials.* 1st standard ed. London, IFLA International Office for UBC, 1977.

51. *Anglo-American cataloguing rules.* 2nd ed. London, Library Association, 1978.

52. American National Standards Institute. *(Draft) American National Standard-Serial holdings statements at the summary level.* ANSI Z39-97.

53. Anable, R. 'CONSER: an update'. *Journal of Library Automation* 8 no. 1 March 1975. 26-30.

54. 'Now add CONSER to your conversation'. (a series of 4 articles). *American Libraries* 8 no. 1 Jan. 1977. 21-7, 42.

55. Berrutti, M. T. and Valenti, M. 'Standardization in the field of periodicals'. *Network* 1 no. 9 Sept. 1974. 19-21.

56. Fayollat, J. 'On-line serials control at UCLA', in Lancaster, F.W. (ed.). *Proceedings of the 1972 Clinic on Library Applications of On-line Computers to Library Problems.* Urbana, University of Illinois Graduate School of Library Science, 1972.

57. Birmingham Libraries Co-operative Mechanisation Project. *MASS manual: input procedures for serials cataloguing.* Birmingham, BLCMP, 1973.

58. Clarke, C. and Wight, T. *MARC acquisition data elements.* Report prepared for BNB Research Fund Committee. London, Aslib Research and Development Department, 1978.

59. Ohio College Library Center. *Serials control subsystem: users manual.* Columbus, Ohio, OCLC, Dec. 1975.

60. American National Standards Institute. *News about Z39: quarterly reports.* January-March 1978. University of North Carolina, Standards Committee Z39, ANSI, April 1978.

61. American Library Association, Bookdealer-Library Relations Committee. *Guidelines for handling library orders for serials and periodicals.* Chicago, ALA, 1974.

62. 'Teleordering: a computerised system for the book trade'. *VINE* no. 22 June 1978. 11-16.

63. Bourne, R. 'Quo Vadis, ISSN?' *Catalogue and Index* no. 44 Spring 1977. 1, 7-8.

64. Groot, E. H. 'Unique identifiers for serials: an annotated, comprehensive bibliography'. *The Serials Librarian* 1 no. 1 Fall 1976. 51-75.

19

The Challenge of Non-Traditional Types of Serial[1]

Malcolm Shifrin

TERMINOLOGY

C hallenge ... traditional ... serial .... To the librarian, each of these words is pregnant with meaning. Or meanings. And therein lies the heart of the problem. For meanings exemplify attitudes of mind.

What is Challenge?

To the librarian who is alive, a challenging problem can 'offer interesting difficulties' — and the implied emphasis is clearly on the interest rather than on the difficulties. To the less lively librarian — or let us be fair — to the overworked librarian who has enough problems already, it is easier to interpret challenge as 'to take exception to', and 'dispute' or 'deny'.[2] But problems in librarianship are not like letters which (according to Mr Disraeli) answer themselves if you leave them long enough. Appropriate action has to be taken.

What is Tradition?

Ashurbanipal's royal collection of 25,000 clay tablets in ancient Ninevah is a reminder that the library (and librarians) were around many years before the arrival of printed books. So were the many libraries of manuscripts. (How did traditional librarians react when it was suggested that printed books might be added to their collections?)

It may be objected that this is irrelevant; that the earliest journals were *Journal de Scavans* (1664 or 1665) and *Acta Philosophica* (1665), both well within the print-on-paper era.

But the earliest equivalent to a present-day newspaper was, arguably, *Acta Diurna* (Transactions of the Day) published daily at Rome between 59 BC and AD 330. In addition to news and official decrees, it included announcements of births, marriages and deaths. But most interestingly, in the present context, it was written on a whitewashed board (*album*), posted in a prominent position and, after removal, stored with other public archives.[3] (So much, incidentally, for the supposed novelty of that modern educational aid, the white-board!)

However, even it if is accepted that 'traditional' serials are printed on paper, most librarians, asked to identify the first non-traditional serials, would probably answer microfilm or microfiche. We shall see below that this is almost certainly incorrect.

What is a Serial?

Perhaps the meaning of this word is the most controversial of all. Carson's analysis of representative definitions[4] demonstrated a singular lack of clarity which did not seem to be remedied by her own suggested definition.

Contributors to the present handbook have been strongly recommended to bear in mind the ISO definition which begins: 'A publication, in printed form or not, issued in successive parts usually having numerical or chronological designations and intended to be continued indefinitely ...' However, in the context of this chapter, the ISO definition can only be considered as a starting point.

SERIALITY

First, as Bourne has earlier suggested[5] (and as will here be repeatedly emphasized), a serial is not a type of material. Serial is an adjective and correctly, if pedantically, can be used only in conjunction with a noun. As currently used by librarians, serial implies an omitted complementary noun such as publication.

Continued use of serial alone encourages cross-classification as exemplified in the chapter headings of AACR2. Part I of this new code 'contains instructions on the formulation of descriptions of library materials'[6] yet the grouping of these 'materials' is by several characteristics: by form of physical object, e.g., books; by content, e.g., cartographic materials; by pattern of publication, e.g., serials etc. Yet seriality is a condition which requires, when appropriate, to be *simply* indicated within the description of *any* type of library material.

The condition of seriality, therefore, must be the topic of our concern.

Second, seriality is a pattern of publication. The concepts which together identify the condition are: succession; numerical or chronological designation; intention of indefinite continuance. These concepts are already expressed in the ISO definition.

Third, the concept of publication must be considered in its broadest sense. It is unduly restrictive to limit the meaning of the verb to publish (as librarians frequently do) to the narrow definition 'issue copies ... for sale to the public'. To publish must also connote 'make generally known' and 'announce formally, promulgate'.[7]

This is not a linguistic quibble to enable *Acta Diurna* to be considered a serial publication (which it undoubtedly is) but to encourage an appropriate treatment of today's equivalent promulgations, disseminations, broadcasts, and transmissions.

Seriality Defined

In order adequately to meet the brief of this chapter it is necessary to extend the given ISO definition but (it is hoped) without in any way changing the *intent* of the definition and its implications:

> Seriality. A pattern of sequential publication resulting in the issue of materials carrying information, or the transmission of programmes carrying information, each issue or programme usually having a numerical and/or chronological designation, and the sequence intended to be continued indefinitely.

If examples of various types of serial publication need to be added to such a definition then it would be important to ensure that they were not all carriers of conceptual treatments of information which suggested the use of the medium of print. Other appropriate types will be indicated below.

TECHNOLOGICAL CHANGE

A new invention or process often triggers a general feeling that one's own professional technology would benefit from its use. The solution searches for an appropriate problem to solve. Perhaps Prestel is such an example of an extremely elegant technology that has not yet found its ideal problem match — which is not to suggest, of course, that it will not eventually do so.

Then there is the problem for which no one has yet found a solution, though work continues and results range from partial success to complete failure.

Most developments lie between the two extremes. These are designed to improve an existing product, to meet a new need, to facilitate a new pattern of use or to improve a technology by making it more cost-effective so as to ensure its survival.

Technological change has a variety of starting points and non-traditional serial publications exemplify this typical pattern of change. Discussion of some of these 'new' types of publication here is intended to increase awareness of their seriality.

It will be impossible to avoid encountering some of the 'new' media of communication, with their equipment and technologies. Yet there is little discussion of problems arising from the technologies themselves since the subject under discussion is seriality and, as will become apparent, any problems relating to the publications do not arise from their seriality. Furthermore, there are now many sources of information relating to the use of these media, and to the organization of those materials which depend on them.[8]

THE FIRST OF THE NON-TRADITIONAL SERIAL PUBLICATIONS

Although newspapers and magazines are by no means the only type of serial publication, most of the developments which have led to the introduction of non-print serial publications have resulted from the use of newly developing media to improve the dissemination of news. The presentation of news, arguably, improves the closer it echoes reality.

In a wholly letterpress world, the engraved illustration shows almost at a glance what has happened, and in doing so replaces several paragraphs of text. On 5 January 1891 the *Milwaukee (Wisconsin) Journal* printed a picture of the United States flag in colour, thereby adding another dimension to its potential for illustrating news.

But illustrations, even colour illustrations, were an enrichment of an existing type of publication. The missing ingredient of the newspaper is action. News happens.

Cinematography instantly changed the traditional approach to the dissemination of news. The Lumière Brothers, credited with the first public showing of films in 1895, soon realized the impact of the news item and their cameramen made a number of very short topical films which were used to demonstrate the Lumière equipment.

Other teams were quick to follow. Early filmed news items were the coronation of Tsar Nicholas II (1896), the Derby (1897), and the funeral of Queen Victoria (1901).[9] Each of these 'topical' films was a separate item and each was very short.

But in 1908 Pathé Frères produced the first newsreel which included several items of news and which was to be issued regularly. This was *Pathé Journal* and it was so popular that before the end of the year a rival newsreel, *Gaumont Actualités,* was already in existence.

Pathé Gazette (1909), later renamed *Pathé News*, was the first British newsreel and the idea spread rapidly round Europe and to the United States.

All these newsreels were, of course, silent and each item was preceded by explanatory titles.

The printed newspaper and the motion picture film are in appearance completely different physical objects. But both are physical objects which carry items of information and are sequentially published; each has a numerical or chronological designation, and each sequence is intended to be continued indefinitely. Those attributes which determine the condition of seriality are all present.[10]

THE ARRIVAL OF SOUND

When the BBC (at that time the British Broadcasting Company) was formed in 1922, news, information, and weather reports were amongst the services to be provided by its broadcasting stations. Yet Briggs has shown[11] that the power of the new company to transmit news programmes was one of the most difficult issues which had to be resolved at that time.

Put simply, the British press (including the agencies, the Newspaper Proprietors' Association and the Newspaper Society) saw broadcasting as a threat even before the Company's first broadcast went out.

Following representations to the Post Office by the press, Sir Evelyn Murray, at that time Secretary to the Post Office, sent a memorandum to the Postmaster-General. He felt that no news should be broadcast until after it had previously been published by the press.

After much negotiation, a six-month trial was agreed whereby the news agencies provided, for a fee, a daily summary of the world's news and the BBC agreed that it 'would not itself collect news from other sources or assist in establishing any other agency for collecting news'.[12]

It is fascinating to follow Briggs's story of the development of BBC news broadcasting, but here it is only necessary to show that from the start, the broadcasting of news was considered by all to be a type of publishing activity.

Even though the BBC Sound Archive does not retain recordings of their news bulletins, all scripts have been retained from the first bulletin onwards and these scripts form an unpublished record of a published transmission.

We must conclude, therefore, that the scripts themselves comprise a permanent record of a serial publication in another form. (Perhaps there is a parallel here with a microform version of an out-of-print newspaper). And, of course any collection of audiotape news bulletins constitutes, for the librarian, a serial publication even if the tapes were not themselves published.

SOUND NEWSREELS AND NEWS MAGAZINES

The year which saw the formation of the BBC, 1922, was also the year when it became possible to record sound on film. Early recording apparatus was difficult to use for synchronized sound but soon the Americans, and then the French, added commentaries to their newsreels. *British Movietone* in 1928 became the first to use sound in this country.

The publication pattern of newsreels in the thirties emphasizes their seriality. In England and America they usually appeared once or twice per week. 'Issues were normally available for three day runs, with the charges decreasing after the third day when a new issue was made available or the news had lost its immediacy. The overall length of an issue was constant at about fifteen minutes'.[13] In make-up also there were parallels with printed equivalents. An attempt would be made to strike a balance between the serious and not so serious. The average issue included about six items.

By this time the news magazine dealing in greater depth with a single topic in each issue was also very popular. The *March of Time*, a monthly first issued in 1934, was one of the most popular and one which was also published (i.e. publicly shown) in countries other than the USA, its place of origin.

The *March of Time* was produced by Louis de Rochement working with the resources and backing of Time-Life Inc. and this direct link with traditional serial publishers gave it a similar style. Barsam[14], analysing its influence notes:

> ... the use of personal interviews and personal portraits of important people, the use of diagrams and charts, and the 'authority' of its narrative presentation and interpretation of the news ... [It] had the undeniable stamp of research and authority that mass-produced journalism can often bring to a story. The marks of research and the tone of authority do not always equal honesty and objectivity, and the films had no reservations about making drama out of fact.

TELEVISION NEWS BROADCASTING

When, in 1936, the BBC started the world's first public television service there was no special television news coverage. Until the war put a temporary halt to the service, the Corporation, by arrangement with Movietone and Gaumont-British Film Companies, screened two newsreels each week.

Exactly paralleling the sound situation, the film industry saw television as a major publishing rival and, after the war, would not renew the arrangements previously allowing the transmission of cinema newsreels.

Schlesinger[15] has described the various phases of the involvement of the BBC (and later, of the independent ITN) in the serial transmission of television news. In January 1948 the BBC produced a twice-weekly newsreel. News at this time consisted of a ten-minute sound only bulletin at the end of each day's programmes. Not until July 1954 did the newsreel develop into a weekday *News and Newsreel*. This was a 20-minute programme starting with the news which was followed by a newsreel of pictures of the current events. Only in the following year was the Corporation's *Television News* started in a form recognizable as a forerunner of today's news programmes.

By this time the newspapers were extremely concerned about their future as a result of the combined onslaught of cinema and television. New techniques of colour printing were becoming available, but not even these appeared to offer competition to the immediacy of the new medium.

Middleton,[16] writing in 1954, describes how a colour photograph of the Coronation was shot on 2 June and, because of the poor weather, was force-developed the same evening. Then a special staff at the printers worked overnight to make the negatives. The following day was spent on retouching and the colour cylinders were etched in the evening so that the machines were able to start printing for insertion in the current issue of *Picture Post*. Middleton remarks: 'A miracle of speed from the printing point of view — but of what interest to the man in the street six days later? He saw it in black-and-white on the day of the event, in colour on the cinema screen three days after the event.'

And we now have colour television and no *Picture Post*.

AUDIOTAPES

Although sound was first recorded on cylinder and disc during the last quarter of the nineteenth century, no early serial publications on disc, designed for general use, could be traced in the library of the British Institute of Recorded Sound.[17]

In the USA, the Audio Digest Foundation started publishing tape journals in the early 1950s, all in medical subject areas. Indeed, medicine, the health sciences, and chemistry seem to have found audiotapes especially suitable for serial publications and, as we shall see below, many of the developments in this area relate to serial publications for the physically handicapped.

But it was the development of the Philips compact cassette during the early 1960s which made it feasible for the person in the street to use audiotape and which encouraged its use for general interest serial publications, in addition to those produced for the physically handicapped.

Lack of adequate materiographical control makes it difficult to trace early examples of this type of publication. Two articles in the *Journal of Chemical Documentation*[18] describe the use of audiotape for a house journal by the Olin Corporation. Port[19] lists 25 audiocasette journals for the health professions available in 1973 on a subscription basis. Ms. Port is quite clear about their categorization: 'Cassettes issued serially … may be considered as audio journals. The contents … may include: interviews with authorities, panel discussions, recent research findings, announcements of upcoming national meetings, recordings of reports of national meetings, etc.' She goes on to note the 'severe handicap to their effective use' due to their omission from the standard periodical indexes.

The early seventies saw the introduction of the first audio journal for general readers, *Audio Arts*. This excellent venture (alas, no longer extant) included in one number a re-issue of the celebrated recording of James Joyce reading 'Anna Livia Plurabelle'. *Audio Arts* was the first audio journal in the UK to be assigned an ISSN.

Another general interest periodical still being published is *International Report*, the first monthly audio journal on current affairs, published by Seminar Cassettes in association with Reuters. The second issue on Pollution and Industry included contributions from Reuter correspondents in New York, Moscow, and Tokyo, in addition to one from *The Guardian* Science Correspondent.

MICROFORMS AND SERIAL PUBLICATION

Microphotography was invented as long ago as 1839 and even the idea of microfiche was suggested in 1906, yet our users are only just beginning to come to terms with microforms in libraries.

Williams[20] has identified three mainstream roles for microforms in libraries: the saving of space, preservation, and increased availability of out-of-print and rare materials by retrospective micropublication. These aspects of microform have been treated elsewhere in this handbook[21] in so far as they relate to traditional serial publications. However, one significant landmark in retrospective publishing is worth mentioning.

In 1939 *The New York Times* made a major commitment to microforms.[22] The newly-formed University Microfilms Inc. was awarded a contract for current filming and Kodak's Recordak Division was awarded a contract for filming the back files to 1851.[23]

This decision is interesting because although there was no intention at that time to initiate a programme of original serial publication, the pattern of technological change in this area is clearly indicated. Line and Williams, writing about book publishing, state with equal relevance here: 'The current phase in which the newer media are ... replicas on a different medium is transient — the newer medium will ultimately introduce substantially changed forms of information packaging.'[24]

This does not just mean that new media soon produce original materials in their own right but also, as we shall see in the final section of this chapter, that they can trigger new approaches to the manner in which the information content is published.

In 1959, *Wildlife Disease* became the first journal to be published in microform alone. It is today still published on microfiche, but was for some time issued on micro-opaques after a questionnaire asking for users' view on the three formats (there were two types of micro-opaques) chosen for the first number.[25]

Teague has noted the advantages of stand-alone microfiche periodical publication[26] amongst which are freedom from the need to edit material into multiples of eight pages for economy in production, and the savings in cost when half-tones are required. This advantage is even greater if colour photographs are necessary.

Many societies and other publishers of learned journals were already publishing 'almost simultaneously' both print and microform editions by the end of the sixties. But when, in 1972, the *New Scientist* announced such a publication pattern, a landmark had been reached since, in the eyes of the public, this was considered a 'popular' magazine. Such simultaneous publications will surely increase with easy-to-read microfiche supplementing the print versions. Microfiche is not always the format chosen though, and the *Geographical Magazine,* for example, is currently available on 35 mm colour film.

1972 also saw the commercial stand-alone publication of *Books in English* (on NCR's PCMI Ultrafiche) although this had already been experimentally published since 1970. It is difficult to imagine that such a comprehensive bibliographical service would have been feasible if print-on-paper had been the publishing medium.

Another first was the choice of microfiche as the primary publication format for conference preprints. Sheppard[27] describes how this was effected prior to the *Rotary-wing Aircraft Symposium,* Melbourne, 24 September 1973. This surely has the advantage, from the speaker's point of view, that listeners are not reading during the proceedings!

SERIAL PUBLICATIONS USING OTHER MEDIA

Data Bases

Data files such as the MARC tapes are another type of serial publication and these are available on a normal subscription basis. Their content can appear in several alternative forms. The file need not itself be published but can be used to generate computer output microform (COM) publications such as the fiche version of *British Books in Print.* Alternatively, the file can be searched on-line. System Development Corporation (SDC) has been providing on-line access to large bibliographic data bases since 1965.

Such data bases are serial publications, each cumulative issue of which is made available for searching. The development of *Chemical Abstracts* from print-on-paper, through cassetted microfilm, to machine-readable data base, reinforces this view.

Most data bases are at present updated by replacing the information carrier by a revised issue, and the frequency of replacement varies from data base to data base. Only when a data base is subject to continuous revision, as when a single 'page' of Prestel data is replaced, does such a data base lose its seriality.

Video Cassette Journals

Originally a French idea, the video cassette journal is a product of the mid-seventies. The Library of Congress *New Serial Titles* includes the US journal *Videotape Theatre* which appeared in 1975 and the first UK publication was launched in August 1976. The *Video Journal of Medicine* is published monthly utilizing the Philips VCR system.[28] It aims to inform doctors of new developments and is distributed in the UK as well as in other English-speaking countries. The journal is partly financed by advertisements, both in the programme itself and also in the accompanying booklet.

Since many might argue that the VCR system is obsolescent and there is no compatibility between any of the major new cassette systems, it is difficult to see how video journals will become popular in the immediate future. This is unfortunate because many subjects lend themselves to the successful use of easy-to-use visual media, and the advantages of standardization can be seen in the example of the standard audiotape cassette.

Portfolios

In 1977, Harvey Miller began the publication (in association with the Courtauld Institute of Art, University of London) of the *Courtauld Institute illustration archives* under the general editorship of Peter Lasko. Four separate archives were initiated. Each archive, on subjects such as *Cathedrals and monastic buildings in the British Isles* and *15th and 16th century sculpture in Italy,* publishes four issues annually and each issue comprises a stiff cardboard portfolio containing approximately 80 half-tone A4 size pictures, together with an introductory booklet.

The content of this type of archive, it should be noted, could equally be carried, for example, in slideset, filmstrip/microfilm, or microfiche format, as digital information on magnetic tape, or on a videotape or videodisc.

SERIAL PUBLICATIONS FOR THE PHYSICALLY HANDICAPPED

The publications described so far use media other than print as enrichment or as alternative means of communication; perhaps a more important development has been the rapid increase in the number of serial publications designed for use by those who *must* use media other than print — the blind and the physically handicapped.

Sturt has described[29] how, on a visit to Sweden in 1968, he saw a copy of *Arosabandet*, a talking newspaper for the blind started in 1962 by the Västerås public library with the local association for the blind. This was recorded weekly on open-reel tape and sent to 130 'readers' on a three-day loan basis.

As a result of the visit, Britain's first tape magazine for the blind, *The Talking Newspaper* was produced and distributed on Mark IV Clarke and Smith Talking Book cassettes. It was a remarkable example of co-operation between libraries, the press, and many other agencies and it was an immediate success.

In the United States, the Library of Congress Division for the Blind and Physically Handicapped (DBPH) plays a major role in producing, and disseminating information about, serial publications for the physically handicapped.

The work of the DBPH is fully described by Cylke and Wires[30] who state that in 1977 there were more than 250 periodical titles available in braille, hard and flexible discs, open-reel and cassette tapes. *Talking Book Topics* is itself published bimonthly in large print and recorded formats. Other recorded titles include *Ebony, Ellery Queen's Mystery Magazine,* and English and Spanish editions of *Good Housekeeping.* Another of their publications *Magazines in Special Media* lists 85 periodical sources outside the DBPH including some from the UK. The DBPH, incidentally, not only loans the periodicals but also (free of charge) loans the appropriate gramophones and cassette players.

The work of the Canadian National Institute for the Blind (CNIB) in Toronto is also important and has been described by Hébert.[31] Four popular Canadian magazines are available for sale on standard cassettes from the CNIB. Their loan collections were originally recorded using the Clarke and Smith system but in 1977 they started a three-year programme to convert to standard 4-track cassettes. The Canadian edition of *Reader's Digest* is one of the four magazines already available in the new format.

NEW APPROACHES TO THE PUBLISHING PROCESS

The 'non-traditional' serial publications so far discussed can be grouped as follows:

    (i) reproduction of existing publications, e.g. in microfilm, braille, or on tape;

    (ii) simultaneous publication with print original, e.g. *New Scientist* on microfiche;

    (iii) stand-alone publications utilizing 'new' media processes resulting in 'new' types of library material, e.g. Ultrafiche, videotape cassette.

These were published:

(i) to make available out-of-print or rare items;
(ii) to minimize storage costs;
(iii) to eliminate binding costs;
(iv) to provide assistance to handicapped users; and
(v) to promote aural and dynamically visual information.

In addition to these types of publication, there have been others, at present few (and mostly still unproven) which result from a look at the publishing process itself. Aitchison, in her 1974 review[32] commissioned by the Office for Scientific and Technical Information (OSTI) writes:

> Criticism of the scientific journal and suggestions for modifying or replacing it occur in the literature as far back as 40 years ago ... In the last few years, there appears to have been a serious drive to find alternatives to the journal, in view of the soaring cost of paper and printing and the undiminished quantity and complexity of the information output.

She identifies as causes for concern pressure on periodical space, high costs, low relevancy of journal content, delays in publication, proliferation of journals, and their format. She concludes by suggesting two categories of alternative methods: those which by-pass the periodical and those which require a fundamental modification of the periodical form.

On-demand Publishing

An example of Aitchinson's by-pass category is on-demand publishing (OD) which is widely used for theses and will perhaps become more popular for highly-specialized monographs.

OD is an example of what Frugé, writing from an American viewpoint,[33] calls 'fractional publishing' when only part of the publishing functions is fulfilled. Articles are abstracted, indexed, stored on microfilm and given a limited amount of specialized publicity. Paper or fiche copies are produced for sale only when specifically ordered: '... articles are, presumably, available forever. As long as the microfilm masters can be kept, the works never go out of print. If they have ever been in print, that is.'

Librarians, Frugé suggests, will increasingly be involved in literature searches, providing bibliographic information and assistance but not the works themselves. These will be obtained by payment made directly to a 'storage agency' from personal or institutional research funds.

Synoptic Journals

The synoptic journal publishes only a short outline of a full-length, fully refereed, paper together with any illustrative matter and important references. The synopsis is prepared by the author (whose typescript is sometimes reproduced) and is intended to be usable without reference to the original.

The Chemical Society's *Journal of Chemical Research* publishes the back-up paper (simultaneously with the synopsis) reproduced from the author's typescript as a negative microfiche.[34]

The Institute of Mechanical Engineers follows a slightly different pattern for its *Engineering Synopses.* If the full-length paper is also published, this is indicated under the synopsis heading. Reply-paid order cards are included and papers supplied as photographically reproduced offprints or in microfilm.[34]

The University of Chicago's *Journal of Modern History* includes full-length articles together with abstracts of further articles which can be purchased through University Microfilms Inc.[33]

Integrated Publication Systems and Editorial Processing Centres

Eakins has highlighted two problems which affect both authors and readers: delays in publication and fragmentation of the literature into increasingly specialized journals. Eakins describes[35] a rational pattern of publication where, in each major subject area, papers could be sent to a single editorial centre which would direct them to the most suitable journal for publication. International Research Communications System (IRCS), the first fully operational centre of this type, is described.

> Papers from a broad field (in the case of IRCS the whole of biomedicine) are submitted to a single editorial office, and, provided they survive scrutiny by editors and referees, published in a variety of alternative forms to suit the differing needs of users; articles are available as individual reprints, or packaged into one or more specialist or general-interest journals according to subject-matter and importance.

An integrated publication system could be combined with the sophisticated type of Editorial Processing Centre (EPC) which is currently the focus of much interest both in the USA and the UK. It is proposed that national EPCs utilize computerized techniques in as many of a journal's editorial and production stages as possible so as to speed up publication procedures and reduce costs. The EPC is a production technique and is not, therefore, treated here,[36] but there is clearly a strong link between the EPC concept and these new patterns of serial publication which is worth following up.

Work in Progress

OSTI's early interest in, and support for, work in this area has been continued by its successor, the British Library Research and Development Department. In the autumn of 1975 they financed a study trip to the USA to discover current thinking on scientific and technical primary journal publication and to identify trends and innovations.

Lea has reported on this visit[37] and was especially impressed by the National Science Foundation project which resulted in the Capital Systems Group (CSG) guide *Improving the dissemination of scientific information: a practitioner's guide to innovation.*[38] This comprises brief user-orientated descriptions of techniques and innovations relating to all types of scientific publication and including important sections treating serial publication. It was (then) a unique guide but is, of course, very US-oriented and Lea recommended that a similar UK/European guide be compiled.

The British Library Research and Development Department followed this up by sponsoring an important workshop on trends in scholarly publication held on 16-17 July 1976 at the University of Leicester. The aims were to bring together librarians, academics, publishers, and booksellers to discuss the problems which beset academic publishing.

Sessions held included ones on Lea's US visit, EPCs, current trends in scholarly publishing, and librarians' reactions to non-conventional publishing methods.[39] Again, the CSG guide was considered impressive, and amongst the specific proposals made were:

(a) a centre or consultancy service to provide publication advice to small societies should be established;

(b) a national focus for gathering data and statistics on scholarly publishing is needed;

(c) a British centre should be established to organize the UK input to the CSG Innovation Guide. This centre should also be responsible for disseminating information contained in the Guide to all sections of the primary publishing industry.

In 1977, the University of Leicester's Primary Communications Research Centre (which organized the workshop), supported by a grant from the British Library Research and Development Department, produced a loose-leaf guide based on the CSG model. *Scholarly publishers guide: new methods and techniques*[40] is not limited to science and technology and is intended for the EEC reader (with special emphasis on the UK). Topics included in the CSG guide are not included in the PCRC guide. Work continues, and it is intended that there will be regular updates and supplements.

REFERENCES

I am indebted to Devra Wiseman for an initial on-line literature search, and also, for interest and assistance, to Jim Ballantyne, British Universities Film Council, Diana Hull, British Institute of Recorded Sound, Chris Mottershead, ILEA Educational Technology Team, and Tony Trebble, BBC Sound Archives.

1. This extremely apposite title was suggested by the Editor.
2. Quotations in this paragraph are from the definitions of 'challenge' in the sixth edition of the *Concise Oxford dictionary*.
3. Entry for *Acta Diurna* in the fifth edition of *Everyman's encyclopaedia*.
4. Carson, D. M. 'What is a serial publication?'. *Journal of Academic Librarianship* 3 (4) Sept. 1977. 206–9.
5. See p. viii of this handbook.
6. *Anglo-American cataloguing rules*. 2nd ed. London, Library Association, 1978.
7. Quotations in this paragraph are from the definitions of 'publish' in the sixth edition of the *Concise Oxford dictionary*.
8. See, for example: Fothergill, Richard and Butchart, I. *Non-book materials in libraries: a practical guide*. London, Bingley, 1978; Shifrin, M. *Information in the school library: an introduction to the organisation of non-book materials*. London, Bingley, 1973; and the contents (especially the bibliographic update) of the *Audiovisual Librarian* published quarterly by the Audiovisual Groups of the Library Association and of Aslib.
9. Information on the history of the newsreel is taken from the entry in *The Oxford companion to film*. ed. by Liz-Anne Bawden. London, OUP, 1976.
10. For information on film and newsreel librarianship see Harrison, H. P. *Film library techniques*. London, Focal Press, 1973.

11. Briggs, A. *The history of broadcasting in the United Kingdom,* Vol. 1, *The birth of broadcasting.* London, OUP, 1961. 127-8.

12. Briggs, A. *ibid.* 132.

13. Entry for Newsreel in the *Oxford companion to film.* 501.

14. Barsam, R. M. *Nonfiction film: a critical history.* London, Allen & Unwin, 1974. 110.

15. Schlesinger, P. *Putting 'reality' together: BBC news.* London, Constable, 1978. 36-42.

16. Middleton, M. 'Colour photography in journalism'. *Penrose Annual* **48** 1954. 86-8.

17. I am indebted to Diana Hull of the British Institute of Recorded Sound for her assistance in this search.

18. Hanford, W. E. *et al.* 'The industrial chemist and chemical information: the human ear as a medium'. *Journal of Chemical Documentation* **11** (2) May 1971. 68-9; Hanford, W. E. *et al.* 'Chemical news via audiotapes: chemical industry news'. *Journal of Chemical Documentation,* **129** (1) Feb. 1972. 3-4.

19. Port, J. 'Audiocassette journals for the health professions'. *Special Libraries* **64** (11) Nov. 1973. 490-2.

20. Williams, B. J. S. *Miniaturised communications: a review of microforms.* London, Library Association; Hatfield, National Reprographic Centre for documentation, 1970. 28.

21. See Chapter 5 of this handbook.

22. Williams, B. J. S. *op. cit.,* p. 45.

23. For information on the librarianship of microforms, see Teague, S. J. *Microform librarianship.* 2nd ed. London, Butterworths, 1979.

24. Line, M. and Williams, B. 'Alternatives to conventional publication and their implications for libraries'. *Aslib Proceedings* **28** (3) March 1976. 109-15.

25. Williams, B. J. S. *op. cit.,* pp. 83-4.

26. Teague, S. J. *Microform librarianship.* 2nd ed. London, Butterworths, 1979. 81.

27. Sheppard, M. O. 'Microfiche preprints for conferences'. *Aslib Proceedings* **26** (11) Nov. 1974. 435-46.

28. Primary Communications Research Centre. *Scholarly publishers guide: new methods and techniques.* Leicester, The Centre, 1977. 63.

29. Sturt, R. 'The talking newspaper'. *Book Trolley* **2** (10) June 1970. 3-12.

30. Cylke, F. K. and Wires, C. 'Periodicals for the blind and physically handicapped'. *Serials Librarian* **2** (1) Fall 1977. 49-65.

31. Hébert, F. 'Magazines for the visually handicapped in Canada'. *Serials Librarian* **2** (2) Winter 1977. 151-3.

32. Aitchison, J. *Alternatives to the scientific periodical: a review of methods reported in the literature.* OSTI Report 5190. London, OSTI, 1974. 5.

33. Frugé, A. 'Beyond publishing: a system of scholarly writing and reading'. *Scholarly Publishing* **9** (4) July 1978. 219-311 and **10** (1) Oct. 1978. 17-35.

34. Further information on these publications can be found in *Scholarly publishers guide* (note 28 supra).
35. Eakins, J. P. 'The integrated publication system: a new concept in primary publication'. *Aslib Proceedings* 26 (11) Nov. 1974. 430–4.
36. For information on editorial processing centres see, for example, Woodward, A. M. *et al. The applicability of editorial processing centres to UK scholarly publishing.* BLRD Report 5270. London, British Library. 1976; and Woodward, A. M. *Editorial processing centres: scope in the United Kingdom.* BLRD Report 5271 HC. London, British Library, 1976.
37. Lea, P. W. *Trends in scientific and technical primary journal publishing in the USA.* BLRD Report 5272 HC. London, British Library, 1976.
38. Capital Systems Group. *Improving the dissemination of scientific and technical information: a practitioner's guide to innovation.* Springfield (Va), NTIS, 1975.
39. *Trends in scholarly publishing.* BLRD Report 5299HC. London, British Library, 1976.
40. Primary Communications Research Centre. *loc. cit.*

20

Education

D. P. Woodworth

Education for all aspects of periodicals control is inferior to that for books and other literature. The number of students bound for public libraries may play some part in this, but whatever the cause, many librarians move into periodicals posts having had very little prior contact with them and being basically ignorant of the many problems that beset the unwary operating in this field.

I have said in another work[1] that the periodical, as a contributor to history, is matchless as a form of publication. It is the essential ingredient for studying or doing research in the history of a subject or of a country, and trends, economic and social, may be discovered from the examination of files of such publications. Additionally, they are sources of much information that is not adequately documented.

Since the end of the First World War and with the rapid technological growth that we have seen during the twentieth century so far, the number of titles has increased enormously, and parallel with this the number of specializing subjects has also mushroomed, and nearly all have turned to the serial as a medium for transmitting their views, news, papers and so on. It is an ideal purveyor of information due to the speed with which it can be produced — where a book may take many months, a journal will take only a fraction of that time.

Because of the ever-increasing number of titles and subjects and the continual spawning of more titles, the vital importance of this literature for the national good, and ultimately its more stringent control, is gradually being recognized by users and librarians alike. The sheer bulk of material previously handled alongside other material soon forced the realization that separate periodical libraries were the only efficient way of handling this material with all its peculiarities and problems. Indeed, their administration, classification, storage and methods of information dissemination are studies in their own rights. These separate libraries were staffed by librarians who began to develop their own expertise solely for their own area of operation.

The growing number of libraries and growing demand for retrospective runs soon saw the birth of a multiplicity of alternatives — electronic journal, microform, reprints, synoptic journal, etc. — to the conventional periodical, and it became evident that a specialized educational area in librarianship was ripe for tapping — almost a science in itself, one might claim.

Admittedly, serials work is a part of librarianship, but, as I have outlined, the sheer amount of work, utilizing massive amounts of staff time, lends itself to special treatment in the syllabus of at least one library school. Others do not agree that there is any need for treatment to be given outside the normal bibliographic administrative axis, but this philosophy is similar to that which pervaded in 1932 and 1956 when, after due consultations for special treatment within the professional body, Aslib and the Institute of Information Scientists were founded. Librarians and their staffs can spend all their professional lives wrestling with the many problems of this area of bibliography, and whereas some are akin to other areas of librarianship there are a multitude of others which need special consideration.

It is early days yet for serials education specifically, and most schools of librarianship sandwich the subject with their general bibliographic courses. However, the School of Librarianship, Loughborough Technical College, with the Department of Library and Information Studies, Loughborough University, have, over the last few years, offered a separate full-time option covering all aspects of serials literature — its history, administration, dissemination, bibliography, storage and disposal — on a basis of two 50-minute lectures plus one seminar per week. 'Take up' for the course was not expected to be high but lately Loughborough staff have almost become embarrassed by numbers opting, which may well reflect the need for such coverage in the real world of librarianship.

There are many bibliographers who maintain that there is nothing of special significance in serial literature to warrant special treatment, but the demand by students, by comment outside and by the formation recently of the UK Serials Group surely underlines the need for such a specialized approach.

The two organizations noted above started the course to meet the need so clearly expressed and to foster the belief that a greater awareness of the potential of this type of material was needed anyway, from those librarians having staffs *solely* concerned with periodicals, right the way down to those small enclaves having a few journals in a corner. In no way is it suggested that the treatment of the subject described is ideal, but it is here outlined to provoke discussion on how it might be improved.

Right at the start it is necessary for a long hard look to be taken at the 'serial' as an entity — what it is and what are its various forms. This, from past experience, usually comes as a shock because of the preconceived idea that one has of this kind of material, e.g. those documents that can be purchased at nearly every newsagent's and what many call magazines — horrible word! But the Americans grade their titles depending on whether they are called magazines, periodicals, or journals — the latter being the most erudite. It comes as quite a surprise when, after the long hard look, it is realized that a good proportion of the literature which we, as librarians, have to deal with is in fact serial, whereas we have previously, for administrative convenience, called them directories, yearbooks, calendars etc.

Having decided what a serial *is* within the definition it is then attempted to categorize them into three groups - Primary, Secondary and Tertiary. 'Primary', as the term implies, is the most important and refers to original material. 'Secondary', on the other hand, refers to the type of publication which monitors material in a number of journals and other sources in a given field and then organizes it for effective dissemination; such a publication may include abstracts, may simply be an index or may take the form of a contents page reproduction. Through this type of serial readers may be alerted to work that they would not otherwise see. A further form of secondary publication is the citation index whereby, if the researcher is aware of certain individuals writing in his field of interest, he can find his way not only to the original articles, but also to articles by the same and other writers, which either prompted the original article or were prompted by it. Finally, 'Tertiary' is used to describe review-type material which may be based on primary or secondary levels, or both. Such publications are often captioned by *Progress in ...*, *Reviews of ...*, *State-of-the-art of ...*, etc.

Having satisfactorily, we hope, defined the everyday serial, the term coined by Osborne[2] — pseudo serial, used to denote a further selection of material like directories and other irregular publications — is introduced. Finally, because of the sheer amount of material now in serial form, the question 'What are the alternatives?' is asked and microforms, synoptics, letters, journals, electronic journals and so forth are discussed.

At this point, having really looked at the definition, and understood the problems involved we stand back and ask the question 'How has it reached this state of affairs?' This basically involves a quick look at the historical development of the serial from its earliest times to date. During the recapitulation, terms mentioned in the discussion on definition tend to crop up again if necessary so that this underlines the understanding and puts everything in perspective, so, it may be hoped, by this time in the course the student is fully aware of the various ramifications and understands points which earlier may have still been hazy.

One might say that the foregoing is a preamble to the main work ahead, for now the primary publication in all its guises is considered in detail: what it is supposed to do, its features, constituent parts, types and purposes. Attention is also focused on what can best be called non-traditional areas — the mechanized services, their scope, number, potential and the related fields of standardization in the guises of the work of the UK National Serials Data Centre, ISO, BSI, and specifically the reasons behind the introduction and growth of ISSN, ISBD, etc.

Wherever possible in the lengthy course of this type we attempt to break it into manageable and interesting divisions, and our belief with any study of the literature, its potential and use, is that there is a place for knowledge of its manufacture. Accordingly outside speakers are invited to cover some of the problems involved in publicity, refereeing, editorial practice, printing and associated financial problems. Wherever possible visits to local firms back up the lectures. Highlighting the librarians' preoccupation with the practical side of storage in later life, attention is also given to the problems of binding and a further visit to a bindery is made to learn at first hand not only the process itself but how the cost structures vary according to cloth used and amount of decoration, etc.

Not forgotten in all these practical considerations is the vexed question of copyright. Most librarians will come across copyright and its implications from time to time, and never more so than in this field. The consideration given is only relative to serials, the current legislation, its implications and moves towards reform.

Finally in this lengthy introductory coverage, a knowledge of the organizations specializing in serials is imparted, culminating in the UK Serials Group formed in 1977 as a direct result of pressure from librarians.

Taking a quick look back a student should now have a reasonable knowledge of what a serial is, or may be defined to be, what its history is and why it is so fragmented today, its potential as an information purveyor, how it is made and what constraints are laid on its use, and be able to argue accordingly. The meat of the exercise is a survey of the bibliographic tools which are used in the day-to-day control of serials themselves and the material in them. What can be called the more 'library oriented' part of the course begins here. Bibliographic activity focuses on two quite clearly defined areas: (1) working with titles of journals and (2) the information in them requiring a knowledge of the various bibliographic tools. Very basically these bibliographic tools divide themselves into two broad categories: (a) works that list journals, into which category can be placed lists of current journals, retrospective lists, catalogues, union lists, etc. and (b) those that index their contents. It is recognized that any treatment is open to personal interpretation but it is suggested that consideration of the following areas should provide a comprehensive coverage in this section of the syllabus.

Books About Serials

In any study of the bibliography of a subject it is useful to have general works covering the area in broad terms, and a variety of works, new and old, are considered in this context. They are the text books of the subject.

Directories/Bibliographies

More important in a working field of librarianship are the tools for the job, and there are many directories of many types both complementary and supplementary to each other and it is difficult to recommend one against the other at times. However the average library should provide a variety of these in order to attempt to meet any contingency, and it is the aim of the Loughborough course to provide an appreciation of the different items of literature in order that a choice be made.

Location Lists

While directories contain material in print at the time of publication,

Education

location lists detail information still available despite its printed state. There are many of these, ranging from those under the Bowker imprint to those produced by local co-operative schemes. But they all have their place in an integrated network.

International Serials Data System

The possibilities of national and international computerized data bases have been considered for some time. To further the efficient running of such systems various schemes have been propounded, abandoned, resurrected and so on, and an attempt is made to survey the major ones, for example the International Serials Data System (ISDS) with comment on their potential.

Newspapers

This is a difficult area to cover within the definition of a periodical but nevertheless it is attempted. Some indication of the variety of coverage of papers in the UK is given, plus comment on the rather patchy way in which news is indexed for posterity. Other types of material are also considered here, each having their own peculiar problems, e.g. reports, conference proceedings etc.

Agents

The better agents are ever increasing the bibliographic scope of their work. The larger ones are now computerized and are able to undertake a considerable amount of bibliographic work via this facility, such as printing of catalogues, bibliographies, select lists etc.

Indexes

A specialized aspect of the bibliographic control of journals concerns the availability of indexes. Indexes appear anything but frequently in a variety of guises, with or without cost, at various times up to many months after the cessation of the volume they are supposed to index. A volume without an index is like a ship without a rudder, but it is surprising how many journals still do not possess them. Very few tools adequately indicate the availability of indexes and there is a crying need for a comprehensive guide.

Abstracting and Indexing Services

These have been defined as continuing bibliographic services — bulletins, journals, card services, microforms, magnetic tapes and search services — offered by many organizations and containing abstracts and/or references to currently published literature including periodical articles, providing on the one hand a current awareness function and on the other hand a retrospective one.

Automated Services

Increasingly these are becoming facts of life, but traditional bibliographic methods will continue to dominate our searching activities in the foreseeable future. The already widely known services of INSPEC, MEDLARS, UKCIS and the potential of the BLAISE and EURONET systems immediately come to the fore for consideration among many others on a broad national and international base. Students are given practical exercises where possible using the University terminals having access to several of these services.

Second-hand Services

One could easily lose sight of the vast trade done in this area. Whilst many of the problems are administrative, there are a few bibliographic services which need a mention, such as the British Library Gifts and Exchange Section, the activities of local co-operative schemes and those bookshops which specialize in this area.

Comparing time for time, bibliography takes up a considerable part of the syllabus in one way or another, but it seems logical, once this has been completed, to move on to the problems of selection and handling. It is recognized that bibliographic control can of course be construed as part of the selection and handling process, but that apart the mechanisms of selection are discussed, personal selection, the use of reviews, trial subscriptions etc. Which proceeds logically to a survey of the sources through which periodicals may be acquired, with an assessment of each. Finally, in the acquisition process, a brief note is made of the various receipt techniques available. So much has been written on this subject that it seems illogical and time-wasting to lecture on an area which (a) can be adequately read about or (b) various examples consulted and assessed individually by students on their visits.

The final section of the syllabus covers the handling techniques variously called exploitation and use. A short course on the basics of abstracting followed by practical work is a useful curtain-raiser here, with similar treatment given to indexing. There follows a review of the various forms of inter-lending and co-operative schemes and services and their relationships within the network of library services in the country. Last but not least, an introduction to bibliometrics is given, leading to a case study covering disposal and de-acquisition.

It should be noted that associated and concurrent course academic work is given, an assessed element towards the end of session examination. During the past few years one part of this assessed work has been the production of a small bibliography which the staff have collated into what is a very valuable course bibliography, fully classified, covering many hundreds of references. Each year students are required to raise further different entries from those on the main list thus ensuring an annual addition to the work. Whilst students are not expected to read every item it has proved to be a most useful reference tool for general use. Additional reading is given where necessary directly associated with lectures. To provide some form of light relief, selected outside speakers are imported to deal with certain major topics for which they are specifically qualified. Also, where notable practitioners appear without warning, which is often the case, they are invited to lecture the students as an added 'perk'.

Several outside visits are made to follow up lectures, and these include, as mentioned earlier, a bindery, publishing firm, a serials agent etc. In this way a greater appreciation is obtained of the various aspects of their work. This is especially useful for students from overseas. Also it acts as a constant reminder that we are basically a very practical profession — something often forgotten from the confines of 'seats of learning'.

I mentioned earlier the use of course work. This is a carefully geared element and forms part of the overall examination attainment. Several pieces are given in order to harness fully the students' understanding of lectures and to bring out their own natural abilities. Towards this latter end an open-ended project is given which it is the responsibility of the student to choose in direct contact with the course tutors.

Whilst it is not possible in one academic year to cross every 't' and dot every 'i', the course outlined briefly above has proved itself to be one which is comprehensive in coverage, taxing to the student, and above all one that is likely to be helpful/useful at a later date. I do not pretend that every single facet of work is included, but this is one way in which a course *is* run and which is open for continual improvement.

REFERENCES

1. Mayes, P. (ed.). *Periodicals administration in libraries.* London, Bingley, 1978.
2. Osborn, A. D. *Serial publications: their place and treatment in libraries.* 2nd ed., revised. Chicago, American Library Association. 1973.

Index

The index contains entries for authors, titles, organisations and subjects. Books and articles listed in the chapter bibliographies are included only when they are specifically mentioned in the text: first authors only are given where present, titles being used for items without authors.

The word 'serial' or 'periodical' has been avoided as far as possible, and has been used only to prevent confusion in subject headings. Titles of periodicals and other serials mentioned in the text are listed with the same capitalization as in the text, viz the first letter of each significant word. Entries for universities and their libraries are given under the name of the university, regardless of the institution's practice.

Filing order is word by word, with abbreviations and acronyms treated as words, and hyphenated words treated as separate words. Generally, abbreviations and acronyms are expanded only where the text does so.

London University Library
  budgets 87
  holdings lists 93
  MASS use 46
  union lists 95, 152, 202
Loughborough library schools, serials
  course 232
Loughborough University Library
  BLCMP–MASS 46, 152
  storage sequences 91
LRCC, union list 152
LULOP 146

McGregor, J.W., on staffing serials
  acquisition 37, 99
Magazines in Special Media 224
main entry, cataloguing 191
Manchester Commercial Library,
  directory provision 77
MARC
  CONSER 6
  discrepancies with MASS 152
  formats 205
  standardization 195–6
  tapes as serial publications 222
MARC-based Automated Serials
  System 46, 151–2
March of Time 218
Marshall, J.K., *Serials for libraries* 6
Martyn, John *and* Gilchrist, Alan,
  *An evaluation of British
  scientific journals* 4
MASS 46, 151–2
Meadows, Prof. J., primary publications research 158
Medical Library Association,
  exchange scheme 20
medical library, Nottingham University, stock arrangement 89
medical profession, audio use 219–
  20
MEDLARS 179, 237
MEDLINE 179, 190
membership subscriptions 14
Metropolitan Special Collections
  Scheme 148
microfiche
  catalogues 45
  sizes 133
microfilm catalogues 45
microfilming, national libraries 71–3

microforms
  govt. dept. libraries 125–6
  industrial libraries 112–13
  learned society libraries 132–3
  legal deposit 68
  polytechnic libraries 104–5
  publications 220–2
  stock integration, university lib-
    raries 90
  storage method 55–7
Middlesex Polytechnic Library, local
  indexing 103
Middleton, M., on journalistic colour
  photography 219
minicomputers, role in systems 207
Milwaukee (Wisconsin) Journal 216
Minnesota Union List of Serials, and
  CONSER 151
mission-oriented services vs.
  discipline-oriented services
  172–3
mobile compact shelving, learned
  society libraries 131–2
monographic series, cataloguing
  41–2
monographs, Regional systems
  definition 145–6
Monopolies and Mergers
  Commission, library service 118
MULS, CONSER 151
multi-site problems, polytechnics
  97–8
multiple copies *see* duplicate subscriptions
multiple output, from single input,
  abstracting and indexing
  services 177

NANTIS
  information services 142
  publications 138, 139
NASA, on-line retrieval system 179
National Central Library 145
National Clearinghouse for Periodical
  Title Word Abbreviations 194
National Committee on Regional
  Library Co-operation, *Report on
  the future pattern of inter-
  lending* 147, 149
national libraries 65–73